Egyptian Cinema and the
2011 Revolution

Egyptian Cinema and the 2011 Revolution

Film Production and Representing Dissent

Ahmed Ghazal

I.B. TAURIS
LONDON · NEW YORK · OXFORD · NEW DELHI · SYDNEY

I.B. TAURIS
Bloomsbury Publishing Plc
50 Bedford Square, London, WC1B 3DP, UK
1385 Broadway, New York, NY 10018, USA
29 Earlsfort Terrace, Dublin 2, Ireland

BLOOMSBURY, I.B. TAURIS and the I.B. Tauris logo are
trademarks of Bloomsbury Publishing Plc

First published in Great Britain 2021
This paperback edition published in 2022

Copyright © Ahmed Ghazal, 2021

Ahmed Ghazal has asserted his right under the Copyright, Designs
and Patents Act, 1988, to be identified as Author of this work.

Cover design: Adriana Brioso
Cover image © HamboT (CC BY-SA 3.0)

All rights reserved. No part of this publication may be reproduced or transmitted in
any form or by any means, electronic or mechanical, including photocopying,
recording, or any information storage or retrieval system, without prior
permission in writing from the publishers.

Bloomsbury Publishing Plc does not have any control over, or responsibility for,
any third-party websites referred to or in this book. All internet addresses given
in this book were correct at the time of going to press. The author and publisher
regret any inconvenience caused if addresses have changed or sites have
ceased to exist, but can accept no responsibility for any such changes.

A catalogue record for this book is available from the British Library.

A catalog record for this book is available from the Library of Congress.

ISBN:	HB:	978-0-7556-0314-5
	PB:	978-0-7556-3542-9
	ePDF:	978-0-7556-0316-9
	eBook:	978-0-7556-0315-2

Typeset by Integra Software Solution Pvt. Ltd

To find out more about our authors and books visit www.bloomsbury.com
and sign up for our newsletters.

Contents

List of figures	vi
Introduction	1
1 Cinema and revolution	15
2 The crisis of the Egyptian film industry	43
3 Representing the national crisis: Films before the revolution, 2006–10	67
4 Constructing cultural memory: Fiction and documentary films that represent the revolution	97
5 Technology and revolution: The continuity of 'independent' films	131
Conclusion	161
Notes	170
Filmography	177
Bibliography	179
Index	192

List of figures

1. Top: Amal delivering food to a luxurious house. Bottom: a hand-held shot of the house from her perspective (*al-Khurug min al-Qahira*, 2010) — 92
2. Top: popular committees. Bottom: the revolution appearing in the background (*Farsh wa-Ghata*, 2013) — 116–17
3. Top: a re-enactment of Rashwan and his kids following the news. Bottom: Rashwan filming the events while protesting (*Mawlud fi Khamsa wa-'Ishriyn Yanayir*, 2011) — 120
4. Underprivileged life and working conditions of characters in *'Asham* (2013) — 142–3
5. A screenshot of *Biy'ulu* (2011) — 152

Introduction

'The people want to bring down the regime' was the main slogan chanted by millions of Egyptians on 25 January 2011. Bread, freedom and social justice were the three main demands of demonstrators, made up of different strata of Egyptian social classes and political affiliations. On 28 January – known as the Friday of Anger – the police attacked the protesters violently through shooting and running over them with their cars. Later that day, the protesters burned the National Democratic Party's headquarters (the ruling party at that time), prisoners escaped after the opening of prisons, the army replaced the police and a curfew was established. Statistics reveal 846 people, at least, were killed and 6,467 were injured (Uwra and Marwan as cited in 'Ali, 2011). The majority of protesters occupied Tahrir Square (literally 'liberation square') in central Cairo and considered it the main symbol of the revolution. However, other protests, demonstrations and marches took place in cities such as Iskindiriya (Alexandria), Isma'ilia, Mansura, Suwis (Suez) and Za'azi'. Scattered all over Egypt, the protesters succeeded in overthrowing Husni Mubarak after his thirty years of rule on 11 February 2011. Subsequently, Egyptian society has encountered profound chaos, including recurrent protests and criminal elements that have monopolized the absence of security and intimidated the public.

During the last decade of Mubarak's rule, Egyptians increasingly suffered from high rates of unemployment, widespread corruption and police brutality. One of the main revolutionary requests was the end of *qānūn al-tawāri'* (emergency law), which was enforced after Sadat's assassination and lasted during Mubarak's rule. 'That law gives executive authorities the right to arrest, interrogate, and imprison any Egyptian for up to six months without a warrant or any legal grounds or even the right to an attorney' (Ghonim, 2012, p. 2). In addition, the state manipulation of the 2010 parliamentary elections, in favour of the National Democratic Party (97 per cent), while ignoring most of the oppositional groups – such as the Muslim Brotherhood and al-Wafd Party – led to a public dissent (Shihata, 2011).

Social media platforms played a significant role in planning for and organizing protests as well as mediating news, photographs and videos of events, which mainstream media channels disregarded. A Facebook group called *Kulina Khalid Sa'id* (We are all Khalid Sa'id) created in the memory of Khalid Sa'id who was beaten to death by secret police in 2010 announced the call for protests on 25 January. By the time of the revolution, the group (moderated by Wa'il Ghunim) had more than 500,000 members. Movements such as Six April Youth and Kifaya (literally 'enough') helped to spread the significance of participating in such an event. Also, Dr Muhammad al-Barad'i – the former chief of International Atomic Energy Agency, known for his oppositional stand against Mubarak's regime – has been one of the main leading figures of the revolution. Mainstream media channels continued to support Mubarak during the early days of the revolution. The Egyptian state-run channels, as well as some privately owned channels, denied the existence of the revolution. They described the events as an attempt by 'a minority of infiltrators' to create chaos and disorder. Due to their obvious bias, many people turned to alternative news sources including social media and non-Egyptian channels (such as Al Jazeera and BBC Arabic).[1]

The fall of Mubarak was the main consequence of the revolution. The Supreme Council of Armed Forces (SCAF) ruled Egypt during the transitional phase from 11 February 2011 to 30 June 2012. Although the army appeared to support the revolution, the protesters experienced catastrophic events – such as the arrest of revolutionary figures, attacking Tahrir Square and obstructing Christian protests at Maspiro – all of which distorted the protesters' view of the army. During the transitional phase, the Muslim Brotherhood gained power through claiming 40 per cent of the parliamentary seats (Farag, 2012), followed by the election of Muhammad Mursi – a leading member in the Muslim Brotherhood – in June 2012 as the president of Egypt. During his first year of rule, Muhammad Mursi received wide criticism for his actions, which included a declaration broadening his legislative power and the enforcement of a new constitution amended by Islamists in November 2012. Protests erupted again by the end of December 2012 at the presidential palace demanding Mursi's resignation. The attacks by Islamists against these protests led to a growing anger and division within the Egyptian community. In April 2013, a campaign named Tamarrud (Rebel) called for protests on 30 June 2013 to overthrow Mursi due to deteriorating economic and political conditions.

On 30 June 2013, millions of Egyptians returned back to the streets and squares calling for Mursi to step down. The following day Marshal 'Abd al-Fattah al-Sisi – Minister of Defense – offered Mursi 48 hours to answer the public demands, before the army's intervention. On 3 July 2013, the army removed Muhammad Mursi from office, shut down the Islamist television channels and called Muslim Brotherhood leaders for arrest. Meanwhile, al-Sisi, together with al-Barad'i and other political leaders, announced a roadmap plan for the new transitional phase, including the suspension of parliament and amending the constitution. This action has led to a controversial debate whether 30 June 2013 was a revolution or a coup. According to the Egyptian constitution, the chief of supreme justice court 'Adli Mansur was appointed as the president of Egypt during the new transitional phase. On 14 August 2013, the army and police attacked the Muslim Brotherhood protest in Rab'a al-'Adawiya, killing hundreds of protesters, whom the regime claimed were armed. In the presidential elections of May 2014, al-Sisi won with more than 95 per cent of the votes, after a public demand that he run in the presidential elections.

Using the term 'revolution' to describe the uprising that took place in Egypt in January and February 2011 has been subject to debates and contestations. Political science and international relations scholars, such as Achcar (2013), have argued that the events of 2011 have only led to the overthrow of the president who dominated the state, but still pending social revolution, democratization as well as change in the constitution and the regime (which seek to maintain continuity with old institutions). However, Achcar does not deny the uprisings that took place in 2011 and articulates them as events within a long-term revolutionary process. The counter-revolutions that followed the uprisings, for example, have complicated the democratization process and formed a 'three-cornered struggle', which Achcar (2016) explains as 'not a binary confrontation between revolution and counter-revolution, as in most revolutionary upheavals in history, but a triangular conflict between one revolutionary pole and two rival counter-revolutionary camps – the regional ancient regime and its reactionary antagonists – both equally inimical to the emancipatory aspirations of the "Arab Spring"' (p. 30). In the case of Egypt, for example, the two counter-revolutionary camps – the Muslim Brotherhood and the ancient regime/military regime supporters – have hindered the sociopolitical transformation that the 2011 uprising aimed for.

In Arabic, the equivalent word for revolution is *thawra*, which is derived from the verb *thara* (to revolt). Many Egyptians have labelled the January and February 2011 events as *thawra* or revolution in the sense of 'a radical upheaval including, at the very least, a change in the political regime accomplished in ways that violate existing legality' (Achcar, 2013, p. 2). The protests, marches and sit-ins demonstrated 'exceptional episodes of high solidarity and sacrifice, of altruism and common will, when a rapid shift in consciousness and momentary change in behaviour takes place' (Bayat, 2013, p. 268). The overthrow of Mubarak by the people ('from below') also qualifies the use of the term 'revolution', in contrast to 'coup d'état' where the army seize the power (as in the case of Egypt in July 2013). Although the millions who went out on the streets during January and February 2011 have toppled the dictator, they did not overthrow the regime, which still dominates state institutions (Mostafa, 2015, p. 120). However, it is yet too early to decide on the 'success' or the 'failure' of the revolution. The release of Mubarak from prison free of charges and the imprisonment of many figures of the revolution since the appointment of al-Sisi as a president are only events within a longer revolutionary process. As Achcar (2013, p. 3) suggests, the uprising has created a 'revolutionary dynamic' which allows radical changes to take place in the future. Thus, I refer to the political movement of 2011 that led to the fall of Mubarak as a revolution in solidarity with the thousands who lost their lives and were injured.

In their study of media communications and the Iranian Revolution, Sreberny-Mohammadi and Mohammadi (1994, p. 19–20) assume that 'all revolutions are communicative processes, including the articulation of sometimes-competing ideologies and demands, the development of leaders and followers, the circulation of information, [and] the exhortations to participation and mobilization'. During the 2011 Egyptian Revolution, cinema was an integral part of this communication process, including the representation of competing ideologies. This book examines the relationship between the 2011 Egyptian Revolution and Egyptian cinema by focusing on the period from 2006 to the present. During this period, Egyptian films and the film industry have demonstrated a complex, yet reciprocal relationship with the revolution. The impact of the uprising on the industry and films and the engagement of films with politics revealed continuities and discontinuities in the relationship between cinema and the revolution. The book reveals the political economy of the film industry during a period of crisis and transformation. I argue that political and economic repercussions of the 2011 Revolution have extended the shortage in film production that started in 2008 and limited post-revolution productions to low-budget films.

On the other hand, this book examines the narratives and social meanings of recent films that address social dissent, political change and revolution. The analysis explores the contribution of film to the growing political activism during the pre-revolution period and argues that films produced from 2006 to 2010 have politicized viewers through representing issues of political corruption and social injustice. I analyse the generic conventions of popular dramas, political satire and independent film style that film-makers used to produce feelings of anger and hope. The analysis also examines the representation of the revolutionary moment in fiction and documentary films, which historicized events of the uprising. These films, I argue, have constructed a cultural memory of struggle against the counter-revolution, which frames the revolution as a conspiracy. In contrast to the film movements that followed political revolutions of the twentieth century, such as the Soviet Union and Cuban revolutions, the post-2011 Revolution period in Egypt did not witness the formation of a film movement. These movements are usually marked by their 'innovative' film techniques used to represent revolutionary struggle. In Egypt, film-makers continued to use independent film style that started before the revolution to represent the marginalization of the working classes, religious minorities and women. However, the conjunction of the revolution and film-making technological developments has encouraged young film-makers to produce films and contribute to the growing 'independent film wave'.

Media studies have reinforced the role of social networking sites in instigating the so-called 'Arab Spring'. The consistent approach to study the 2011 revolutions in relation to social media has undermined the role of other cultural artefacts such as film. While earlier studies have credited social media for connecting social actors and organizing protests before and during the 2011 Revolution (Eltantawy and Wiest, 2011; Howard and Hussain, 2011; Lim, 2012; El-Nawawy and Khamis, 2013), more recent studies have examined the role of citizen journalism and social media as alternative outlets that resisted the state's monopoly of information (Elghamry, 2015 and Radsch, 2016). Only a few scholars have analysed the role of pre-revolution films in exposing corruption to the broader public (al-Zubidi, 2011; Armbrust, 2012; Tabishat, 2012; and Tartoussieh, 2012). Tartoussieh (2012) and Armbrust (2012) scrutinize *'Imarat Ya'qubiyan* (*The Yacoubian Building*, Marwan Hamid, 2006) – a popular drama about political corruption and fundamentalism – and *Rami al-I'tisami* (*Rami the Protester*, Sami Rafi', 2008) – a comedy revealing a protest organized through a Facebook group and joined by different classes, ages, genders and political and religious backgrounds. Similarly, Tabishat (2012) analyses film scenes exposing revolts, such as *al-Irhab wa-l-Kabab* (*Terrorism and Kebab*, Shirif 'Arafa, 1992) and *Hiyya Fawda* (*Chaos, This Is*, Yusif Shahin and Khalid Yusif, 2007).

Although the attention has been centred around social media, cinema has played a significant role in contributing to and representing the 2011 Revolution. Egyptian popular films, including sociopolitical texts, have been widely viewed by mass audiences in Egypt and the Arab world. The circulation of these films on television channels has exposed them to a wider public. Social media users have used screenshots of some of these films as memes to comment on current political events and actions. However, putting aside Gabriel's (1982, p. 25) view of Third Cinema as provoking and leading the audience to action, Tabishat (2012, p. 395) believes that films produced prior to the 2011 Egyptian Revolution did not trigger the uprising. Instead, he describes them as portraying the frustrations of inequality experienced by low-income groups and women – feelings of fear, distrust and anxiety – in addition to the turmoil experienced within Egyptian society as a whole at the time. In expressing the role of pre-revolution films in the revolution, Tabishat (pp. 382–3) reveals,

> I have met and talked to many viewers of films in the last few months, some of whom were very involved in the protests. All insist that cinema played a major role in the *sawrah*, or uprising. Most of them are able to list films by title, year of production, plot, and main political message. Some could even cite the names of the protagonists and interpret the characters as representing major issues, problems, and institutions.

Film has also been a significant mode of documenting revolutions. Although digital cameras and video sharing websites have offered an alternative space to document and archive events, films have contributed to the cultural memory of the collectively experienced struggle during the 2011 Revolution. In addition to historicizing events, these films have represented the roles of other forms of media including the state's television denial of the revolution and the use of social media as an alternative source of news. They also integrated some of the footage shot by protestors and witnesses on mobile cameras within their narratives.

Moreover, revolutions have been associated to film movements that document and narrate revolutionary struggles. Several studies and manifestos have examined films that promote revolutionary change, including Third Cinema, anti-colonial, decolonizing and nationalist and indigenous movements (Solanas and Getino, 1970; MacBean, 1975; Gabriel, 1982; Willemen, 1989; Youngblood, 1991; Balaisis, 2010; Naficy, 2011; and Roncallo and Arias-Herrera, 2013). These researchers have examined the significant role of cinema in constructing new cultures based on ideologies of revolutions. Post-revolution film movements have also introduced new film-making styles such as Eisenstein's use of montage following the Soviet 1917 Revolution. The ways in which the 2011 Revolution is going to influence film styles in Egypt was one of my initial research interests. Although film-makers did not develop a radical film style, they represented struggle through various creative and realist approaches that deserves attention.

Along with economic deterioration confronted by the state since the revolution, Egypt's film industry (the leading film industry in the Arab world) has been facing its own crisis. The recurrent curfews and insecurity have exacerbated the financial difficulties that started after the 2008 global financial crisis. Film-makers have appeared on television channels to address the characteristics and implications of the crisis as well as call for government support. The crisis in producing high-budget films has meant that low-budget films have dominated Egyptian cinema since the revolution. While a few studies have explored independent film-making in relation to the 2011 Revolution (Lebow, 2016) or in the context of new cinemas of the Arab world (Schwartz, Kaye and Martini, 2013; Jarjoura, 2014; and Armes, 2015), the crisis of the film industry has not yet been covered in any academic text.

Meanwhile, the 'Arab Spring' has been one of the most globally discussed topics in the past few years. One of its major events – the Egyptian 2011 Revolution – is a turning point in history. It is vital to examine its impact on social, economic and cultural aspects, as it is critically important to historically document and archive political film-making practices during this period in Egyptian history. This project contributes to the experience of Egyptian cinema during the 2011 Revolution through examining the engagement of films with dissent and political change and exploring the impact of the revolution on the film industry and film texts.

While the actual uprising lasted for eighteen days from 25 January to 11 February 2011, this book covers the period from 2006 to the present. The pre-revolution period dating from 2006 to 2011 represents the rise of political anger and dissent in Egypt expressed through protests and strikes, organized by labour unions and professional syndicates. As Shihata (2011) explains, 'Over the last five years [2006–2011], the Mubarak regime began to violate this implicit agreement [with oppositional parties], by imposing renewed constraints on the ability of political parties and movements to organise and to contest elections' (p. 29). Political movements such as Six April – one of the largest youth movements – was created in 2008. Simultaneously, the people's escalating anger appeared on film screens during this period. Popular high-budget dramas and political satire films depicted the rising tide of anger and anticipated an upcoming revolution. Films such as '*Imarat Ya'qubiyan, Hiyna Maysara* (*When Convenient*, Khalid Yusif, 2007) and *Dukkan Shihata* (*Shihata's Shop*, Khalid Yusif, 2009) are examples of the high-budget popular dramas that depicted issues of corruption, poverty and police brutality. Comedy films including *Rami al-I'tisami, Zaza* ('Ali 'Abd al-Khalik, 2006) and *al-Diktatur* (*The Dictator*, Ihab Lam'i, 2009) portrayed themes of dictatorship and economic inequality. They set their plots in imagined countries to circumvent censorship.

The pre-revolution period has also witnessed the inception of the wave of independent films. Film directors such as Ibrahim al-Battut, Ahmad Rashwan and Ahmad 'Abd Allah used digital cameras, new actors and personal savings to fund their films. al-Battut's films *Ithaki* (2005) and *'In Shams* (*Eye of the Sun*, 2008), as well as Rashwan's *Basra* (2008) and 'Abd Allah's *Hiliaupulis* (*Heliopolis*, 2009), disregarded commercial market considerations. They signalled a rebellion against predominant ideologies through their non-traditional narrative structures, creative modes of production and resistance to mainstream film-making styles. Although these films did not aim to mobilize their audiences, they used alternative aesthetics and realist approaches to relate to their viewers. They represented social issues that mainstream cinema tends to dramatize in melodramatic fashion and narrated interrelated stories about issues such as unemployment, cronyism and the structural transformations of popular districts in Cairo.

The post-revolution period, dating from 2011 to the present, reveals the ways in which film-makers represented the revolution in their narrative and documentary texts. Films such as *Ba'd al-Mawqi'a* (*After the Battle*, Yusri Nasrallah, 2012) and *al-Midan* (*The Square*, Jihan Nujaim, 2013) are forms of representation of history through visual images, which White (1988) dubs as historiophoty, and they contribute to the construction of the visual memory of the 2011 Revolution (Rastegar, 2015). These films narrate the revolution through depicting opposing 'voices', popular discourses and ideologies that competed during the 2011 Revolution (Shohat and Stam, 1994).

In contrast to the lack of government support for the film industry in Egypt during a period of crisis, post-revolution governments in the Soviet Union, China and Cuba have encouraged the production of educational and scientific films. Post-revolution governments in these countries realized the significant role of film in disseminating 'revolutionary' ideologies and creating new cultures. In China and Cuba, mobile projection units showed films in rural and countryside areas. Film-makers also used alternative aesthetics to engage with the 'revolutionary reality', social changes and historical themes of struggle. In his notes about economic crises and political transformations, Antonio Gramsci emphasized the need for a new culture in opposition to the traditional artistic approaches, 'one must speak of a struggle for a new culture, that is, for a new moral life that cannot but be intimately connected to a new intuition of life, until it becomes a new way of feeling and seeing reality and, therefore, a world intimately ingrained in "possible artists" and "possible works of art'" (Gramsci as cited in Forgacs, 2000, p. 395). For Gramsci, the significance of this new culture resides in its formation of a 'hegemonic attitude' (p. 395) that counters dominant ideologies.

The independent film-making wave that started in 2005 has flourished after the 2011 Revolution. The conjuncture of technological developments of film-making tools and the 2011 Revolution, which allowed a momentary sense of freedom and urged artistic forms of self-expression, has encouraged the production of more independent projects. Films such as *al-Khurug li-l-Nahar* (*Coming Forth by Day*, Hala Lutfi, 2012),[2] *'Asham* (Maggi Murgan, 2013) and *Harag wa-Marag* (*Chaos, Disorder*, Nadin Khan, 2013) have engaged with sociopolitical issues and themes, such as marginalized communities. These films continued the earlier styles of independent films rather than developing a 'revolutionary' film style. One of the reasons that hindered the creation of a post-revolution film movement is the struggle of the revolution to make radical changes in social and state institutions. However, despite their employment of traditional realist approaches, such long takes and casting new actors, I argue that these films represent feelings of frustration and hope during a period of social change.

The book determines the relationship between Egyptian cinema and the 2011 Revolution through examining the different sectors of the Egyptian film industry (production, distribution and exhibition) and film texts during the revolution. I argue that the film industry has transformed due to the revolution and a production crisis. An oligopoly of production, distribution and exhibition has dominated the Egyptian film industry since the late 1990s. After the global financial crisis in 2008, major film companies such as al-'Arabiya and al-Nasr wa-l-Masa wa-Auskar have reduced their production of films. Repercussions of the 2011 Revolution such as recurring curfews, insecurity, extended piracy and unexpected censorship have extended the shortage in film production. Thus, many popular film-makers moved to television production, where a higher profit is guaranteed. Since then, Egyptian film productions have been mainly limited to low-budget popular films released in the high seasons of *'īd al-Fitr* and *'īd al-Adhā*. These films depend on a fixed formula of a belly dancer, popular song and mediocre comedy and action scenes.

On the other hand, a few film-makers have used digital technologies and non-traditional narrative structures to engage with sociopolitical themes of social deprivation and frustration. A few film producers, such as Muhammad Hifzi, together with funds offered by international film festivals have supported these films – labelled as 'independent films'. In addition, the development of film-making technologies, such as inexpensive digital cameras and the use of video sharing websites as screening spaces, encouraged the production of a diversity of film styles and blurred the distinction between professional and amateur film-making. Digital technologies are not the only reason behind the emergence of these films or style, since film-makers developed realistic styles and approaches since the 1960s in Egyptian cinema, but the availability of inexpensive digital cameras and video sharing websites as screening spaces have facilitated and expanded the production and screening of films. Only a few blockbusters have been recently produced due to the demands of other television networks – MBC and OSN. Film producers and directors have been calling for state support as the main way out of the crisis. Although a governmental committee was set to discuss the crisis, the state gives a minimal consideration to the film industry issues. These forces, I argue, have *limited the post-revolution film productions to low-budget popular and independent films.*

The book also examines how Egyptian films addressed political crisis, dissent and social change in revolutionary times. Since 2006, films have gradually represented political anger and dissent in Egypt. Film-makers used popular dramas, comedies and independent film style to represent issues of social inequality, freedom of expression and police brutality. These sociopolitical conscious films did not mobilize the audience but raised awareness regarding the public's discontent and showed images of protests and marches that inspired the audience and took place a few years later.

Fiction and documentary films have also represented the revolutionary moment to historicize and construct a cultural memory of struggle. Films such as *al-Shitaa illy Fat* (*The Winter of Discontent*, Ibrahim al-Battut, 2012) have represented events of the revolution in relation to state security and the state's media, while films such as Ahmad 'Abd Allah's *Farsh wa-Ghata* (*Rags and Tatters*, 2013) and Johanna Domke and Marwan 'Umara's *Crop* (2013) focused on under-represented cities, districts and themes. In contrast to the coverage of mainstream media of the events, the latter films engage with the revolution without revealing images from the iconic Tahrir Square. I argue that film-makers used stylistic elements of both fiction and documentary to construct and historicize the events in an authentic manner that validates their arguments.

Since the revolution, a few films have addressed issues of marginalization of working classes and social deprivation such as *al-khurug li-l-Nahar*, *'Asham* and *Harag wa-Marag*. These films resist the Hollywood film-making style that dominates Egyptian cinema. They reveal a day (or more) from the lives of their characters to convey their social struggles. Young film-makers have also produced short films about communication and political conflicts within the context of the revolution and, in some cases, uploaded them online. I confirm the argument of film scholars such as Lebow (2016) and critics including al-'Umari (2014) that these films do not constitute a post-revolution film movement due to the lack of a common aesthetic approach. However, I also add that these films have engaged subtly with the revolution. They represented themes of struggle, frustration and hope through diverse styles (including realism and fantasy) during a period of social and political change.

Chapter 1 explores the relationship between cinema and revolution. It reviews the literature on film politics and examines studies by Kellner (1995), Street (1997) and Wheeler (2006) to explain the intimate and reciprocal relationship of cinema and politics. I also draw upon studies by scholars such as Solanas and Octavio (1970), MacBean (1975), Gabriel (1982) and Naficy (2012a) who contributed to the articulation between film and revolution in other national contexts such as the Latin America, Iran, China and the Soviet Union. I classify the approaches of these studies to examine the relationship between cinema and revolution into four interrelated categories including the use of film as a political activism tool before revolutions, the role of film in documenting the revolutionary moment, the impact of revolution on the political economy of film industries and the influence of revolutions on film texts and styles. I argue that film has been a significant mode of resistance and documentation during times of social and political change, which produced political affect and contributed to cultural memories of revolutions. I also contend that the role of post-revolution governments in supporting film industries (through providing funds and/or regulations or censoring films) was vital in shaping the style and content of films produced after revolutions. It is through these practices that post-revolution films have experimented with film techniques and produced 'innovative' film-making styles.

Chapter 2 examines what the mainstream media have been calling 'the crisis of Egyptian film industry'. It explains the characteristics and implications of the crisis based on interviews with film-makers in Cairo during December 2014, January 2015 and January 2016. After the global financial crisis in 2008, Rotana Cinema and ART Aflam – Gulf television channels and the main financiers of Egyptian films since the late 1990s – retreated from buying new films. The repercussions of the 2011 Revolution, such as piracy, curfews and lack of security, exacerbated the crisis. Ahmad Badawi, the producer of *Sonia fi Masr* (*Made in Egypt*, 'Amr Salama, 2014) – a film featuring one of Egypt's leading comedy star Ahmad Hilmi, states that they lost a minimum of 15 million Egyptian pounds due to the piracy of the film (CBC Egypt, 2014a). Although a ministerial committee was formed to discuss the crisis, film-makers argue that the state does not support film-making. Moreover, unpredicted censorship and an oligopoly of production and distribution have increased the risk of producing a film. These forces have led to the migration of film-makers to television production after the 2011 Revolution. They justify the domination of low-budget films as well as the curbing of politically engaged films during the post-revolution period.

Chapter 3 argues that films produced during the pre-revolution period contributed to the growing political activism and anticipated the revolution. It mainly concentrates on the films released before the revolution (2006–2010) and analyses how directors portrayed dissent and anger through specific scenes and sequences of demonstrations and marches against the regime. I argue that these films raised awareness and politicized viewers through different genres and narrative styles. High-budget popular dramas, political satire and independent films have represented issues of unemployment, absolute poverty and bribery, which were prevalent during the pre-revolution period. However, these films did not mobilize audiences as changing Mubarak's regime seemed impossible at that time. I analyse high-budget dramas that featured film stars such as *'Imarat Ya'qubiyan*, *Hiyna Maysara* and *Dukkan Shihata*. I also analyse political satire films including *Rami al-I'tisami*, *Zaza* and *al-Diktatur*. These films used comedy as a genre to circumvent censorship. The chapter ends with an analysis of 'independent films' such as *'In Shams*, *Basra*, *Hiliaupulis* and *al-Khurug min al-Qahira* (*Cairo Exit*, Hisham 'Issawi, 2010). Although these independent films did not reveal scenes of a revolution, they represented political and social oppression during the pre-revolution period.

Chapter 4 examines post-revolution fiction and documentary films that focus intensely on the 'revolutionary moment'. Feature films include *Ba'd al-Mawqi'a*, which depicts the 'Battle of Camels' – one of the famous events in the revolution, where some inciting agents attacked the protesters at Tahrir Square while riding horses and camels. In addition, *al-Shitaa illy Fat* which started with some shots of the revolution, filmed by the documentary director Ibrahim al-Battut, then shifted into a feature about police brutality during Mubarak's era. I also analyse Ahmad 'Abd Allah's independent feature *Farsh wa-Ghata*, which follows a prisoner who was set free during the eighteen days of the revolution. These films used footage from the revolution, re-enactments and improvised scenes to narrate their experiences or reflect on events in an authentic sense. They portray the obvious bias of state-run media during the revolution as well as the significant role of international and digital media outlets in covering the events. In addition to historicizing events of the revolution, I argue that these films constructed the cultural memory through representing experiences of dissidents, marginalized districts and oppositional political views that were under-represented by the media during the revolution.

This chapter also provides an analysis of documentary films, which became a popular means and mode of production after the revolution. Focusing on documentaries discussing the revolution, the analysis includes *Mawlud fi Khamsa wa-'Ishriyn Yanayir* (*Born on the 25th of January*, Ahmad Rashwan, 2011), which narrates the director's personal experience during the revolution. The discussion on documentaries also includes *al-Tahrir 2011: al-Taiyyib, wa-l-Sharis, wa-l-Siyasi* (*Tahrir 2011: The Good, The Bad, and The Politician*, Tamir 'Izzat, Aytin Amin and 'Amr Salama, 2011). This film, divided into three parts, interviews and discusses the protesters (as the good), the police (as the bad) and profiles Mubarak (as the politician). The last film I analyse in this chapter is the independent documentary *Crop* (Johanna Domke and Marwan 'Umara, 2013). *Crop* is a creative documentary that narrates a fiction story of a photojournalist during the revolution without showing any images from Tahrir Square. These films represent a sample of the style and modes of documentaries that depicted the 2011 Revolution. While some documentaries used a first-person film-making style to narrate the revolution experience, others engaged with multiple perspectives on the events. Both fiction and documentary films represent the revolution in the form of binary oppositions: pro- versus anti-revolution, upper- versus lower-classes and police versus protesters. Only a few films have creatively narrated the revolution unaccompanied by visuals from Tahrir Square. My analysis is supported by interviews made with the directors of these films – Ahmad 'Abd Allah, Ahmad Rashwan, Aytin Amin and Marwan 'Umara.

Chapter 5 focuses on the continuation of new production formats and film styles introduced before the revolution. One of these forms is *āl-āflām āl-mustaqilla* or 'independent films' as classified by critics, curators and a few film-makers. I draw on interviews with independent film-makers who recount the brief history of independent film-making in Egypt. The chapter provides an analysis for films that used independent production modes such as *al-khurug li-l-Nahar*, *'Asham* and *Harag wa-Marag*. These films employed relatively new actors and depended, in many cases, on improvisation to evoke a sense of authenticity to their narratives about marginalization of working classes. The independent wave did not develop into a revolutionary film movement due to the lack of a clear and consistent aesthetic approach. However, I argue that film-makers used different approaches including cinematic realism to represent themes of frustration, ambition and hope. These films represent the revolutionary struggle collectively and resist mainstream film-making styles.

The chapter also examines the contribution of the 2011 Revolution and technological developments to the independent wave. Technological developments have facilitated film production and screening among youth. Young film-makers produced short digital films and used digital screening tools to reach a wider audience. However, these films did not develop a radical film-making style. They remediated traditional short film styles using digital technologies. The conjunction of the revolution and technological developments also allowed a space for self-expression. Artists used various forms including film, music, graffiti and poems to resist and represent resistance. Misr International Films and individuals such as Hala Lutfi, Tamir al-Sa'id and Khalid 'Abd Allah started production and screening initiatives to support independent film-making. It also explains the state's recent practices and attempts to prevent the screenings of independent films for the oppositional ideologies they carry.

The concluding chapter synthesizes the main findings of the research. The relationship of Egyptian cinema and the 2011 Revolution started in 2006 when film-makers used multiple genres to represent dissent and produce political affect. Film-makers continued to engage with politics and during the revolution, they constructed a cultural memory of events and political views through fiction and documentary films. These films historicize the revolutionary moment, which the counter-revolution aims to alter through mainstream media. Economic and political changes during the revolution have extended the crisis of the Egyptian film industry and limited post-revolution films to low-budget popular and independent films. Although film-makers did not develop a post-revolution film movement, they represent the revolutionary struggle in their own styles.

1

Cinema and revolution

Popular culture is a form of political activity, that it involves the expression of political ideas and the inspiration of political actions. (Street, 1997, p. 121)

Films have played a crucial role as agents of revolutions. They have contributed to social change through raising awareness and by resisting dominant ideologies. Films have also played a significant role in documenting revolutions. Fiction and documentary films that represented revolutions have historicized events and developed visual memories of struggles. In *The Political Unconscious*, Fredric Jameson prioritized reading texts politically and adopted a Marxist philosophy to emphasize the political role of texts in historicizing class struggles: 'It is in detecting the traces of that uninterrupted narrative, in resorting to the surface of the text the repressed and buried reality of this fundamental history, that the doctrine of a political unconscious finds its function and its necessity' (Jameson, 1981, p. 20). Thus, films about revolutions have contributed to the histories of nations and complemented previous historical narratives about the oppressed and their oppressors. Revolutions have also impacted film industries and influenced film style and content. Post-revolution governments prioritized the support for film industries, due to the significance of film as a tool of education and propaganda. Post-revolution film movements have contributed to the construction of 'revolutionary values' through innovative film language.

This chapter reviews the conceptualization of the relationship between political conjunctures and cultural production in previous scholarship. It considers the understanding of scholars such as Kellner (1995), Street (1997) and Wheeler (2006) who articulated the dialectical relationship between film and politics, with an emphasis on Hollywood. MacBean (1975) took a more narrowed approach and emphasized the presence of revolutions in film forms as well as content. The chapter then examines studies of film-making during revolutions in the Soviet Union, China, Latin America and Iran to provide a framework for the relationship between cinema (as an art form and as an industry) and revolution. I consider multiple aspects of the relationship between cinema and revolution including the role of film in mobilizing audiences and historicizing uprisings as well as the influence of revolutions on film content and style and film industries.

Scholars have studied several models of film-making during revolutionary times. These studies and cases have shaped our understanding of the relationship between cinema and revolution. I classify these aspects into four main categories: (1) film as a form of political activism, (2) documenting revolutions on film, (3) the impact of revolutions on film industries and (4) the impact of revolutions on film content. Under the first category, film-makers used film as a form of political expression. They conveyed political 'messages', whether explicitly or implicitly, in their film content. These films did not only emerge after revolutions, but they also appeared before and contributed to revolutions through politicizing viewers. Film-makers produced these films, the first type of 'revolutionary films', to represent the oppression and resist the dominant ideologies. The second category considers the role of film in documenting revolutions. These 'revolutionary films' developed the cultural memory of the events of revolutions. One of the best examples of this type of film is *The Battle of Algiers* (Gillo Pontecorvo, 1966), which records the struggle of Algerians against the colonial French government. The third aspect of the relationship focuses on the political economy of film-making during post-revolution periods. Governments have supported and nationalized film industries to support the construction of revolutionary ideologies. The fourth aspect of the relationship suggests the emergence of alternative film movements that oppose mainstream film-making styles.

The framework embraces the examination of the Egyptian cinema during the 2011 Revolution. It provides an understanding of the development of the relationship between cinema and revolution through history, as well as the continuities and discontinuities in relation to the 2011 Egyptian case. Egyptian films have actively engaged with sociopolitical issues during the pre-revolution period and were a significant mode of documentation during the uprising. The development of digital technologies facilitated the production and distribution of independent films since the revolution. The political and economic consequences of the 2011 Revolution exacerbated the crisis of the film industry that started shortly before the revolution. In contrast to other cases, the post-2011 governments did not support the film industry. Also, the rise of a counter-revolution and the lack of a clear and consistent aesthetic framework during the post-revolution period have hindered the development of a 'revolutionary cinema'. Film-makers did not constitute a post-revolution film movement that followed a particular aesthetic approach due to the counter-revolution that grew with the Muslim Brotherhood in 2012 and that prevailed with the 2013 Coup. Instead, film-makers represented struggle through expressing their personal experiences and using their own styles, which in many cases depended on traditional realist approaches.

The context in which Gramsci wrote his prison notes (1929–35) after the defeat of socialist revolutions is similar to the situation in post-revolution Egypt. Gramsci described this post-revolution period as a moment of crisis that 'creates situations which are dangerous in the short run, since the various strata of the population are not all capable of orienting themselves equally swiftly, or of reorganising with the same rhythm' (Gramsci as cited in Forgacs, 2000, p. 218). The political instability in Egypt after the revolution has created a state of confusion among the public. The Censorship of Artistic Works was uncertain of the political directions that it will support (pro- or anti-revolution). In the meantime, film-makers were striving to produce their films, using digital technologies, within a growing anti-revolution environment. However, after the 2013 Coup and the retention of power by the traditional ruling class (as Gramsci explained) a new equilibrium was found. Although the current regime recognizes the events of 2011 as a revolution, it suppresses oppositional voices and allows a counter-revolutionary discourse to dominate mainstream media. The challenges set by the current regime and forced through the Censorship of Artistic Works limit artistic freedom, which Gramsci emphasized as a determinant of a new culture and was evident in cases such as Latin America.

After the Cuban Revolution and the political mobilization of Latin America in the 1960s, films, interviews, discourses and manifestos proposed the integration between cinema and revolution. These texts have coined terms such as 'political cinema' and 'revolutionary films' in different contexts, and thus produced different definitions and generated ongoing debates around them. For example, film directors, such as Solanas and Getino, issued manifestos calling for a 'revolutionary cinema' – a sociopolitical conscious cinema that opposes the traditional/mainstream styles of film-making and adheres to the values of the revolution. Meanwhile, studies that have focused on the relationship between cinema and revolution in particular contexts include Kenez (2001) and Malitsky (2013) in the Soviet Union's case, Pang (2002) and Yau (1997) in the Chinese case, Hernandez (1974) and Balaisis (2010) in the Cuban case and Naficy (2012a) and Behnam (2014) in the Iranian case. These studies have explored changes in the film industries and the texts of the countries they focus on during revolutionary times. Examining the common political and film-making practices among these models will form an understanding of the dynamics of the relationship between cinema and revolution. For example, the intervention of post-revolution governments in regulating and deregulating film-making processes and the use of film as a popular instrument of education or as a tool for propaganda are evident in almost all cases. However, before examining the relationship in different national contexts, it is crucial to explain how cinema and revolution are connected.

One of the fundamental theories that can be used to understand how cinema and revolution cohere together within political and cultural discourses is Stuart Hall's articulation. According to Hall, articulation is,

> the form of the connection that can make a unity of two different elements, under certain conditions. It is a linkage which is not necessary, determined, absolute and essential for all time. You have to ask, under what circumstances can a connection be forged or made? So the so-called 'unity' of a discourse is really the articulation of different, distinct elements which can be rearticulated in different ways because they have no necessary 'belongingness'. The 'unity' which matters is a linkage between that articulated discourse and the social forces with which it can, under certain historical conditions, but need not necessarily, be connected. (in Grossberg, 1986 p. 53)

However, the articulation of cinema and revolution is not a simple connection between two distinct elements but an assemblage of political, social, cultural and technological forces. In the case of the 2011 Revolution, films were used to represent political dissent and document social change. Technological developments facilitated the production and distribution of films and offered wider opportunities for expressing rebellion. On the other hand, post-revolution governments have shown interest in cinema and met film-makers to discuss the crisis of the industry, but they never took any further actions to solve the confronted problems such as piracy. The Censorship of Artistic Works does not issue screening permits for films that criticize police or military officers, and the state encourages the production of propaganda films. Such forces have hindered the production of radical texts that engage with the sociopolitical situation in Egypt after the revolution and construct a new 'revolutionary' culture.

In articulating the relationship between film and politics, scholars have emphasized the reciprocity of both elements. In his work on popular culture and politics, John Street (1997, p. 10) contended: 'Popular culture's ability to produce and articulate feelings can become the basis of an identity, and that identity can be the source of political thought and action.' Street has examined the 'intimate relationship' between politics and popular culture through two perspectives: from popular culture to politics and from politics to popular culture. While the first perspective looked at how we read popular culture politically, the second considered the use of popular culture by politicians (e.g. associating themselves with popular culture icons). For the purpose of this text, I will be focusing on the first perspective, where popular culture holds a political significance. Under this view, Street argued that we engage with politics through producing or consuming popular culture. He noted,

> 'Politics' [...] refers to many dimensions of social interaction – from the mediating role of institutions, to the expression of ideals, to the relationship between interests and identities. Politics extends beyond the formal boundaries of the constitution and the political processes as they are conventionally understood. It extends to the ways in which people see themselves and those around them. And it is this broader view of politics that establish the place in politics occupied by popular culture, making the consumption and production of popular culture a political act. (Street, 1997, p. 42)

Street used a wide variety of examples, from music and films, to demonstrate popular culture as a form of political engagement including pressure to resist or reinforce a certain ideology. He referred to the role of East German rock musicians bringing the Berlin Wall down in 1989 as an example of how popular culture 'can function as an instrument of political change, not merely reflecting reform, but actually prompting it' (Street, 1997, p. 28). Street's suggestion of viewing popular culture texts as political statements, whether in their explicit intentions or interpretations, confirms the political role of cinema. Films, songs and plays that engage with sociopolitical issues, through supporting a position or requesting change, become a part of the political discourse. Street's argument of producing and consuming popular culture as a political act also reinforces the relationship between film and politics. In the Egyptian case, pre-revolution films have raised awareness or reinforced popular discourses about the corruption of Mubarak's regime. Their depiction of scenes of revolt suggested the possibility of overcoming social struggle.

Street (1997) also examined the political management of popular culture. He considered the role of government in regulating and deregulating censorship, subsidies, legislation and copyright protection to constitute cultural policy and 'fashion' culture. Street's argument of how popular culture stimulates political action serves as a strong base for theorizing the relationship between cinema and revolution. His discussions of film as a political statement that motivates action and the political management of film industries explore relevant characteristics of the relationship between cinema and revolution.

During the process of examining the relationship between cinema and politics, it is hard not to acknowledge *The Battle of Algiers* as one of the most significant 'political films'. The film, based on Saadi Yacef's memoir, is a lyrical representation of the oppression and struggle of Algerians for independence against the French colonial government. For Rastegar (2015), the film developed the cultural memory of and recognized colonial struggles. Several studies have considered the film's aesthetics for producing a sharp depiction of struggle and oppression (Mellen, 1973; and Solinas, 1973; and Harrison, 2007). These analyses provided some of the characteristics of political film as a genre. For example, Mellen (1973) analysed Pontecorvo's employment of hand-held camera shots, natural light, black and white film stock and grainy image to produce newsreel style. She argued Eisenstein and Rossellini inspired Pontecorvo's cinematic style, particularly in terms of mise-en-scène and editing techniques. Pontecorvo's focus on the masses rather than a single hero and defining the characters according to their social conditions linked the film to earlier political film styles. However, Mellen criticized the film for not representing the historical events accurately (1973, p. 60). Political criticisms of the film also indicated its favourable characterization of one side of the struggle. The examination of the film's aesthetics and the critique of the 'accuracy' of depiction construct a critical base for analysing 'revolutionary films'. Film theorists and critics examine the perspective, which the narrative is told through, as well as its stylistic approach. The film techniques identified by these studies demonstrate how some theorists understood the styles of 'revolutionary films'.

The articulation of cinema and politics is not limited to the revolutionary context. Ryan and Kellner (1988) and Wheeler (2006) have examined the reciprocal relationship between Hollywood and politics. They focused on the engagement of films with social movements, their celebration of Reaganite ideologies and the support of the governments for the film industry.

In *Camera Politica: The Politics and Ideology of Contemporary Hollywood Film* (1988), Ryan and Kellner argued that popular Hollywood films produced between the 1960s to late 1980s are closely related to political struggles and movements of the time. Many of the late sixties films responded to social movements that were widespread during the Cold War such as civil rights, poverty, feminism, counterculture and militarism, as well as taking positions within the debate over the Vietnam War. Ryan and Kellner argued that these films 'debate significant social issues, and many, operating from a left-liberal perspective, attempt to use the traditional representational formats and conventions for socially critical ends' (p. 2). They used examples such as *The Graduate* (Mike Nichols, 1967), which represented the alienation of younger generations, and *Easy Rider* (Dennis Hopper, 1969) focusing on the hippie counterculture. In addition to the radical and social movements of the 1960s, industrial movements as well influenced the critical and stylistic modes that Hollywood adopted (and characterized European and Third World film-making). The waning of the influence of studio system gave film-makers more control over their projects, which helped them produce more socially conscious films.

Ryan and Kellner's argument demonstrates the engagement of films with social and political matters, which can be represented through traditional and conventional forms and are not limited to radical film-making style. Their argument also reinforces the role of the political economy of film industries in shaping film content and style. The influence of political management of film industries on the content of films produced was also evident in the case of Egyptian cinema. While some fiction and documentary films have represented the 2011 Revolution, only a few films have engaged with the post-revolution conditions due to state censorship pressures.

Kellner expanded on the relationship between media and politics in *Media Culture: Cultural Studies, Identity and Politics between the Modern and the Postmodern* (1995). He suggested that we should read media cultures politically as they are intensely ideological and political. Media cultures depict relations of power through reinforcing or resisting dominant ideologies. Kellner contended that media culture texts take either a progressive or a reactionary position to representations of gender, sexual preference and race. According to Kellner,

> The representations of popular cultural texts constitute the political image through which individuals view the world and interpret political processes, events, and personalities. The politics of representation thus probes the ideological images and figures, as well as discourses, which transcode dominant and competing political positions in a society [...] Moreover, it is through the establishment of a set of representations that a hegemonic political ideology is established, such as New Right conservativism. Representations thus transcode political discourses and in turn mobilize sentiment, affection, perception, and assent toward specific political positions. (1995, p. 60)

To support his argument, Kellner (1995) examined some examples from Hollywood film in relation to political debates and struggles during the presidency of Ronald Reagan. He assumed that Hollywood films celebrated conservative and militarist values, which included limiting the role of government, supporting individual entrepreneurialism and the invasion of Grenada and the bombing of Libya. Kellner's analysis of *Rambo* (1982, 1985 and 1988) and *Top Gun* (Tony Scott, 1986) affirmed that they 'articulate conservative imperialist/militarist fantasies which in turn transcode Reaganite anti-communist and pro-militarist discourses' (1995, p. 74). The analysis of *Rambo* also included the character's success over the 'evil communists', which is portrayed as a 'mythic redemption' (Kellner, 1995, p. 69). Kellner viewed this 'mythic redemption' as similar to Reagan's use of violence in resolving political conflicts. Thus, Kellner suggested that Hollywood films and franchises, such as *Rambo*, *Top Gun*, *Indiana Jones* (1981, 1984, 1989) and *Star Wars* (1977, 1980, 1983), complement the Reaganite conservative ideology and provide propaganda for his militarism. Kellner's work considered the role of films in normalizing and reinforcing political ideologies, which represents one important aspect of the relationship between politics and cinema.

This view can be applied to Egyptian cinema history, which reinforced the ideologies of political leaders such as Nasser's socialism in *Bur-Sa'id* (*Port Said*, 'Izz al-Din Zu-l-Fuqqar, 1956) and *Rudda Qalbi* (*Return My Heart*, 'Izz al-Din Zu-l-Fuqqar, 1957). Even after the 2011 Revolution, a few films have supported the state's view in depicting police officers as heroes including *al-Maslaha* (*The Deal*, Sandra Nash'at, 2012) and *al-Khaliyya* (*The Cell*, Tari' al-'Irian, 2017) or military officers in *Al-Mamar* (*The Passage*, Shirif 'Arafa, 2019). Also, *Gawab I'ti'al* (*An Arrest Letter*, Muhammad Sami, 2017) criminalized Islamists and portrayed them as terrorists to support al-Sisi's regime ideologies. Meanwhile, the censorship body did not issue a shooting permission for films such as *illy Hasal fi-l-Niyl Hiltun* (*The Nile Hilton Incident*, Tari' Salih, 2017), which depicts corrupt police officers before the revolution. The film was shot in Morocco and police officers have prevented audiences from attending the screening of the film in Egypt ('Police Reportedly Prevents Screening', 2017).

Understanding the relationship between politics and cinema requires examining the role of governments in supporting film industries. The degree to which a government supports its film industry reveals the state's economic dependence on the industry as well as the nature of the relationship between state and cinema. Different forms of support include tax breaks, financial subsidies and regulation and deregulation. Hollywood is one of the examples where governmental support helped its transformation from an industry to a global business. US governments understood the significance of Hollywood's contribution to their economy as one of the largest exporters of American products and in terms of income, it adds to the gross domestic product.

In *Hollywood Politics and Society*, Mark Wheeler (2006) examined the political economy of the motion picture industry – production, distribution and exhibition – and the role of American governments in establishing and developing the industry. He related the revival of the industry in the 1970s (after the introduction of television and decline in audiences in the 1950s) to the internal reorganization of the industry as well as the government's reform of the tax system (2006, p. 36). The reintroduction of investment tax credits boosted productions, employment and increased profits. Wheeler (2006, p. 37) also signalled Reagan's opposition to anti-trust rulings and favouring the vertical integration of film production, distribution and exhibition as the reason behind the industry's growth. However, government intervention in the film-making process is limited not just to economic support but also to content regulation. Street (1997) discussed the political control of popular culture through censorship. Advocates and critics of censorship view popular culture as either a 'source of dangerous or anti-socialist ideas and practices' (Street, 1997, p. 32) or a progressive medium respectively. Censorship departments in some countries, including Egypt, allow the release of films based on vague rules such as protecting 'public morals'.

In addition to these studies, which illustrated the nature of the relationship between cinema as a popular form of culture and politics, other scholars narrowed their scope to the connection between cinema and revolutions. James Roy MacBean's *Film and Revolution* emphasized the significance of the revolutionary film form, as well as its content. He focused on Godard's work to demonstrate the use of innovative narrative structures in representing revolutionary themes.

As signalled in the introduction of this chapter, the literature does not provide a clear definition of a 'revolutionary film'. Scholars have used the term to refer to films that clearly resist dominant ideologies (through the film's content or form) and encourage revolutionary action or films that document the events of a revolution. In *Film and Revolution* (1975), James Roy MacBean applied Marxist ideas to Godard's work in order to examine the connection between film and revolution. He did consider not only militant/revolutionary films such as *British Sounds* (Jean Luc Godard, 1969) and *La Hora de los Hornos* (Fernando Solanas and Octavio Getino, 1968) but also films like *La Prise de Pouvoir par Louis XIV* (Roberto Rossellini, 1966) where revolutionary ideologies can be traced.

MacBean argued that such films raise revolutionary consciousness through developing materialist and class analysis of political attitudes. He contended that these films exceed the mere provision of emotional support for revolutions, unlike *The Battle of Algiers* for example.

MacBean (1975) did not classify films into Second (European art) Cinema and Third Cinema, but examined films that engage with revolutionary struggle and liberation to form an understanding of the relationship between film and revolution. From MacBean's perspective, the relationship involves

> not artificially separating content and form, and then privileging content by simply noting that a given film takes sides either for the ruling capitalist bourgeoisie or for the proletarian and Third World forces of liberation. Instead, whether writing on individual films or examining the theoretical foundations of film criticism, I have found it necessary to concentrate on the whole range of relations between film and ideology that are manifested as much in the relations between images and sounds on celluloid as in the filmmaker's (or the theorist's) selection and treatment (or omission) of political themes. (1975, p. 10)

Thus, MacBean did not consider every single film that has engaged with a revolution as a 'revolutionary film'. A film's form is as significant as its content in representing a revolution.

The discourses of the relationship between film and politics (including MacBean's study) have involved, in a way or another, ideology at the centre of their discussions. They may have referred to Althusser's (1971, p. 145) ideas of considering the arts as one of the cultural 'ideological state apparatuses', which function by ideology rather than violence. MacBean (1975) reiterated the ruling class' use of cinema as a popular vehicle to reinforce its ideologies, to accept and adapt to the current circumstances as well as suppress questions of reform. He asserted that revolutionary work must consider deconstructing dominant ideologies and constructing new realities. Similar to the Third Cinema strategy of deconstruction and reconstruction, MacBean confirmed:

> The creation of a revolutionary work of art must be an act of simultaneous destruction and creation; that revolutionary art must destroy the accepted artistic values at the same time that it creates, out of the rubble and debris of the old, new artistic values which will be truly revolutionary because they will challenge the prevailing mystification and repression in art itself. (1975, p. 74)

In this instance, film acts as an agent of a revolution. It serves as a cultural vehicle that disseminates revolutionary values and resists pre-revolution dominant ideologies. In terms of creating new artistic values, MacBean considered Godard's work to be 'revolutionary'. Through MacBean's perspective, Godard has contributed to the revolution in society through making a revolution in art as he did integrate themes of revolution not only in the subject of his films (fighting bourgeois ideologies) but also in the form through freeing them from the traditional narrative structure. Godard sought to raise awareness of the sociopolitical circumstances as well as prompting change and emphasizing people's responsibility. MacBean affirmed Godard's contribution to the revolution through his 1967 films, such as *Weekend* and *La Chinoise*, where he 'revolutionize[s] the way people look at art and [...] stimulate[s] people to look at things in new ways' (1975, p. 59). MacBean also considered films such as *La Hora de los Hornos* (1968) to be a working definition of revolutionary cinema. The film developed a close relationship between film and revolution as it required bringing militant groups together which had never met before. 'Thus, the film inserted itself in the revolutionary praxis, and the revolutionary praxis inserted itself in the film, causing the filmmakers to rethink again and again their conception of the film and their conception of the revolution' (MacBean, 1975, p. 184). According to MacBean, the film's rhythmic cutting and use of quotes that call for liberation (some of the techniques of Third Cinema films) manipulates the audience's feelings and invites them to take the position of the protagonists (1975, p. 188–9).

Therefore, revolutionary values are expressed not only through film texts but also through style. Innovative film-making practices that engage with politics and resist dominant ideologies are fundamental to 'revolutionary films'. In the case of the Egyptian 2011 Revolution, film-makers have utilized digital technologies to produce their films freely, disregarding commercial market constraints. However, feature and short films produced after the revolution did not produce radical film styles. They engaged with political issues but through using film styles that were developed before the revolution. Although a few film-makers have been creative in representing the revolution and expressing themselves, we can only consider their attempts individually due to their various techniques and production modes.

MacBean's discussion on the relationship between content and form of revolutionary films can also be applied to cinemas in different national contexts such as Soviet Union, China, Latin America and Iran. Post-revolution governments in these countries supported film industries to construct 'new' cultures and produce films that celebrate revolutions. Film-makers including Eisenstein and Vertov in the Soviet Union, and Solanas and Getino in Latin America have experimented with film techniques (such as montage), which were considered 'revolutionary' at that time. Examining the relationship of cinema and revolution in national contexts demonstrates the continuities such as the use of film as a form of political expression and documentation of historical moments.

The cases examined hereafter, in this chapter, delineate the relationship of cinema and revolution in national contexts in relation to the Egyptian 2011 Revolution. They demonstrate the historical role of films in resisting dominant ideologies, which continued during the Egyptian 2011 Revolution. The cases inform us that revolutions were followed by film movements, such as Third Cinema, which represented revolutionary struggle through innovative film language including fast and rhythmic editing techniques. Although post-revolution films in Egypt did not employ common aesthetics, they used similar modes of realism cinema such as the non-dramatic narrative structures and long-takes. The cases also reveal the role played by post-revolution governments to support film industries to construct 'revolutionary values' and educate people, which was absent after the Egyptian 2011 Revolution.

The model of the Soviet Revolution demonstrates the role of post-revolution governments in using cinema to disseminate values of revolutions. In contrast to the 2011 Egyptian case, the Soviet post-revolution government industrialized the film industry and encouraged the production of educational films and films that construct a new society. However, post-revolution economic hardships have led to the decrease in the number of audiences in both models – the Soviet Union and the Egyptian cases. Despite the use of cinema as a form of propaganda in the Soviet Union case, film-makers innovated a distinctive film style to represent the revolution and engage with politics.

After the 1917 Revolution, Lenin supported film production as a powerful medium for propaganda. However, film directors and private film studios continued to produce entertainment films through 1918 until film production ceased due to the Civil War and the First World War. Although the Soviet government did not nationalize the film industry during this time, they consistently intervened in cinema, particularly for protection from ideologies that foreign products carried. In addition, film censorship was limited to the anti-Soviet and pornographic films (Kenez, 2001). After the nationalization of the industry in 1919, Soviet leaders sought to educate and unify the masses through newsreels and documentary films. Similar to the case of the post-revolution Cuban cinema, these educational films were easier to produce for their economic efficiency. The nationalization of the Soviet cinema coupled with the New Economic Policy revived the film industry. However, due to the economic hardships in the early 1920s, the government imposed higher taxes on film tickets leading to a lower number of audiences (Kenez, 2001).

The complexity of the relationship between the Soviet Revolution and cinema is also comparable to the Egyptian model. Both revolutions were followed with confusion and chaos on the political and cultural fronts (the Civil War and the First World War in the Soviet case, and the rise of the Muslim Brotherhood and the 2013 Coup d'état in Egypt). These events have led to economic crises that impacted film production. However, in contrast to the Soviet case, Egyptian post-revolution governments did not nationalize or support cinema. al-Sisi's regime has prioritized economic development and 'fighting terrorism', disregarding the role of cinema in achieving these objectives. The case of Soviet cinema demonstrates the impact of revolutions (as well as wars and economic reformations) on film industries, which consequently shapes the type of films produced.

Similar to other revolutions that came later on in histories, such as the 1959 Cuban Revolution, Soviet cinema aimed to complement the 1917 Revolution goals through building a new society and a new man. According to Malitsky, both Cuban and Soviet post-revolution cinemas 'sought to forge a nation by carving a space for a national and international consciousness alongside particular local identities' (2013, p. 4). However, the Soviet Union's involvement in local and international political conflicts delayed its development of a unique film language and style until 1925. Film directors such as Eisenstein, Pudovkin and Vertov shaped the 'Golden Age' of film through their experimentation and acknowledgement of the medium's political significance. During this period, at least one-third of the films produced incorporated the revolution (Kenez, 2001, p. 54). Some of these films, which Kenez (2001) dubbed as 'revolutionary spectacle', focus on symbols rather than characters and stories. The Soviet Union's interest in and support for cinema, during the post-revolutionary period, reinforces the idea of recreating national culture and identity through film. It also correlates with Third Cinema's concept of deconstructing pre-revolution dominant ideologies and constructing a new culture based on values of the revolution. Soviet leaders used cinema as a form of propaganda for socialist values and as an instrument of education.

The current military regime in Egypt has also started to encourage the production of propaganda films that promote its ideologies. Recently, films such as *al-Khaliyya* (*The Cell*, Tari' al-'Irian, 2017), and television series such as *Kalabsh* (*Handcuffs*, Peter Mimi, 2017) and Al-Ikhtyar (The Choice, Peter Mimi, 2020) represent the 'sacrifices' that policemen made to save and secure Egypt from terrorism. These texts support the counter-revolution aim to reinstate the powerful and respectful status police officers had before the revolution. Also *Sirri li-l-Ghaia* (*Extremely Confidential*, Muhammad Sami, in production) is depicting the period from 25 January 2011 to 30 June 2013, including the 'heroic' action of al-Sisi against the Muslim Brotherhood. However, these texts are produced using the generic conventions of action films and feature film stars, whereas the Soviet post-revolution propaganda films (supported by the state) engaged innovatively with political themes and events. The Soviet Union's post-revolution support for cinema was also evident in other cases, such as China. The 'new' film-making style started in China even before the revolution to resist the dominance of American films.

Political film scholarship emphasized the significance of the contribution of films to revolutions. Similar to the Chinese case, a few films have always attempted to resist dominant political ideologies and/or mainstream film-making styles throughout Egypt's history. However, the criticism of political ideologies in Egypt before the 2011 Revolution was not limited to a left-wing film-making movement, as in the case of China. In Egypt, mainstream films used popular genres of drama and comedy to meditate on political corruption, poverty and dictatorship. On the other hand, the different prioritization of film by both post-revolution governments has encouraged the growth of the film industry in the Chinese case and the decline of revolutionary cinema in the 2011 Egyptian case. The realization of the post-revolution Chinese government of the significance of cinema in educating the public was translated to financial support for the film industry. By contrast, a few independent initiatives in Egypt have spread new film-making styles among the public due to the lack of post-revolution governmental support. For example, Wagih al-Laqani started *sinima fi kul makan* (Cinema Everywhere) to screen independent and alternative films in cafes, local clubs and schools, similar to the mobile cinema projects in the Chinese and Cuban cases.

China is among a few countries where a 'revolutionary cinema' started before the revolution. Pang (2002) explored the Chinese left-wing cinema movement that started in 1932 to resist the domination of commercial films popular for their violent and pornographic scenes. The movement, which developed after the Japanese invasion of China in 1931, included films that engaged with issues of class struggle and social criticism – such as *Kuangliu* (*Torrent*, Cheng Bugao, 1933) and *Chengshi zhi ye* (*City Nights*, Fei Mu, 1933). Pang (2002) examined the realist and sentimentalist approaches of the films of this movement. She argued that these stylistic practices were shaped by the complex interactions of the cultural, social and political contexts (Pang, 2002, p. 197). The left-wing cinema movement, and the popularity of its films among mass audiences as Pang (2002) argued, confirms the claim of Solanas and Getino (1970) that revolutionary films come before and contribute to revolutions. Also, the resistance of the movement to mainstream and dominant films confirms our understanding of 'revolutionary cinema' as defying traditional film forms and styles and engaging consciously with sociopolitical issues.

Similar to other post-revolution governments, the Chinese government prioritized the development of the film industry after the revolution. Yau (1997) noted the Chinese film industry's dramatic growth within the first decade of the revolution. The increase in numbers of films, film theatres, audience, studios and film personnel translated the expansion of the film industry. Films produced during this period included feature-length dramas, animation, newsreels and (similar to the Soviet post-revolution cinema) science education shorts addressing issues such as healthcare. Chinese mobile film projections circulated these films to rural and countryside areas. Films about peasants, workers and soldiers replaced Hollywood and Hong Kong films to support 'a socialist reconstruction of the country' (Yau, 1997, p. 694). However, the various backgrounds of the film-makers (such as members of the left-wing film movement and employees of private studios) led to the representation of the revolutionary struggle through different film forms. The strategies varied from traditional Hollywood narrative styles to 'revolutionary realism', which Yau describes as 'classical realism as they [filmmakers] took up traditional dramatic patterns and an organization of space and time according to the principle of verisimilitude' (1997, p. 695). However, before the Cultural Revolution in 1966, many officials who sought reformism started to attack post-revolution films that represented class struggles and labelled them as 'poisonous weeds' (p. 695).

Although the Cultural Revolution has brought forward the political significance of film, as argued by Gabriel (1982, p. 65), it is crucial to recognize the development of the Chinese film industry in the post-revolution period. The film industry, which the Japanese invasion had destroyed, was reconstructed within the ten-year period after the revolution. The post-revolution government's aim of reviving institutions has nurtured the film industry, and its prioritization of cinema has confirmed its understanding of the significance of cinema as an educational instrument. By contrast, Egyptian post-revolution governments have underestimated the power of film in constructing new cultures and supporting economic and social development. Since the 2011 Revolution, Egyptian film-makers have been calling for governmental support and post-revolution governments promised to take serious actions towards supporting the industry, but they never did. Only individual film production or screening initiatives, such as Hassala, Zawya and Cimatheque, have attempted to support independent and alternative films.

Despite the contrast in the support of post-revolution governments for the film industries, the Chinese and Egyptian cases have some commonalities. Both revolutions were preceded by films that represented social criticism; however, the Chinese left-wing movement had a clear approach to film style and aesthetics, whereas pre-revolution Egyptian films that engaged with politics included popular dramas, political satire and independent productions. Also, both revolutions were followed by a variety of styles and approaches to represent revolutionary struggles. Egyptian film-makers have represented their experiences and feelings of hope, ambition and frustration through classical realism styles, which they used shortly before the revolution to resist mainstream film styles.

In contrast to the melodramatic Hollywood film style that dominated Egyptian cinema since its inception, a few film-makers represented social issues through realist approaches such as natural lighting and shooting in real locations. Although many of these stylistic elements are relevant to Third Cinema style, independent films in Egypt do not fit into this category. Third Cinema refers more to a collective film-making style, rather than the individual aesthetic approaches applied by Egyptian film-makers. Third Cinema also encourages revolutionary action, whereas independent films express the feelings of their makers and represent subtle political critiques due to censorship restrictions. However, similar to the conception of Third Cinema by several scholars, independent productions are socially conscious films that engage with themes of class struggle, discrimination and marginalization.

The term 'Third Cinema', coined by Fernando Solanas and Octavio Getino (1970), has given birth to one of the most significant film movements. In the 1960s, the movement aimed to oppose the domination of the Hollywood system and distinguish itself from the European cinéma d'auteur through reconsidering film content, aesthetics and means of production and distribution. In their manifesto *Towards a Third Cinema* (1970), Solanas and Getino defined Third Cinema as

> the cinema that recognizes in that struggle the most gigantic cultural, scientific, and artistic manifestation of our time, the great possibility of constructing a liberated personality with each people as the starting point – in a word, the decolonization of culture. (p. 2)

As film directors, Solanas and Getino advocated the creation of a revolutionary culture to end capitalist society. In doing so, they suggested deconstructing the image created by neo-colonialism and constructing a new image based on a 'living reality'. They denied the role of cinema as pure entertainment (referring to the Hollywood film model) and encouraged diverting it into a more sociopolitically conscious form. Jorge Sanjines, a Bolivian film director, also confirmed Third Cinema's definition as a revolutionary cinema, which 'proposes to create consciousness for liberation' (1970, p. 13). Sanjines reiterated the responsibility of film-makers for exposing the 'truth'. *Towards a Third Cinema* offered a view of cinema as a means of liberation in opposition to imperialism. It proposed a conceptual framework of the relationship between cinema and revolution. More specifically, Solanas and Getino proposed an alternative style and sociopolitical topics that cinema should consider within the context of struggle. Sanjines (1970) also suggested the distinguishing of 'revolutionary cinema' from other mainstream 'commercial films' through a refusal to participate in the star and profit system. He maintained that Third Cinema's main objective is the war against imperialism.

Many other studies have examined Third Cinema and New Latin American cinema through articulating the relationship between cinema and revolution and/or politics (Gabriel, 1982; Willemen, 1989; Wayne, 2001; and Roncallo and Arias-Herrera, 2013). In search for a definition for 'revolutionary films', Gabriel (1982) reviewed the different approaches of Latin American directors. He compared Jorge Sanjines definition of revolutionary films that reveal the truth and call for action, in opposition to Miguel Littin, who considered a 'revolutionary film' requires an audience engagement in order for the action to take place. Unlike the earlier studies, which examined Third Cinema within the Latin American context, Gabriel (1982) analysed sociopolitically engaged films in other Third World countries (such as Senegal, China and India) as well as Latin American countries (such as Cuba). He argued, 'A film's validity as a "revolutionary" film resides in its cultural intonations, historical context and ideological dimensions' (p. 38). Thus 'revolutionary films' have different characteristics in different parts of the world. However, in *Third Cinema in the Third World* (1982) and *Towards a Critical Theory of Third World Films* (1989), Gabriel identified the common aesthetics and ideological approaches of Third Cinema. He indicated the concern of Third Cinema with themes of class, culture, religion, sexism and armed struggle.

Gabriel (1982) also discerned the stylistic approaches of Third Cinema, which opposed traditional cinematic language and aligned with revolutionary aims.

The approaches to style vary from hand-held shots, fast pace editing and a collage of words and photographs in Latin American films to moments of silences, long takes, wide shots and slow pace in African films. The revolutionary aims of Third Cinema were not only limited to content and style but also included alternative means of distribution and exhibition. Film-makers such as Sanjines and Ousmane Sembene, Senegalese film director, took film projectors to screen their films at the countryside villages. However, Willemen (1989) criticized Gabriel's attempt to unify the non-Euro-American aesthetics, claiming that it is problematic in the sense that 'Third Cinema is once more defined in terms of its difference from Euro-American cinema, thus implicitly using Hollywood and its national-industrial rivals as the yardstick against which to measure the other's otherness' (p. 15). Willemen addressed the question of the national (which Gabriel does not consider substantially) as a major factor that distinguished cinemas of the Third World from one another. He argued that social and cultural contexts shape specific (and distinctive) practices.

The various assumptions of scholars about Third Cinema can be extended to encompass the relationship between Egyptian cinema and the 2011 Revolution. Themes of struggle, liberation, deconstructing the dominant pre-revolution ideologies and constructing new values based on the goals of a revolution are major characteristics of cinema within a revolutionary context. To a certain extent, independent films in Egypt have engaged with themes of class, culture, religion and sexism. They refused to be mere entertainment and liberated themselves from commercial market constraints (such as casting new actors instead of film stars). Films such as Hala Lutfi's *al-Khurug li-l-Nahar* (2012) and Ahmad 'Abd Allah's *Farsh wa-Ghata* (2013) used long takes, non-traditional dramatic structures and a few dialogue lines to evoke a sense of authenticity. These films, among others, engaged with themes of social deprivation and marginalization of lower socio-economic classes, but in contrast to the Third Cinema movement, Egyptian film-makers expressed their feelings and views based on a personal basis rather than a collective practice. The representation of the revolutionary struggle in Egyptian films was also limited by censorship restrictions and a sense that the Muslim Brotherhood and the military regime have 'defeated' the revolution.

Solanas and Getino noted the lack of equipment and technical difficulties as obstacles for developing 'revolutionary cinema'. They argued that the accessibility to film-making tools among different social groups helped to encourage the production of guerrilla films. Recent technological developments have facilitated the production of low-budget films that do not conform to the mainstream formulaic genres. However, with the rise of the counter-revolution, censorship has limited the screening opportunities of these films (which also reinforces their – the films and their makers – strong relation to the revolution).

Similar to the perspective of viewing film as a form of expression and resistance, Solanas and Getino's manifesto realized the role of revolutionary films before revolutions. They contended that films do not only come after revolutions, but they also come before and contribute to revolutions. Sanjines (1970) added:

> The work of revolutionary cinema must not limit itself to denouncing, or to appeal for reflection; it must be a summons for action. It must appeal to our peoples' capacity for tears and anger, enthusiasm and faith; we must participate in the effort to remove them from the slumber and confusion to which oppression and misery have submitted them; we must contribute to shaking away the apathy which pseudo-revolutions, failure and frustration have sown in popular consciousness. (p. 14)

This claim allows us to view the role of films in prompting revolutions, besides the well-developed aspect of the impact of revolutions on cinemas (as art and industries). Reinforcing Solanas's and Getino's argument, Gabriel (1982) confirmed that not only liberated countries produce revolutionary films but they can also appear in other colonial countries. For example, Argentina, Bolivia and Senegal have produced 'revolutionary films' without a revolution (Gabriel, 1982). He drew upon some examples such as 'New Wave' or 'Left Cinema' in India; 'Cinema al-Shabab' in the Arab world; 'Parallel Cinema' in Sri Lanka; and 'Engaged Cinema' in Senegal. Disregarding the Hollywood model, these cinemas aimed to present sociopolitical conscious films that highlight developing world struggles. Before the 2011 Revolution, films in Egypt revealed images of protests and marches as potential consequences of injustice.

Third Cinema also emphasized the role of films in documenting revolutions as an integral part of cultural memory. Documenting revolutions on film served as a historical evidence of a group of people's struggle against an oppressor. Solanas and Getino (1970) suggested that documentary films are the basis of revolutionary cinema. They noted, 'Every image that documents, bears witness to, refutes or deepens the truth of a situation is something more than a film image or purely artistic fact; it becomes something which the System finds indigestible' (Solanas and Getino, 1970, p. 6). However, they argued that it is not sufficient for revolutionary films to merely document events but to intervene and provide rectification.

In his recent study, Kamran Rastegar (2015) accentuated the role of cinema in contributing to the cultural memory in relation to social conflicts. Rastegar demonstrated his argument with a specific focus on the Middle East. Although Rastegar questioned the cinema's ability to continue to develop cultural memory along with the development of new media and digital technology, he mentioned Jihan Nujaim's *al-Midan* (*The Square*, 2013) as one of the films that constructed the memory of the Egyptian 2011 Revolution. Rastegar's argument of cinema's contribution to cultural memory is relevant to other post-revolution narrative and documentary films that represented the 2011 Revolution such as *al-Shitaa illy Fat* (*The Winter of Discontent*, Ibrahim al-Battut, 2012) and *al-Tahrir 2011: al-Taiyyib, wa-l-Sharis, wa-l-Siyasi* (*Tahrir 2011: The Good, The Bad, and The Politician*, Tamir 'Izzat, Aytin Amin and 'Amr Salama, 2011). These films have contributed to the construction of a visual memory of the struggle experiences during events of the Egyptian 2011 Revolution. They engaged with digital media, within their texts and/or to retrieve footage, in their narratives about the revolution. However, these films have used traditional forms and styles of representing the revolution. Only a few films such as *Farsh wa-Ghata* (*Rags and Tatters*, Ahmad 'Abd Allah, 2013) and *Crop* (Johanna Domke and Marwan 'Umara, 2013) have creatively represented the revolution without showing images of protests and demonstrations.

The case of the Egyptian cinema and the 2011 Revolution is comparable to the characteristics of Third Cinema on several levels. Independent productions resisted popular film-making styles through using alternative film language. They are socially conscious films, however, in the Egyptian case; independent films are not popular among audiences. They participate in international film festivals and attract a minority of intellectuals and cinephiles locally. Similar to Solanas and Getino's argument of the contribution of films to revolutions, Egyptian films have actively participated in the pre-2011 Revolution political dissent. Film-makers have represented themes of social injustice and political oppression in mainstream and independent films since 2006. These films did not mobilize the audience, as Sanjines (1970) suggested, but they represented dissent and anger and evoked feelings of hope. A few fiction and some documentary films have also represented the 2011 Revolution, where they historicize the events of the revolution and construct an audio-visual memory of the uprising through different perspectives. However, the anti-revolutionary attitude of post-revolution governments did not encourage the production of films about the revolution or its values.

Similar to the Soviet and Chinese cases, the Cuban model affirms the role of post-revolution governments in supporting film industries. The financial and regulatory support that governments provide demonstrates their recognition of film power in creating new cultures. In the Egyptian case, the discontinuation of support of post-revolution governments for the film industry was due to the underestimation of the significance of cinema. Also, the post-revolution political instability and the rise of the counter-revolution have discouraged the support for a revolutionary cinema. Only a few film-makers and curators have initiated projects to support and screen alternative films. These independent initiatives aim to spread a new film culture, which was enabled through governmental support and nationalization in other cases such as the Cuban Revolution.

The Cuban 1959 Revolution was the main inspiration for the political mobilization in Latin America during the 1960s and the Third Cinema movement. In addition to its influence on the New Latin American cinema, the Cuban Revolution had a distinct impact on Cuban cinema in particular. Hernandez (1974) offered an analysis of the post-revolutionary Cuban cinema's role in achieving the revolution's goals of transforming the society and 'building a new man' (p. 360). He examined the Cuban pre-revolution cinema's status in order to determine the impact of the revolution on the industrial factors (production, distribution and training of film-makers) and the content and form of narrative and documentary films. Hernandez referred to the nationalization of the film industry and the formation of the ICAIC foundation after the revolution as the main reasons behind the dramatic increase in film production. In their attempt to use cinema in achieving revolutionary goals, ICAIC nationalized the film industry in 1959 to mobilize and educate the masses as well as 'to improve the quality level of Cuban films and to further the appreciation of good cinema among the masses, whose taste had been manipulated and debased by the profit-oriented pre-revolutionary industry' (Hernandez, 1974, p. 365). The nationalization of private organizations expanded the film industry's assets including film equipment and personnel. In addition, nationalizing film theatres resolved a pre-revolution issue of foreign control on distribution. ICAIC also had an imperative role in training and developing Cuban film-makers. ICAIC's actions represent the interest of the Cuban revolutionary government in cinema. It develops the understanding of the relationship between cinema and revolution through recognizing the support of governments for film industries during post-revolution periods.

The Cuban Revolution also had a direct impact on film form and content. Hernandez (1974) noted the change in genre from musicals and American detective and romantic melodramas during the pre-revolutionary period to educational documentaries after the revolution. A few feature films engaged more with themes of revolution and political struggle. The reasons behind the increased focus on documentary productions after the revolution were not limited to the politics of mass mobilization and education. Technical reasons, such as the inexpensive production requirements, prompted the proliferation of documentaries. On the other hand, the revolution instigated movements, which helped to expand film culture. Mobile projection units helped to extend film education activities to the countryside and mountainous regions (Hernandez, 1974; and Balaisis, 2010). Universities started integrating film education as part of their curriculum. Further film activities included the initiation of 'Cinematheque' to show and discuss classics and contemporary art films. Most of these movements showed documentary films to raise awareness and educate people. The revolutionary goal of 'improving the audience taste' and incorporating the marginalized rural Cubans were the main motivators behind the change in film form and content and initiation of movements.

The use of film to achieve revolutionary goals develops our understanding of the intimate relationship of cinema and revolution. The impact of revolutions on film form and content as well as the governmental efforts to support expanding film industries and culture are some of the characteristics of this relationship. The nationalization of the Cuban film industry and the formation of the ICAIC supported the cultural transformation of society and the production of socially conscious films. By contrast, post-revolution governments in Egypt disregarded the crisis of the film industry and underestimated the power of cinema to propagate the values of the revolution or their political ideologies.

The previous cases have demonstrated that post-revolution governments used cinema to disseminate their ideologies. Similarly, in the case of the Iranian 1979 Revolution – where cinema opposed the beliefs of Mullahs and clerics – Ayatollah Khomeini supported film to spread Islamic ideologies. In response, a collective of film-makers used a distinctive style and challenged the Islamic regime. Despite the different ideologies of the Islamic and military regimes in Iran and Egypt during the post-revolution periods, groups of film-makers have expressed resistance through film texts and language in both countries. In Egypt, a few films have resisted dominant political and social ideologies fed through mainstream media. They represented social oppression through the internal conflicts and struggles of their characters. In both cases, the Iranian and the Egyptian, post-revolution governments have marginalized these films for their oppositional ideologies. The Egyptian 2011 and Iranian 1979 cases have also demonstrated the role of film and technologies to document the revolutions. The filming of events and their utilization in documentary and fiction films that historicize revolutionary struggles were evident in both cases.

In the 1970s, a new wave of Iranian cinema was formed as a response to the commercial Iranian cinema, which critics often denounced for its poor quality and repetition of popular themes. The new-wave film-makers including Reza Allamehzadeh, Hushang Baharlu, Hajir Dariush, Bahman Farmanara, Ali Hatami, Abbas Kiarostami, Masud Kimiai, Dariush Mehrjui and Kamran Shirdel focused on the originality of their screenplays as well as 'realistic' development for their characters (Naficy, 2011, p. 327). These film-makers collaborated with secular and leftist writers and introduced a new generation of theatre actors, which Naficy (2011, p. 335–6) contends have added to the realistic quality of these films. The pre-revolution new-wave films engaged with issues of modernity, patriarchy, religion, fear of the totalitarian state, foreign powers and internal enemies. For example, one of the earliest films of the new wave Darius Mehrjui's *The Cow* (1969) exposed rural impoverishment. Iranian film scholars, such as Naficy (2011) and Mirbakhtyar (2006), have analysed the film for its lead in challenging the aesthetics of commercial films. According to Naficy (2011), the film's focus on rural locations countered the urbanization of Iranian mainstream films. Also the film's portrayal of villagers, in contrast to the popular tough-guy genre, was considered a 'return to the authentic bedrock of Iranian society and psychology' (p. 339). Although the censorship department banned the film, it was smuggled and screened in the Venice Film Festival. The film's success caused the censorship to lift the ban and led to the support of the government to new-wave films.

After the 1979 Revolution in Iran, Ayatollah Khomeini emphasized the educational role of film. The Islamic state understood the role of cinema as a powerful propaganda tool. It sought to legitimize cinema since Mullahs viewed it as a 'godless symbol' before the revolution, which led to the burning down of several film theatres. Before the revolution, anti-cinema clerics adopted a media effects approach and argued that cinema interpellated individuals with its 'corrupt' ideologies. However, Khomeini's regime banned most of the foreign films, which opposed 'Islamicate values', and constructed an 'Islamicate Cinema' (Naficy, 2012a).[1] The process of Islamicizing cinema included its purification from all the pre-revolutionary unwanted morals and replacing them with 'true' Islamic ideologies. The purification process included changing the name of some film theatres from Western to Islamic or revolutionary names. Pre-revolution films and posters were re-edited to comply with the 'Islamicate values'. The Ministry of Culture and Islamic Guidance accepted or rejected films based on the degree of their conformity to Islamic beliefs. While the Islamic regime negotiated the practices of film-making with some film-makers, they prosecuted, executed and exiled many film-makers for their connection with the pre-revolution government and accused them of other moral charges. Khomeini's regime plan to 'cleanse' pre-revolutionary dominant ideologies through building a new Islamicate culture confirms the post-revolution process of deconstruction and reconstruction evident in previous experiences. It also reaffirms the use of post-revolution governments of film as an instrument for propaganda and the interference in the process of film-making to assure its compliance with ideologies of revolutions.

An independent film-making movement,[2] led by Abbas Kiarostami and consisting of a collective of film-makers, challenged the regime. The new-wave movement, which engaged with sociopolitical issues through a distinctive film style before the revolution, continued after the revolution (Behnam, 2014).[3] The independent films during the pre-revolution period focused on themes of social injustices and rebelled against oppression. Behnam (2014) argues that films such as *Tangna* (*Impasse*, Amir Naderi, 1973) anticipated the 1979 revolution through revealing a narrative about revenge. Many of these films, including *The Cow* (1969), were screened in public cinemas as they were deemed suitable for the revolutionary time. Post-revolution independent films, including art-house and experimental films, criticized Iran's social structure and the post-Iraq war circumstances and questioned Islamic laws such as the banning of suicide and the existence of the afterlife. Their film style, a mix between documentary and fiction, succeeded sometimes in circumventing censorship. In order to limit the threat of oppositional ideologies that these films carry, the government classified them as 'underground'. This term 'embodies both the subversive function of this alternative film culture and its reactionary/artistic function against the censorship and restrictions in contemporary Iran' (Behnam, 2014, p. 33). Naficy (2012b, p. 176) dubs these films as 'postal' as they are considered a post-Islamicate, ethical and spiritual cinema, but also 'in the way some films reject the exclusionary high culture, authoritarian certainties, and politicised aesthetics of modernism for the more nuanced, open, ambiguous, self-reflexive, self-inscriptional, intertextual, pluralist, playful, and humanist ethics and aesthetics of postmodernism'.

Post-revolution independent films confirm the concept of 'liberating cinema' after revolutions. As in other similar models, alternative film movements originated to challenge economic and ideological/censorship constraints. These movements either criticize post-revolution regimes through depicting social inequalities and oppression, as in Iran, or support constructing a new national identity, such as Third Cinema. In Egypt, a few films used an independent style to represent social and political critiques of contemporary Egypt. Similar to the Iranian case, mainstream media and some film-makers in Egypt marginalized alternative film-making by referring to it as 'independent'. The connotations associated with this term include the complexity of the narrative and addressing intellectuals and film festivals rather than the mass audience.

In *A Social History of Iranian Cinema*, Naficy (2012a) examines films that documented the revolution. He describes professional film-makers, such as Kamran Shirdel, and amateurs filming of revolutionary moments and events (on 16 mm and Super 8 cameras). These events included the Shah's departure and Khomeini's arrival. Naficy (2012a) also notes the exhibition of this unedited footage in spaces such as hospitals, mosques and streets. Some of this footage was assembled in what Naficy (2012a) calls compilation films. Unlike historical documentaries, compilation films did not situate the events within a historical context. Shahdust edited some footage into the feature-length film *The Pulse of History* (*Tapesh-e Tarikh*, 1980). Film-makers exchanged footage with one another of events that they needed for their films. Other film-makers used the demonstrations within their fiction films. Naficy explains how Haritash filmed actors in anti-Shah demonstrations and used them in his movies. After the revolution, the government requested that it hold of all the archival footage of the revolution. While some film-makers turned in their footage, others sent it out of the country. The experience of documenting the Iranian Revolution has many similarities to the documentation of the Egyptian 2011 Revolution. Film-makers and amateurs used technology (digital and mobile cameras in the Egyptian case) to film the protests and demonstrations, utilized footage in short and feature documentary and fiction films and exhibited these films in public spaces in both revolutions. In the case of the 2011 Revolution, the internet served as an archival platform, where the footage is more widely accessible to film-makers and audiences.

Similar to post-revolution governments in other cases, Khomeini used cinema to disseminate his regime's (Islamic) ideologies. The lack of dominant political ideologies, during Egypt's post-revolution period (from 2011 to 2013), and the unclear political attitudes towards the 2011 Revolution (due to the rise of a counter-revolution) discouraged the production of a revolutionary cinema. However, a few film-makers represented their feelings of frustration in independently produced films. Post-revolution governments, in Iran and

Egypt, marginalized these films through labelling them as 'underground' or 'independent'. The similarities also include the strategies of film-makers to film and integrate parts of the revolutions in their fiction and documentary films. In the case of the 2011 Egyptian Revolution, digital technologies have decentralized film-making and allowed the production of a few indigenous films.

* * *

Political film scholarship has examined the relationship of revolution and cinema through four main aspects. The first one views film as a form of political activism. Film-makers use film as a form of political statement to express the public's dissent. They represent themes of oppression and colonialism and resist dominant ideologies. In some cases, such as the Egyptian 2011 Revolution, these films are produced before, and contribute to, revolutions. Studies have also considered the significant role of film in documenting and historicizing revolutions. These films develop cultural memories of the experienced struggle. Technological advancements helped to develop these films as evident in the case of Iran. Documentaries about the Egyptian 2011 Revolution used footage of events that people filmed with their digital and mobile cameras. Technology has also enabled a number of amateur films about the revolution, where young film-makers expressed their feelings towards the uprising.

Periods of economic development/deterioration have usually followed revolutions and in some cases civil wars and chaos such as the Soviet Union case. These consequences had a direct impact on film industries and consequently have shaped film texts and styles. In the case of the 2011 Egyptian Revolution, elements of insecurity, chaos leading to curfews and economic deterioration created a film production crisis. Political management or governmental interference in the process of film-making is another aspect of the impact of revolutions on film industries. The different understanding of the post-revolution regimes of the role of film in educating and unifying the masses has led them to regulate or deregulate film industries accordingly. In most of the studied cases, governments had a significant role in supporting and/or controlling film industries. This support came in several forms, such as nationalizing and denationalizing the industry, providing financial support (subsidies and tax breaks) and generating legislations (copyright protections). Censorship departments, representing the post-revolution governments, confirmed the compliance of film industry and film-makers to the ruling ideologies.

Following revolutions, film-makers have 'revolutionized' traditional film-making techniques through initiating film movements and new film waves. These films addressed sociopolitical topics and called for a conscious cinema. In most of the cases, these film movements opposed mainstream film-making styles. They invented an alternative film language and style, sometimes perceived as 'realistic', and used new actors to defy the star system. These films aimed to deconstruct pre-revolutionary dominant ideologies and construct a new culture based on the values of revolutions. Films utilized these aesthetics to celebrate revolutions or, such as in Iran, to resist ideologies of post-revolution regimes. In the latter cases, governments attempted to suppress new film movements and film-makers by marginalizing them. In addition, revolutions escalated film activities such as showing and discussing art-house films in cultural centres and educational films in suburbs. Film enthusiasts carried out these movements in the case of the absence of governments from cultural activities.

The four dimensions of the relationship outlined in this chapter were evident throughout the history of Egyptian cinema. Political events and regimes have had a direct impact on the Egyptian film industries and influenced film content. Egyptian film-makers have gradually used film to voice discontent and resist dominant ideologies. Film has been a persistent mode of documentation for the main social and political phases in Egyptian history. Fiction and documentary films were consistent with historicizing political events such as the 1952 Coup and the 1973 War. The Egyptian film industry, which was dominated by foreigners during the colonial period then nationalized under the rule of Gamal Abdel Nasser, encouraged a shift in production from musical and comedy films to more sociopolitical conscious films. Egyptian cinema has also witnessed multiple 'new' film waves that resisted the (Hollywood style) popular productions of the time and approached more realistic representations of society. As a result, many Egyptian film scholars have periodized the history of Egyptian cinema according to the political periods, due to the distinguishable characteristics of cinema during each of the periods.

The aspects of the relationship of film and revolution also apply to the 2011 Egyptian context. Films have contributed to the pre-revolution political activism through representing the public's anger and dissent. Film was also a significant form of historicizing events of the 2011 Revolution in documentary and fiction narratives. Film-makers selected from the hundreds of hours of footage available, enabled by digital technologies, to produce films about the revolution.

The repercussions of the 2011 Revolution and the lack of state support have impacted the political economy of the film industry and limited production to low-budget popular and independent films. Meanwhile, young film-makers have used digital technologies and represented struggle through creative and realist approaches. These practices continue the entanglement of politics and Egyptian cinema, which has existed since its inception.

2

The crisis of the Egyptian film industry

The structure of the Egyptian film industry has always had a role in shaping the content and style of films produced. In order to examine the engagement of films with the 2011 Revolution, it is important to understand their production context, which includes the transformation of production, distribution and exhibition factors during the time of social change. Since the late 1990s, an oligopoly of production and distribution companies – al-'Arabiya, al-Aukhwa al-Mutahadiyn and al-Nasr wa-l-Masa wa-Auskar – has dominated the Egyptian film industry. They produced and distributed films that were funded by Gulf television networks. For example, Rotana – a television network owned by the Saudi al-Waliyd bin Talal – invested at least USD 20 million annually, almost 50 per cent of the total annual expenditure for Egyptian films (M. Hifzi, interview, 25 January 2015). But the 2008 global financial recession, which started with the subprime mortgage market in the United States and developed into an international banking crisis, severely affected the funding of Egyptian cinema. As multinational companies cut their advertising spending, the Gulf television channels reduced their purchase of new films. The inflation of costs for equipment, crew salaries and payments for stars in a relatively small national film market also hindered the volume of production. In 2009, production rates decreased by about 30 per cent; most of the films completed had been initiated before the financial crisis, and very few new projects were started (M. Hifzi, interview, 25 January 2015). Films did not profit from their theatrical release, due to the insufficient number of film screens and the relatively expensive price of tickets. Film piracy through the internet and television channels that broadcast films (often within a week of their theatrical release) has also drastically reduced film revenues. The government has been ineffective in preventing piracy, even when a few producers identified the culprits (CBC Egypt, 2014b).

Since the 2011 Revolution, Egypt's economy has gradually deteriorated. In *Crisis and Class War in Egypt*, McMahon (2017, p. 27) argues that the events that took place in Egypt in 2011 were an 'expression of the ongoing crisis of global neoliberal capitalist relations and processes'. McMahon contends that the crisis, in its broader sense (politically and economically), continues to take place even after the revolution and will impact Egyptian workers. Moreover, political instability represented in recurrent protests, curfews, insecurity and terroristic attacks had a direct impact on sectors such as tourism – one of the main sources of Egypt's income. The withdrawal of several major investments and continuous inflation discontinued the improvement of economic indicators that started slightly before the revolution. The repercussions of the 2011 Revolution have also impacted the film industry and extended the decline in film production rates. Multiple curfews and the lack of security prevented audiences from moviegoing and exacerbated the political economy of the film industry leading to a crisis in film production. Thus, many film-makers shifted to the more secure production of television series for private networks such as CBC (Capital Broadcast Center) and MBC leading to the production of a limited number of mostly low-budget films. These films depend on the high seasons of cinemagoing or a circulation in international film festivals and/or online release.

In the meantime, the state has been inconsistent in its intervention and support for cinema. Governments have focused on issues of security and economic development disregarding the role of cinema in such processes. The Censorship of Artistic Works has also reflected the 2011 political crisis, where a state of ideological confusion has led to random acceptance and rejection of films. These forces have led to the domination of formulaic productions that consist of a popular song, a belly dancer and a set of poorly produced action and comedy scenes. Film distributors released these popular films only during high seasons such as 'id al-Fitr and 'id al-Adhā. However, within the economic, political and social crises, some film-makers managed to engage with sociopolitical themes and document narratives of the revolution. They used several strategies including setting films in one primary location such as a villa in *Villa 69* (Aytin Amin, 2013), a factory in *Fatat al-Masna'* (*The Factory Girl*, Muhammad Khan, 2014), a public school in *Lamu'akhza* (*Excuse My French*, 'Amr Salama, 2014) and a police van in *Ishtibak* (*Clash*, Muhammad Diab, 2016). Also, digital technologies enabled hours of footage of the revolution, which facilitated the production and screening of a number of documentaries and low-budget films.

This chapter examines the crisis of the Egyptian film industry since 2008, drawing on research interviews with film producers and directors conducted in Cairo in December 2014, January 2015 and January 2016. Some of these film-makers have drawn attention to the industry's problems and helped to articulate them as a crisis by using the media to address the public, ministerial committees and President al-Sisi himself to encourage state support. Due to the 2008 global financial crisis and declining advertising revenues, television channels retreated from buying new films. As well, film-makers have emphasized that piracy through other television channels contributed to further decline after the 2011 Revolution. The many curfews and lack of security during the political upheaval severely impacted filmgoing. Film censorship has been unpredictable and susceptible to the idiosyncrasies of government organizations. In articulating what they called a crisis, mainstream film producers foregrounded the lack of support from post-revolution governments. However, they disregarded fundamental issues that contribute to the crisis such as the oligopoly of producers, distributors and exhibitors, which limit opportunities for innovative and experimental film styles. The oligopoly has reduced production in a risky marketplace and enabled low-budget popular films after the revolution.

This chapter draws upon interviews with film industry personnel. These interviewees represent different sectors of the industry, as well as a range of film production modes and aesthetics. Due to the scarcity of public documents and industry statistics, I depend to some extent on the interviewees as trusted sources. These film-makers represent a wide segment of the industry, but inevitably, they view the issues through their specific interests and position in the industry. Film producers articulate the lack of state support as the main reason for the crisis. They emphasize the role of the state in supporting the industry to fight piracy and facilitating the government-related procedures of film-making. On the other hand, film-makers associated with independent film-making style have focused on the oligopoly of production, distribution and exhibition, which marginalizes their films. They found the decline in producing mainstream films a logical consequence of the incurred losses after the revolution. The dramatic shift to television production supports the argument of these independent film-makers that mainstream film producers are pure investors who seek profits rather than creating art.

The interview sample includes film producers from major and independent companies who have represented the industry in government organizations and on television. Muhammad al-'Adl is one of the owners of al-'Adl Group, a significant production house established in 1997 that introduced many current stars, such as Muhammad Hiniydi and Ahmad al-Sa'a. Producer-director Shirif Mandur owns Film House Egypt, which has produced films since 2002, including *'In Shams* (*Eye of the Sun*, 2008) and *Hiliaupulis* (*Heliopolis*, 2009), two low-budget releases that explored the decline in their respective Cairo neighbourhoods using digital cameras and new actors. Mandur is also Vice President of the Chamber of Film Industry, an NGO for producers and distributors. He is also a member of two government organizations, the National Centre for Cinema and the Supreme Council of Culture. Producer and screenwriter Muhammad Hifzi is the owner of Film Clinic, a production company founded in 2006, a board member of the Chamber of Film Industry and known for his support for 'independent film-making'. He co-produced *Mikrufun* (*Microphone*, 2011), which profiled the underground music scene in Egypt, and *Ishtibak*, which depicts detainees from many backgrounds in the back of a police van. Hifzi is currently the president of the Cairo International Film Festival. Ahmad 'Abd Allah directed *Hiliaupulis*, *Mikrufun* and *Farsh wa-Ghata* (*Rags and Tatters*, 2013). al-'Adl, Mandur and Hifzi were involved in consultations with the ministerial committee formed in 2013 to address the industry crisis.

Hisham Suliman, owner of Hama Productions, produced two commercially successful comedy films before the revolution – *Itsh Dabbur* (*H Dabbur*, Ahmad al-Gindi, 2008), about a rich young man who sees how the 'other half' lives, and *Tiyr Inta* (*It's Time to Go*, Ahmad al-Gindi, 2009), a version of the *Bedazzled* films (1969 and 2000). Suliman was the chairman of the DMC television network.

Muhammad Samir is a young producer, director and editor who established Daydream Art Production in 2007 to support the growing independent cinema wave. Although most of his productions are limited to short films and documentaries, he produced the feature *Fatat al-Masna'* through raising local and international funds for this story that explored the subjugation of women. Veteran director Khan was a major figure in the new cinema wave of the 1980s, and this film went on to win international awards.

Producer-director Hala Lutfi made her first independent feature *al-khurug li-l-Nahar* (*Coming Forth by Day*, 2012) with new actors (rather than stars) after several years of funding it through personal savings and small grants. Her Hassala Films (founded in 2011) supports young film-makers with their first features. Lutfi's interview highlighted the marginalization of independent film-makers by the state, mainstream producers and distributors.[1] Hala Galal is also a film director and founder of SEMAT – the first Egyptian institution established in 2001 to support independent productions. Hala Galal explained the origins of independent productions in Egypt and their relation to the mainstream production.

Ahmad 'Abd Allah narrated his experience of directing the near-silent film *Farsh wa-Ghata* after the revolution. Aytin Amin, director of *Villa 69* (2013), confirmed the retreat of major film producers after the revolution and their partial return in 2013. Ahmad Rashwan, director of *Basra* (2008) and *Mawlud fi Khamsa wa-'Ishriyn Yanayir* (*Born on the 25th of January*, 2011), emphasized the oligopoly that dominates the industry as well as the lack of state support. The co-director of *Crop* (2013), Marwan 'Umara, discussed the proliferation of independent films as a result of the revolution and the internet. These filmmakers discussed the oligopoly dominating the film industry and the conflict of interest in the Chamber of Film Industry.[2]

Director Samih 'Abd al-'Aziz made the commercially successful films *Kabarih* (*Cabaret*, 2008), *al-Farah* (*The Wedding*, 2009) and *al-Lila al-Kibira* (*The Big Night*, 2015), each of which is an ensemble drama set in one night in a particular Cairo neighbourhood. Egypt's former prime minister Ibrahim Mahlab ordered the withdrawal of 'Abd al-'Aziz's *Halawit Ruwh* (*Ruwh's Beauty*, 2014) due to its apparent sexual content.

This chapter examines the main aspects of the film industry crisis. Firstly, I shed light on the shifts in the mediascape in relation to the economic and political changes during the 2011 Revolution period. That time witnessed the inception of several private television networks such as CBC and al-Nahar. The investment of these channels in *musalsalāt ramadān* (television series broadcasted during the Holy month of Ramadan) supported the cinematization of television productions. I also explain how mainstream media have reported and addressed the problems of the industry as a crisis. The chapter describes the structure of the Egyptian film industry (production, distribution and exhibition) since the late 1990s. It outlines problems related to theatrical exhibition and television, including the oligopoly of production, distribution and exhibition and the number, location and outdated technologies of film theatres. The emphasis then shifts to the impact of the 2011 Revolution on the crisis of the industry. I explain how the repercussions of the uprising such as curfews and insecurity had a direct impact on filmgoing and film production costs. Filmmakers shifted to television production, as it has been a safer medium since the revolution. The chapter uncovers the inconsistent role of the state in dealing with issues of the industry such as piracy. The state's intervention has been mainly limited to censorship, and film-makers are calling for state support. It ends on a note of a limited recovery from the crisis, which some film-makers claim is now taking place.

Egyptian cinema scholarship has tended to focus on film texts, exploring issues of national cinema, different styles of film-making, cinema and politics, gender and class (Gordon, 2001; Shafik, 2007b; Armbrust, 2011; and Armes,

2015). Relatively few scholars have concentrated on political economy, but none has yet examined the situation in the last decade (Gaffney, 1987; and Flibbert, 2007). Since the late 1990s, television channels determined the volume of film production in Egypt. During that time, film-makers did not emphasize the issue of insufficient number and outdated technologies of film screens due to the stability of their major revenue source – television networks. Unlike cinema since the January 2011 Revolution, television has flourished with new channels such as CBC and al-Nahar launched in 2011 and DMC in 2017. With many talk shows that cover current affairs, Marwan Kraidy argues that television channels have received the 'unexpected ratings boosters' of turbulent political events (2014, p. 18). The increasing interest of audiences in politics encouraged television channels to produce more talk shows and buy fewer films. Film producer Shirif Mandur explains,

> A talk show fills up four hours of the airing time each day, unlike films, which are costly and only fills a 90 minutes slot. Every channel now is based on one or two talk shows, subsequently, they are less interested in buying films, and thus film production decreased. (S. Mandur, interview, 25 January 2015)

After the revolution, television channels continued to invest in television series during the Holy month of Ramadan – when advertisers have been directing most of their spending (Kraidy and Khalil, 2009, p. 116).[3] Due to the few films in production, many film-makers shifted to television production. They used digital cameras, such as Alexa, and post-production techniques, including colour grading, to develop the image quality of television series. They also focused on art direction and fashion styling, which were among the competitive advantages of, the very popular in Egypt, Turkish series. The cinematization of television series has increased the demand for Egyptian television productions and maintained the competition with Syrian and Turkish series. The Saudi-owned and Dubai-based television network MBC launched a free-to-air channel (MBC Masr) with a particular focus on Egyptian matters. MBC Masr has funded the most expensive television productions such as 'Adil Imam's television series and Ramiz Galal's celebrities' prank shows. The interest of Saudi channels, such as MBC, in Egyptian media is due to the available market opportunities, and their investment supports the political alliances between both countries.

Kraidy (2014) explored shifts within the production of Egyptian media during the uprising due to security issues and political conflicts. He described how the deteriorating security situation in 2013 led to the delay of pop star albums by 'Amr Diab and Shirin 'Abd al-Wahab. Kraidy (2014) also explained the increase of drama series production in Egypt since the revolution because of the security conditions in Syria, which was leading the production of drama in the Arab world before the revolution. Moreover, Kraidy (2014, p. 19) noted the Egyptian-Turkish dispute over the 2013 military coup leading to the boycott of the popular Turkish drama series by Egyptian television channels.[4] The boycott, and the crisis of film production, has encouraged film-makers to develop the image and narrative qualities of local television productions. The cinematization of television drama included an engagement with sociopolitical topics, which were limited to films before the revolution. Kraidy (2014) explained how television series in Ramadan 2013 (during the rule of the Muslim Brotherhood) criticized clerics. They discussed 'boldest-yet themes and scenes of featuring sexuality, addiction, drugs, rape, the marriage of minors, and radicalism' (Kraidy, 2014, p. 18). The growth of television drama has in return impacted film production, so now there is only a limited time for shooting films during the year (after the Holy month of Ramadan) due to the busy schedules of casts, crews and equipment.

Since 2013, Egyptian mainstream media have devoted special attention to these aspects of the crisis. The private TV channel CBC, ON E and the magazine *Egypt Today* have referred repeatedly to *āzmit sināʿat āl-sīnimā āl-Masrya* (the Egyptian film industry crisis). Film-makers have appeared on many live programmes to discuss the crisis and used these forums to call for government support. In October 2013, the evening talk shows *al-Sada al-Muhtaramun* (ON E) and *Bath Mubashir* (CBC) interviewed film producer Gabi Khuwri in episodes titled 'Crisis of the Egyptian Film Industry' (CBC Egypt, 2013b; ON E, 2013c). They discussed piracy, lack of financial support from the state and the formation of a ministerial committee in October 2013 to consult with members of the film industry. But due to the ineffectiveness of this committee, film producers Muhammad Hassan Ramzi, Gabi Khuwri and Hisham Suliman approached popular talk show *Cairo 360* hosted by Usama Kamal in order to reach President al-Sisi.[5] Broadcast on the *al-Qahira wa-l-Nas* channel in November 2014, the episode focused on piracy and lack of government support (*al-Qahira wa-l-Nas*, 2014). Ibrahim 'Issa also hosted film producer Muhammad al-'Adl and director Magdi Ahmad 'Ali on his show *25/30* (ON E) in January 2015. In a speech earlier that day, al-Sisi had directly addressed actors Ahmad al-Saʿa and Yusra in the audience, telling them to 'give people hope for tomorrow and enhance our values and ethics,' alluding to the criticisms of *āflām āl-subki* – the films associated with producer Mohammad al-Subki that feature thug heroes, belly dancers and popular songs. al-'Adl put the ball back in the government's court, stating that the 'political will' is the president's will: 'It is the state's problem, represented by the president because the state views us as a funfair' (ON E, 2015).

Print journalists have also commented extensively on the nature of this crisis. In an *Egypt Today* article in December 2013, Sherif Awad recommended crowdfunding to encourage more moderate budget films, the easing of bureaucratic hurdles for foreign film-makers shooting in Egypt and the creation of pay-per-view websites, despite the still-nascent online retail culture (Awad, 2013). By the end of 2015, several journalists had reported various interpretations of the crisis. Hadiyr al-Mahdawi focused on the bureaucratic restrictions of the Cinematic Syndicate (a film-makers' organization) and state censorship that restricts shooting permissions to graduates of the state-sanctioned High Institute of Cinema (al-Mahdawi, 2014). Samar Samir addressed the 'mafia' or oligopoly over production and distribution since the late 1990s and the inflated payments to stars of popular films (Samir, 2015). Sarah Ibrahim focused on the small market size for films and the government's ineffectiveness in curbing piracy (Ibrahim, 2015).

The crisis relates to the broader political and economic crises in Egypt, but also to a cluster of specific problems in the Egyptian film industry. As Pendakur (2013, p. 125) argues for the Indian case, the shift to neo-liberal economic policies has led to key structural changes, including the privatization of telecommunications and media industries. Indian and Egyptian governments have also encouraged the investment in film industries through, for example, facilitating the construction and ownership of multiplexes. The building of these multiplexes coincided with the emergence of shopping malls that comprised a number of retail stores directing middle and upper classes. In the Egyptian case, since the late 1990s, a few major distributors and exhibitors – al-'Arabiya, al-Aukhwa al-Mutahadiyn and al-Nasr wa-l-Masa wa-Auskar – have dominated film production for theatrical release. These companies entered the sector to meet the shortage in the number of Egyptian films for the growing number of urban multiplexes, especially during the 2000s. During this period, the launch of new movie TV channels such as Rotana Cinema in 2005 increased the demand for and financial investment in new films. Producers began to use *sulfit tawzi'* (distribution loan) to fund new films. Shirif Mandur explains, 'This is when you as a producer go to a distributor before actually shooting the film and present your project, including the budget and actors. The distributor then lends you money for production' (S. Mandur, interview, 25 January 2015). This process has been relatively uncomplicated if projects involve stars such as Ahmad al-Sa'a or Ahmad Hilmi since the television networks ART and Rotana will buy them.

However, the high demand for new films had led to inflation in film-making costs, with payments to stars in particular often accounting for 70 per cent of a film's total budget.[6] According to Mandur, this means that most films do not break even in a small national market, thus producers only profit from selling their films to television channels. Consequently, the retreat of television channels from buying new films after the 2008 global financial crisis has dramatically affected the number of high-budget films produced.

On the other hand, director Samih 'Abd al-'Aziz (despite his engagement in mainstream and popular films) believes the real crisis is the lack of access to equal screening opportunities. He blames the oligopoly of companies such as al-'Arabiya and al-Aukhwa al-Mutahadiyn that owns many film theatres, produces and distributes films. These distributors classify the films into commercial and independent categories, allowing more screening opportunities for commercial films. For example, Ahmad 'Abd Allah's *Farsh wa-Ghata* was released for only one week. According to 'Abd Allah, 'They gave us the smallest screens in their multiplexes because they thought the film has no audience, but eventually they found that the film attracted some people' (A. 'Abd Allah, interview, 31 January 2015). Moreover, popular film producer Muhammad al-Subki has argued that al-Aukhwa al-Mutahadiyn prioritize their own films when it comes to distribution and exhibition (Rotana Masriya, 2014). The major distributors are also members of the board of the Chamber of Film Industry, which regulates and manages the subsectors of the industry. Film producer Muhammad Samir has raised his concern about the conflict of interest in the Chamber of Film Industry. He explains, 'They take a decision based on votes, the more film theatres you have, the more votes you get. If I own 100 film theatres, I rule' (M. Samir, interview, 27 January 2015).

The deteriorating economic situation also had an impact on filmgoing. Muhammad Hifzi pointed out that only 10 per cent of 55 million Egyptians within the age demographic for cinemagoing can afford to spend much on entertainment (M. Hifzi, interview, 25 January 2015). The ticket price has increased with the construction of air-conditioned multiplexes and the necessary upgrading of sound and picture quality. Producer Muhammad Samir explains,

> I asked a taxi driver once if he goes to the cinema. He replied that he loves cinema but it is very expensive. I told him that there are tickets for only 10 Egyptian pounds (EGP). He then said that he has three kids, so it will cost 50 EGP [for the family] to go to the cinema. Then he will have to buy them a canned drink (2 EGP each) which means another 10 EGP. Therefore, he has to pay around at least 60 EGP in a day that he has not worked on the taxi, which is a great loss for

him. So, it is much better to buy a dinner and watch the film on TV. (M. Samir, interview, 27 January 2015)[7]

The location of film theatres, their inadequate number and outdated technology are significant problems for the industry. Cairo and Alexandria account for most of the theatres with very few in other cities. Cairo's urban development and lack of planning have hindered filmgoing. Director Samih 'Abd al-'Aziz describes film theatres as scattered along 6 October Bridge, an elevated highway in central Cairo, which means that 'some people do not have access to film theatres through direct transportation' (S. 'Abd al-'Aziz, interview, 22 December 2014). Film producer Gabi Khuwri has also addressed the issue of outdated booking system set by the Ministry of Finance for film theatres. The system includes different sets of tickets for each show, which complicates the booking process and prevents the exhibitors to make special offers on tickets, such as over 60 and student discounted tickets (CBC Egypt, 2013b). The total number of screens in Egypt is also only 400, which sets a limit to the revenue of films (S. Mandur, interview, 25 January 2015). Many of the interviewees thought this number would drop with the need for technological upgrades that threaten older film theatres, which still project 35 mm film and have insufficient capital for the transition to DCP (Digital Cinema Protocol), which costs about 70,000 USD per theatre (S. Mandur, interview, 25 January 2015; and M.al-'Adl, interview, 27 January 2015).

During the interviews, film-makers articulated these issues as challenges that limit their creative productions and accessibility of audiences to their films. They narrated their experience and struggle to explain that a crisis was already taking place since the late 1990s. However, major film producers approached the media and articulated their problems as a crisis only after the dramatic impacts of the 2008 global financial crisis and the 2011 Revolution. These film-makers emphasized the need for the government to support the transition to digital cinema screening, for instance, through loans, partnerships or foreign funding, the latter which it has consistently rejected without stating its reasons. The government could expand the size of the domestic market by providing land and tax breaks for investors who are willing to build film theatres.

The political turbulence and civil disturbances of the 2011 Revolution exacerbated the film industry's crisis. In order to eliminate protests, Mubarak's government set a curfew from 28 January that lasted for ten weeks. Films released on 25 January, such as *Mikrufun*, incurred excessive losses in this environment. After the election of the Muslim Brotherhood government in

June 2012, President Muhammad Mursi's policies received wide criticism and protests demanding his resignation. In July 2013, Minister of Defence and head of the military 'Abd al-Fattah al-Sisi offered Mursi 48 hours to answer the public's demands after huge demonstrations. On 3 July 2013, the army removed Mursi from office and imprisoned him. This coup d'état led to Muslim Brotherhood protests in Raba'a al-'Adawiya in Cairo. On 14 August 2013, the army and police attacked Rab'a, killing over 800 protesters and a second curfew was introduced. Both curfews were set from early evening to the next morning, which impacted ticket sales during two important show times (9 p.m. and midnight).

The losses incurred on films shown after the January 2011 Revolution practically shut down production. Producer Hifzi explains, 'The absence of security and curfews frightened people who thought they might produce a film and release it in theatres, and the next day a disaster happens and they [the Muslim Brotherhood and military governments] re-set the curfew. Many people were confused, and many people actually stopped producing' (M. Hifzi, interview, 25 January 2015). Producer Hisham Suliman confirms, 'I was planning to produce, but I couldn't find any distributor. When I said that I will do a comedy film, the first thing the distributor told me was do you guarantee that you will bring an audience to the film theatre?' (H. Suliman, interview, 27 December 2015) The absence of security did not only impact the sale of tickets but also increased production costs. Director Ahmad 'Abd Allah explains that while shooting *Farsh wa-Ghata* in 2012/2013, 'the police had little control over the places we shot, so we had to arrange other security options' (A. 'Abd Allah, interview, 31 January 2015). Resident families and individuals in the neighbourhood where the film was shot provided security for hefty payments. The recession of film production represented the broader political and economic crises during the 2011 Revolution.

During this period more film-makers, crews and actors largely abandoned feature production for theatrical release to work instead on television series broadcast on privately owned television channels during the peak season of Ramadan. In fact, newly launched channels after the revolution such as CBC and MBC Masr increased the demand for *musalsalāt ramadān* (Ramadan series). When sometimes over sixty series screen during the month, film-makers have turned towards television channels as their primary source of revenue. For example, well-known film director Kamla abu Zikri made the successful series *Bint Ismaha Zat* (*A Girl Named Zat*, 2013) and *Sign al-Nisaa* (*Women's Prison*, 2014), both with film producers turning to television. However, producers have been using the post-revolution recession as an excuse to pay fewer wages to film-makers. Film director Samih 'Abd al-'Aziz explains,

Producers have been using the term *revolution* to decrease one's wage while contracting. Instead of producing revolutionary texts, the revolution has been exploited for profits. I have seen this, they are producing the same TV series they used to make before the revolution [using the same themes, without referring to the revolution], but they are contracting with 50% reduced wages, using the revolution and its subsequent recession as an excuse. (S. 'Abd al-'Aziz, interview, 22 December 2014)

For reasons of cost and security, television has also become a less risky medium for film producers and audiences.

The levels of insecurity have provided opportunities for small criminal organizations and individuals to benefit from film piracy. Pirated films are widely available on CDs and DVDs, online and on more than eighty television channels. Altok tok, Cima Aly Baba, LCD and other channels broadcast films, sometimes as soon as the day after their theatrical release. Theatre attendance has therefore dropped and Gulf television networks are increasingly disinterested in buying these films for further broadcast across the region because they are no longer exclusive to their channels. Producer Muhammad al-'Adl explained that these legal channels that broadcast pirated material are the result of an agreement made in 2006 between Egypt's Nilesat (satellite) and the French Eutelsat. After Nilesat reached its maximum capacity, former minister of information Safwat al Shirif suggested initiating a second satellite (M. al-'Adl, interview, 27 January 2015). But instead of buying a new satellite, he rented some transponders (each transponder contains a number of channels' frequencies) from Eutelsat. This agreement was made in return for placing Eutelsat's satellite over the Nilesat to gain reach over the MENA (Middle East and North Africa) region for the French company. The distribution company Noorsat bought most of the remaining transponders on the same satellite. According to Muhammad al-'Adl, 'You call them [Noorsat] over the phone and request a frequency. They tell you it is worth 10,000 USD per month, you pay and they give you the frequency to air whatever you wish' (M. al-'Adl, interview, 27 January 2015). Although this agreement was contracted for the period 2006–16, the government subsequently extended it to 2022. The Chamber of Film Industry has attempted to stop these channels through contacting officials in Jordan (where Noorsat's office is located), but the company reopened in Cyprus.

Since the 2011 Revolution, film-makers have repeatedly called for government support to curb film piracy and have been frustrated at the little action in response. The current government's stance on Eutelsat's agreement is contradictory and perplexing. Although al-Sisi ordered the shutdown of any channels on Nilesat that were sympathetic to the Muslim Brotherhood, most of these networks reopened in Turkey and bought frequencies from Noorsat, taking advantage of its agreement with Eutelsat. Ironically, this agreement not only impacted the film industry but also restored the oppositional voices that al-Sisi attempted to eliminate. The government – which in other policies aims to seize control over media – has not worked to amend this ongoing agreement. The state produces public service announcements to encourage the payment of taxes, yet ironically these ads are placed on channels to which the government turns a blind eye to piracy.[8] The state clearly does not value copyright, since government-operated buses often show pirated films for extra charges. Although the average cost of a film in Egypt is 4–6 million EGP, the government views films as a low priority in the Egyptian economy, even though it has made some public statements about the ideological value of the arts.

The state has also been unconsciously encouraging piracy by neglecting laws to protect films and intellectual property. According to Shirif Mandur, the pirates exploit the lack of laws protecting films and transfer the ownership of any film copyrights to themselves. He explains,

> We can go now to the notary records and you can transfer your ownership of 'Adil Imam, Ahmad Mikki and Ahmad Hilmi's new films to me, and they will do it! They do not ask for any proof of your ownership to these films. If you are selling a telephone, they will ask for a proof of ownership, but not the film. (S. Mandur, interview, 25 January 2015)[9]

The notion of normalizing piracy, and viewing films as less important products, has dispersed from the state to the public culture. Film director Ahmad 'Abd Allah confirms, 'When I promote my films on Twitter and invite people to watch it in theatres, I usually receive a comment or two asking for the YouTube link to the film. They think that films are made to be shown on YouTube, and it is normal to watch it from home' (A. 'Abd Allah, interview, 31 January 2015). It is clear that post-revolution governments and political parties have paid less attention to cultural developments and focused more on political conflicts.

In his pre-election meeting with personnel in the cultural industries in May 2014, al-Sisi asserted, 'Art has a huge role, especially in the current situation after the past few years ... when there is art and awareness, there will be no opportunities for extremism' (Sada al-Balad, 2014). However, government support for the film industry has been minimal, due to the prioritization of other issues such as security and economic development in other larger sectors. While al-Sisi has paid lip service to the idea that cinema might contribute to the ideological well-being of the nation, film-makers are disillusioned with direct government support. For example, one of al-Sisi's priorities is fighting terrorism, but as Muhammad al-'Adl argues, 'The state is still not aware that if they are fighting terrorists, we are the ones who fight terrorism through cinema, theatres and books' (M. al-'Adl, interview, 27 January 2015). Moreover, film producer-director Shirif Mandur has emphasized the economic benefits that cinema can offer to the state, such as its positive impact on tourism. In their interventions in cinema, governments have tended to focus on the traditional taboos of sex, politics and religion.

The interviewed film-makers stated that the censorship regime has not changed significantly since the revolution due mainly to bureaucratic inertia. The censorship staff members still accept or reject films, scenes and lines based on unclear criteria. The priorities of employees are often to protect themselves, their bosses and the censorship's reputation. They fear that if they approve a controversial film, they may lose employment. al-'Adl explains, 'This has previously happened with censorship of *al-Muznibuwn* [*The Guilty*, Sa'id Marzu', 1975], when the whole censorship department was dismissed when it approved the film' (M. al-'Adl, interview, 27 January 2015). After the revolution, the censorship department was confused and 'shaky' (the term that Samih 'Abd al-'Aziz used to describe the censorship department) since the political direction was still unclear. The absence of a clear ideological agenda in the years following the revolution, until al-Sisi removed the Muslim Brotherhood from power, led to a random acceptance and rejection of films. Many films that celebrated the revolution were accepted, excluding the ones that criticized the military such as *al-Midan* (*The Square*, Jihan Nujaim, 2013). The censorship department rejects films that depict a corrupt military police officer or judge, without giving reasons or a written ruling.

Historically, the organization's practices have also been shaped by the imperatives of its chairperson. For example, Dr Ahmad 'Awwad, a relative liberal, who was the chair of the censorship department after Mursi's year in power, took some major decisions during his short period (less than one year) at the helm. He sanctioned the release of *Lamu'akhza* – a satire about sectarianism between Muslims and Copts – without modifications when the censorship department before the 2011 Revolution had previously rejected the script. After 'Awwad's resignation, due to the prime minister's interference in his job, al-'Adl describes the following manager of the censorship body as 'an employee who wants to keep his position' (M. al-'Adl, interview, 27 January 2015).[10]

After the revolution, other government bodies and officials, such as the Ministry of Endowments and the prime minister, have also acted as censorship authorities. One of the scenes in Ahmad 'Abd Allah's *Farsh wa-Ghata* – a near-silent experimental film about a fugitive who escapes prison during the 2011 Revolution – was set in a mosque. During Mursi's period, when the shooting was taking place, the Ministry of Endowments declined to issue a permit to shoot in a mosque. 'Abd Allah explains,

> Usually, it is very easy to get such permission, just a routine process, as long as you are not disturbing the rituals and respecting the sacredness of the place. The ministry does not own the mosque, they just manage it, so they do not really have the right to permit or reject a shooting … Without giving any clear reasons, they kept on postponing the permission – in a state of fear – because we were not the 'usual crew' they are used to deal with. In the meantime, they gave permissions to TV series starring famous celebrities, because they knew they were under their control, and we are not. During Mursi's period, the people in the ministry told us mosques are not shooting locations, and not for that type of work. (A. 'Abd Allah, interview, January 31, 2015)

In the case of Samih 'Abd al-'Aziz's *Halawit Ruwh*, the prime minister ordered the film withdrawn from theatres a few days after its release. Inspired by *Malena* (Giuseppe Tornatore, 2000), the film narrates the story of Ruwh – a beautiful widow played by the Lebanese singer Haifaa' Wahbi – who becomes the obsession of a Cairo district's men and boys. The prime minister's decision was made in response to the public debate over the film's sex scenes and apparent violation of Egyptian morals. The film's release had been accepted by the censorship department with a 'for adults only' rating. 'Abd al-'Aziz claims that government officials had not even watched the film and took the decision based on the trailer. The film's producer filed a case, and the film was released again after adjudication in December 2014. These instances were among the attempts of the governments to impose their conservative ideologies over cinema. However, the film industry has continued to express concerns about producing and releasing films when the parameters for censorship are vague and unpredictable.

While large sectors of the public call for extra censorship on film, music and television productions, film-makers have called for changes in the structure of the censorship department. In 2014, a Freemuse study by Ezzat, al-Haqq and Fazulla analysed the legal framework that governs the censorship of artistic expression in Egypt. They proposed a rating system for different age groups, rather than the acceptance or rejection of films.[11] They also argued for amendments to the vague and elastic vocabulary in censorship laws to make them more specific. For example, Article 1 of the decree 220/1976 'defines the goal of censorship as the protection of public morals, public order, and children from deviance' (Ezzat, al-Haqq, and Fazulla, 2014, p. 30). Such ambiguous laws give the right to censorship employees to accept or reject lines, scenes and films based on their personal judgements. Conservative audiences have criticized the censorship department for allowing al-Subki films, which have dominated the film scene after the revolution, for their excessive portrayal of violence.

As well as more consistent and transparent guidelines on censorship, film-makers want the government to take a more active role in supporting film production and cinema culture. There is as yet no clear public funding system for cinema. During the past six years, the Ministry of Culture has offered an inadequate subsidy of 40 million EGP (less than one million dollars a year), which is inconsistently disbursed. Film director Ahmad Rashwan narrated his experience in applying for the fund, 'They announced a second round for funding in February [2015], and while it should take a month or two, the results are not announced until now [January 2016]. They keep on saying we'll announce the results next month. Recently, I heard that it has been cancelled' (A. Rashwan, Interview, 5 January 2016). Rashwan also contends the Ministry of Culture funds a number of poor festivals, such as the Alexandria International Film Festival, despite the multiple reports demanding to discontinue it. Among members of the public, there is a longing for Egyptian cinema to reach the heights of its 'golden age' in the 1960s. But that era of film production had a stronger commitment to the state of cinema than today. The state's economic crisis, since the 2011 Revolution, has dramatically decreased the priority of supporting film-making.

Film-makers argue that the post-revolution regimes of the Muslim Brotherhood and military have been exploiting the industry. In other words, these governments have dealt with film companies as commercial enterprises rather than industrial institutions. For example, the government charges film theatres for electricity and water at full price as commercial stores and homes, not offering any special industrial rate. al-'Adl believes the state has always dealt with the film industry as equivalent to 'cabarets and nightclubs'. He explains, 'Before the revolution, the electricity cost for a cinema ranged from 5,000 to 6,000 EGP. Electricity now can reach up to 70 to 80,000 EGP per month.' He adds,

In some sectors, officials are convinced that filmmakers generate high profits, which is not true anymore. Therefore, when you plan on shooting, the Ministry of Interior charges a fee, the airport requires a fee and so on. These fees add up to a bulk, which makes you quit producing. (M. al-'Adl, interview, 27 January 2015).

While shooting permission fees were required before the revolution, filmmakers indicate that these have increased significantly after the revolution. Director Hala Lutfi says, 'It is even worse. We are now charged for "facilities protection", since 2014, where we pay 4,000 EGP to the Ministry of Interior in order to shoot in the street' (H. Lutfi, interview, 17 January 2015).

The film-makers have noted that particular government officials can have a significant influence on the direction of the film industry. Several interviewees mentioned Dr Ziad Bahaa' al-Din's (Deputy Prime Minister July 2013–January 2014) attention to the industry crisis. He formed the special ministerial committee for cinema, which included seven ministers and key film-makers (including Muhammad al-'Adl, Muhammad Hifzi and Shirif Mandur) to address chronic problems. On its first meeting in October 2013, the committee issued important rules, including *āl-shibbāk āl-wāhid* (literally 'the one window'). This 'one window' issues all the shooting permissions for foreign shootings, which had been limited due to the numerous permissions required, and clearance of film content by the censors. Morocco generates more than USD one billion a year through foreign shootings. The new 'one window' policy streamlined the process in Egypt. However, the Hollywood blockbuster *Exodus: Gods and Kings* (Ridley Scott, 2014) has been the only major foreign film shot in Egypt after this rule came into force. In fact, the rule was discontinued after the film was banned in Egypt due to 'historical inaccuracies' (*Egypt Bans 'Zionist' Film*, 2014). In the wake of the controversy, the government changed the ministries that oversaw particular sectors of the film industry. For example, the committee decided that the management of cinema palaces would return to the Ministry of Culture from the General Authority of Investment, but this transfer of jurisdiction has not yet been implemented.

However, the state has been effective in supporting film-makers in other respects. In July 2016, Prime Minister Shirif Isma'il issued decisions that increased the state subsidy from 20 million EGP to 50 million EGP and reduced the fees for shooting at archaeological sites (Mukhtar, 2016). He proclaimed the urgency of protecting films from piracy. But given the ineffectual statements of past government meetings and lack of new legislation and regulation, there is little confidence that this political discourse will translate to tangible change.

Among the few producers who continued producing films after the 2011 Revolution are the brothers Muhammad and Ahmad al-Subki. Popular for owning butcher stores, al-Subki brothers have been involved in film production since the mid-1990s. Along the new wave of comedy films that took over in the Noughties, al-Subki produced several box-office hits, such as *al-Limbi* (Wa'il Ihsan, 2002). They have focused on producing low-budget comedies such as *Kallim Mama* (*Talk to Mum*, Ahmad 'Awwad, 2003) and *Haha wa-Tufaha* (*Haha and Tufaha*, Akram Farid, 2006), which unfolds a conflict between a brother and his sister over the possession of their parent's house.[12] After the revolution, al-Subki continued to produce low-budget films, targeted mainly at middle- and lower-class audiences. They release these films during the high seasons of 'īd al-Fitr and 'īd al-Adhā to accumulate the highest profits possible during a short time period. Films such as *Shari' al-Haram* (*al-Haram Street*, Shura, 2011) and *'Ish al-Bulbul* (Husam al-Guhari, 2013) which delves into the world of Cairo's nightclubs, have been a hybrid of comedy, romantic and musical scenes. *'Abdu Muta* (Isma'il Faru', 2012) and *Qalb al-Asad* (*The Lion's Heart*, Karim al-Subki, 2013) are action films dealing with the drug and entertainment industries starring Muhammad Ramadan.[13]

The al-Subki family use similar approaches in promoting their films, such as including popular songs shot with music-video styles (including belly dancers). They insert songs, such as *Ah Law Li'ibt ya Zahr* (meaning a lucky roll of dice) by Ahmad Shiyba, in films as well as release them on television. Film producer Muhammad Samir appraises their innovative marketing techniques,

> My office is just on the other side of his [Muhammad al-Subki's] office and butchery. In 'īd al-Adhā he sells meat for 25 EGP per kilo, which is why you find long queues in front of the butchery. Next to the queue, he puts a screen and two large speakers on a truck showing the trailers of his film released during the 'īd. He was the first to write on his trailers, this is the season's film, starting Thursday … and the date so people can memorise. He knows whom he is talking to. (M. Samir, interview, 27 January 2015)

Since al-Subki became the dominant film producer after the revolution, due to the retreat of other producers, audience have imagined the post-revolution film crisis as the content produced by al-Subki. The wide conservative segments of the audience, together with film critics and some film-makers, have criticized al-Subki for the mediocre films they produce. Film critics, such as Tari' al-Shinnawi, have described some of their films as 'tacky' in their film reviews (al-Shinnawi, 2015). Mainstream media outlets have also contributed to the growing moral panic and accusing al-Subki films of 'deteriorating the public taste' and 'urging moral corruption'. Television shows, such as *al-'Ashira Masa'an (10 pm)* broadcast on Dream TV, blamed al-Subki films for 'destroying the younger generation' (Dream TV, 2015). These shows support their argument with vox pops and images of young people re-enacting violent scenes from al-Subki's films such as *'Abdu Muta*. Audiences have thus created Facebook groups calling for the boycott of al-Subki's films and sometimes criticize the censorship department for allowing the release of such films.

On the other hand, some film-makers have defended al-Subki for maintaining the flow of film production during the time of recession (post-2011), regardless of the content they present. They suggest, rather than abolishing these films, the state should support producing other types of films (CBC Egypt, 2013b). Film-makers have also engaged in debates about the relationship between cinema and society. In response to the claims that al-Subki films will affect the public behaviour and impact the younger generation's morals, film-makers have discussed the reciprocal relationship between film and society (M. al-'Adl, interview, 27 January 2015, and S. Mandur, interview, 25 January 2015). Muhammad and Ahmad al-Subki have emphasized that they produced 'good' films such as *al-lila al-kibira* and *Min Dahr Ragil* (*Born to a Man*, Karim al-Subki, 2015), which have participated at the Cairo International Film Festival.

Many of the arguments criticizing al-Subki films have disregarded that their films were popular and attracted large audiences. al-Subki targeted audiences who desired pure 'entertainment films', especially during the news-saturated post-revolution period. The popular and *mahragānāt* (or electronic music genre) songs included in these films became music hits heard by a wide range of audiences of different social classes. The commercial success of al-Subki's films encouraged other production companies, such as New Century, to produce films of similar themes such as *al-'Ashash* (Isma'il Faru', 2013) – an action film about a young man who is accused of murder and falls in love with a belly dancer.[14] Film critics, media personnel and some audiences have described these films as low-culture products that lessen 'public taste' and called for further censorship restrictions to limit al-Subki's productions. Meanwhile, film-makers have called for state support to increase film production and provide a variety of film genres and styles.

After the dismissal of the Muslim Brotherhood's government in July 2013, al-Sisi's government and state media have conveyed the impression of security and economic stability. While the highest revenue for a single feature in Egypt had been 30 million EGP for *X-Large* (Shirif 'Arafa, 2011), in 2014 three films surpassed this record: *al-Harb al-Alamiya al-Talta* (*Third World War*, Ahmad al-Gindi), *al-Fiyl al-Azra'* (*The Blue Elephant*, Marwan Hamid) and *al-Giziyra2* (*The Island 2*, Shirif 'Arafa). This comedy, psychological thriller and action film as political allegory gave producers hope for the rejuvenation of box-office revenue. According to Hifzi, 'There are a lot of film projects starting, and some television channels started buying films again in 2013, which is positive, together with the entry of channels such as MBC and OSN which bought some films, and gave a boost to the industry' (M. Hifzi, interview, 25 January 2015). The commercial success of recent films such as *Hepta* (Hadi al-Baguri, 2016), an ensemble film about romance, might encourage further production.[15] However, this sense of recovery is weakened by a broader tendency of fewer producers making feature films for theatrical release, since most of them have shifted to producing less risky and more profitable television series.

* * *

The film industry has been in a crisis even before 2008. The oligopoly that dominated the film industry has limited production of alternative film styles. Producers depended mainly on profits from Gulf television channels due to a limited number of film theatres and declining audiences because of ticket prices. After the global economic crisis in 2008, the multinational corporations reduced their advertising expenses, which impacted the Gulf television networks' purchases. After the revolution, the recurring curfews and insecurity have led to financial losses. The absence of security has also led to the expansion of piracy; films are recorded in film theatres and broadcast on television channels after a day or two of their release. According to film-makers, consultation with governments has inspired little confidence in the prime minister's plans to prevent piracy and support the industry financially. In practice, the government has increased the electricity and water bills for film theatres, as well as raising fees for shooting permissions. The state has intervened largely in film content, with censorship guided by some vague rules. Film-makers have shifted to television production and defined the film production situation as a 'crisis'. Producers are risk aversive in the unstable political and economic environment. The crisis in the film industry, as the film-makers project it, is primarily a production crisis of mainstream films. They address the crisis as the lack of high-budget popular genre films featuring stars in comparison to the high volume of production from the late 1990s to 2008. However, they ignore issues of oligopoly and underestimate the value of independent productions.

Film-makers remain surprisingly optimistic about the future of the industry, even with the lack of positive signs. While producer Muhammad al-'Adl admitted the lack of a strategic plan to sustain the industry, he considers the current decline as part of the 'natural' and continuous fluctuations of the industry since its inception. Producer Muhammad Hifzi argues, 'The revolution happened in the downside of the cinema's cycle, which made it longer and harder, and we are still suffering from its consequences. But I am sure that it is a cycle, and that we will experience a vogue period' (M. Hifzi, interview, 25 January 2015). Through his more frequent interactions with the government, producer Shirif Mandur gives greater importance to the direct intervention of President al-Sisi himself rather than ministerial meetings:

> In Egypt, the government is not a decision maker. That is why you will not find the term 'the political will' except in Egypt, which is another word for the president's will. It is either the president wants it or not, no matter how many committees you go through. The new constitution has made a balance between the president and the parliament, but we do not have a parliament yet, so the decision can only be taken by the president regardless what the government thinks. This includes all the governments: [of Prime Ministers] 'Issam Sharaf, al-Biblawi, Ganzuri and Mahlab. We have met all these governments. However, we are lucky enough today to have a political leadership (as a president) who is very interested. He is the first president in Egypt's history to mention 'we want back our old cinema' in his speech (S. Mandur, interview, 25 January 2015)

Although the current government has suggested that it will intervene in the crisis, in the first year of his rule, al-Sisi's priorities were economic development and security. The state has been working on mega projects, such as the New Suez Canal, with negligible attention to the film industry or entertainment more broadly. Dominant ideologies in Egyptian society, supported by the military, give the cinema minor consideration as industry and culture. Meanwhile, the way out of the crisis is not only in the government's hands. Key players in the film industry have a part to play in reforming industry practices. Film stars, who often account for up to 70 per cent of a film's budget, might reconsider their wages to support more productions. The distribution and exhibition oligopoly has 'killed' (according to Samih 'Abd al-'Aziz) many projects during their development or in their limited release. Supporting the more serious-minded low-budget, independent, 'quality' or 'art' films, which have viable middle- and upper class, young and urban audiences could improve the situation. Egypt also needs more screens for both feature and short films. Such changes might help the film industry retain its leading position in the Middle East and encourage film-makers to make films for theatrical release, rather than investing most of their capital and labour in the lucrative Ramadan television series.

Interviewing film-makers revealed that they have made the strategic decision to take their problems to the media and have had considerable influence in articulating them in the terms of a 'crisis'. However, film-makers must negotiate the commonalities and differences among themselves as an industry sector. In general terms, they tend to see themselves as belonging to either more popular film-making or more independently minded film-making. The latter finds its audiences at international film festivals rather than Egyptian film theatres or television. Each of these groups supports its own film-makers. These borders are porous. But the vertical integration of the industry means that an oligopoly dominates production, distribution and exhibition. Most feature-film producers are members of the Chamber of Film Industry. In many cases, the board members of this organization support their own films through government processes and in the marketplace, rather than those of the wider membership. Interviewing film producers and directors of different film-making style has helped understanding how they view the crisis differently. Major film producers have appeared on television channels as representatives of the film industry. In the interviews, they addressed the lack of state support as one of the main aspects of the crisis. They also rationalized their retreat to the increasing risks, such as the vague guidelines of censorship. On the other hand, the domination of the oligarchy of production and distribution companies is the real crisis for 'independent film-makers'. The major film producers did not include this issue in their construction of the film industry crisis in the media.

The structure of the industry does not encourage new creative talent to enter the field. Egypt still only has one film school – the Higher Institute of Cinema. Graduates from this school can join the Cinematic Syndicate. Other film-makers have to pay a hefty sum to join this organization. Film-makers outside this production system – the growing numbers of self-taught producers and directors involved in the small-scale independent production with digital equipment – rely on the distribution-exhibition networks of international film festivals and the internet. The political instability and turnover of government officials make the situation of film-makers more vulnerable and unpredictable. This period of crisis seems an important transitional moment towards a new 'equilibrium' in Egyptian cinema and its imbrication in the communication landscape of television and new media. The crisis may open up spaces for new modes of film-making and experiments in film aesthetics. The variety of recent critically lauded independent films testifies to some of these developments. The interviewees all ended on an optimistic note about the future of film-making in Egypt. We will have to see if and how these shifts are enabled or hindered in the complex interactions and negotiations between film-makers, media industries and governments.

The crisis of the film industry and the broader national crisis did not obstruct the production of sociopolitical films. Among the few films produced during this period, film-makers have engaged with socio-economic and political themes. Since 2006, films started to depict issues of poverty, corruption and police brutality. High- and low-budget films have mainly used comedy and drama genres to portray the dissent and suggest the possibility of an upcoming revolution. During the uprising, several documentary and fiction films have focused on memorializing the revolutionary moment. The footage recorded in Tahrir Square during the eighteen days of the revolution (supported by technology and digital and mobile cameras) facilitated the production of narratives about the revolution. Some film-makers were creative in representing the revolution without showing the popular images of Tahrir Square. The crisis also advantaged 'independent film-makers', since their films achieved better exposure to the lack of mainstream films. A number of film-makers did not surrender to the production crisis and considered it a challenge to the wider national crisis.

3

Representing the national crisis: Films before the revolution, 2006–10

The revolution does not begin with the taking of political power from imperialism and the bourgeoisie, but rather begins at the moment when the masses sense the need for change and their intellectual vanguards begin to study and carry out this change through activities on different fronts. (Solanas and Getino, 1970, p. 1)

The years 2005–6 witnessed an expansion in the number of political movements in Egypt. In 2004, a year before the re-election of Mubarak to a new presidential term, a movement named Kifaya (literally 'enough') started to call for democratic reform in Egypt. However, the re-election of Mubarak to a fifth six-year term in 2005 instigated public discontent. Sakr (2013, p. 333–4) argues the increasing expression of anger through online blogs intensified the discussion of politics on television shows. The discussed issues included the presidential and parliamentary elections as well as Egypt's foreign relations with the United States (Sakr, 2013, p. 333–4). Furthermore, in 2008 a group of political activists formed Harakit shabab sita ibril (April Six Youth Movement) to support the strike of the workers in al-Mahalla al-Kubra on the same day. Harakit shabab sita ibril and Kifaya are among the main political movements that called for and supported the 2011 Revolution. Concurrently, film-makers were keen to represent the major political and social concerns of the public on screen. Although film-makers had depicted social and political corruption during Mubarak's era as early as 1992 (Tabishat, 2012, p. 378), many films focused on criticizing Mubarak's regime during his fifth six-year term (starting in October 2005).

This chapter examines the role of films released in the immediate years before the 2011 Revolution, focusing on the films released from 2006 to 2010. It argues that some pre-revolution films contributed to the political activism that was growing during this period. These social problem films were offered among a wave of comedy, romantic-comedy and action films that started in the late 1990s. A few popular dramas engaged with issues of poverty, police brutality and political corruption using high budgets and film stars. For example, director Khalid Yusif incorporated sequences that reveal increasing violence and conditions of absolute poverty along the main romantic drama lines of his films. Comedy films have also imagined consequences of a revolution in *al-Diktatur* (*The Dictator*, Ihab Lam'i, 2009) and the election of a young middle-class man as the president in *Zaza* ('Ali 'Abd al-Khalik, 2006). These films have set their plots in imagined countries to circumvent censorship, but they made clear references to Egypt's social and political situations. A few film-makers have also meditated on marginalized communities and engaged with such themes as class struggle. However, these film-makers sought a more realist approach through employing alternative aesthetics, such as filming on digital cameras, shooting in real locations, casting new actors and using improvisation, to convey a sense of spontaneity and authenticity. These films include *'In Shams* (*Eye of the Sun*, Ibrahim al-Battut, 2008), *Basra* (Ahmad Rashwan, 2008), *Hiliaupulis* (*Heliopolis*, Ahmad 'Abd Allah, 2009) and *al-Khurug min al-Qahira* (*Cairo Exit*, Hisham 'Issawi, 2010).

Since 2006, films started to represent dissent based on political oppression and civic mobilization that were evident during this period. Before the re election of Mubarak in 2005, the police detained oppositional leaders, such as the chairman of al-Ghad Party Aiman Nuwr. They convicted him of forging the party's establishing documents. The 2005 presidential election (the first multi-candidate election in Egypt) was limited to candidates from licensed parties. The regulations favoured the domination of Mubarak's National Democratic Party (NDP) and prevented the banned Muslim Brotherhood members and independent candidates for nomination. After several strikes and sit-ins by the workers of the state-run textile company in al-Mahalla al-Kubra (an industrial city in Egypt) in 2006, they called for mass protests on 6 April 2008. This protest was calling for increased wages and better living conditions. Also in April 2006, several bombs exploded in Dahab – a town on the southeast coast of Sinai and were attributed to Islamist extremists. Mubarak used these bombings as an excuse to extend the Emergency Law, which suspended constitutional rights, limited protest and gave the right to police and armed forces to detain civilians. Egyptian journalist Ibrahim 'Issa was sentenced to prison in 2006 and 2007 for 'defaming' Mubarak and reporting his health issues.

Political activist and blogger Wa'il 'Abbas started to upload photos and videos of protests and police brutality incidents since 2004. Sakr (2013, p. 328) notes the politicization of television talks starting in 2005. The launch of *al-Ashira Masa'an* (*10 pm*) in 2005 on Dream TV (a private channel owned by Ahmad Bahgat) besides the already-established *al-Qahira al-Yuwm* (*Cairo Today*) and the state-run television's *al-Biyt Biytak* (*Make Yourself at Home*) have intensified political talks on television. Sakr also argues, 'Camera phones, YouTube, and blogs contributed to the circulation of television images that testified to the dysfunctionality of governance in Egypt' (2013, p. 330). The increasing access to the internet in Egypt and the introduction of Arabic blog sites and the Arabic interface of Facebook in 2009 eased the circulation of uncensored articles that opposed the regime. Ahmad Mahir and Israa 'Abd al-Fattah gathered more than 70,000 on their Facebook group, which supported the general strike on 6 April 2008. Simultaneously, films contributed to the growing anger through realizing issues of political corruption and poverty and attempted to participate in mobilizing audiences.

During this period, the Censorship of Artistic Works has continued to prevent any direct criticisms of the president. Films that included the president as one of the characters showed him as a kind and generous person surrounded by corrupt advisors. For example, in *Tabbakh al-Ra'iys* (*The President's Chef*, Sa'id Hamid, 2008) the Egyptian president employs Mitwalli, a street food vendor, as his personal chef to tell him the real problems the country.[1] Otherwise, films had to be creative in engaging with politics and portraying the president. Popular films, such as *'Imarat Ya'qubiyan* (*The Yacoubian Building*, Marwan Hamid, 2006) and *Hiyya Fawda* (*This Is Chaos*, Yusif Shahin and Khalid Yusif, 2007), achieved the censorship's approval due to their association with prominent film-makers – 'Adil Imam and Yusif Shahin. Banning these films would have attracted international media's attention, especially in Shahin's case, and started discussions about freedom of speech in Egypt. Mubarak's regime allowed these films to avoid controversies and to claim democracy. Comedy films that represented a rebellion against the president, such as *Zaza* and *al-Diktatur*, have set their plots in imagined countries but made clear references to Egypt. On the other hand, independent film-makers ignored censorship approvals as a part of their rebellion against mainstream film-making styles and the state oppression. Some productions have shot their films secretly (due to the lack of shooting permissions, which are granted after the approval of a film's script by the censorship department). However, some independent film-makers released their films, such as Ibrahim al-Battut's *'In Shams*, after negotiations with the censorship department. These popular and independent films have represented dissent and anger through drama and comedy genres.

In *Unthinking Eurocentrism* (1994, p. 208), Shohat and Stam highlight genre as one of the key mediation elements. In addition to the narrative structure, cinematic style and music, generic conventions are significant when considering the social portrayal in a film. They discuss, for example, how realist-dramas attempt to critique stereotypes through representing complex 'three-dimensional characters' (p. 210). Shafik (2007b) examines the complexities of genres, namely melodrama, realism and action, in representing class struggle in Egyptian cinema. She argues:

> What in my view has helped melodrama in the Egyptian context to transcend itself into a kind of 'rhetorical' realism [after the 1952 Coup] is the emergence of the idea of confrontation, or the rejection of consensus, and the motivation to expose social and political injustice allegorically (Shafik, 2007, p. 266).

A wave of comedy and action films have dominated Egyptian cinema after the commercial success of a few comedy films in the late 1990s. *Isma'iliya Raiyh Gaiyy* (*Returning to Isma'iliya*, Karim Diaa' al-Din, 1997), a comedy-drama that narrates the success story of a popular singer, and *Si'idi fi-l-Gam'a al-Amrikiya* (*Upper Egyptian at the American University*, Sa'id Hamid, 1998), a comedy film about an Upper Egyptian who gets a scholarship to study at the American University in Cairo, were the films that started the comedy wave. However, with the rising political dissent in 2006, film-makers represented the crisis in drama, political satire and independent films. The latter films have expressed their rebellion on mainstream Hollywood–filmmaking style and used realistic approaches to represent social and political injustice.

This chapter analyses the different genres and forms that film-makers used to voice the public's discontent before the 2011 Revolution. Using mainly drama and comedy genres, popular high-budget films (featuring stars) and independent productions intersect in their meditations on dictatorship, poverty, police brutality, corruption and fundamentalism during the pre-revolutionary period (al-Zubidi, 2011; Armbrust, 2012; Tabishat, 2012; Tartoussieh, 2012; Gordon, 2013; and Hassan, 2015). Some of these films capture revolutionary-like images and project an upcoming revolution. For example, *Hiyya Fawda* engages intensely with issues of bribery and police brutality. The film ends with an attack by demonstrators on a police station against a corrupt police officer, which reoccurred during the 2011 Revolution.

Popular dramas such as *'Imarat Ya'qubiyan* and Khalid Yusif's Films – *Hiyna Maysara* (*When Convenient*, 2007) and *Dukkan Shihata* (*Shihata's Shop*, 2009) – garnered many audiences due to their featuring of prominent stars and extensive promotions. Audiences and film critics appreciated the films' denunciation of the government and the acknowledgement of the people's anger; however, the latter criticized the films for their mediocre cinematic language (in particular Khalid Yusif's films). Leftist artists view them as mainstream films that only present a soft criticism of the government. Film director Aytin Amin said that *'Imarat Ya'qubiyan,* 'does not strike anything that shakes the constants. It was going with the trend of relieving people. They were saying that there are such and such things happening but in the way that relieves the people' (A. Amin, interview, 30 December 2015). Although popular films are usually not considered for their political practices like alternative or independent films, Brunow argued, 'Mainstream productions play an important role in the struggle over the power of interpretation and they are performative in creating reality through repetition' (2009, p. 52). Many audiences have watched Egyptian popular dramas produced before the revolution. Their engagement with issues of political corruption, police brutality and poverty has contributed to the political discourse.

On the other hand, political satire and independent films discussed in this chapter did not achieve commercial success. The limited popularity of the comedy stars – Ahmad 'Id, Khalid Sarhan and Hani Ramzi – and their engagement with politics (which was uncommon in comedy films at that time) have restrained the audiences from watching them in film theatres. In addition, their release among other comedy films of popular stars such as Muhammad Hiniydi, Ahmad Hilmi and Muhammad Saa'd have impacted their commercial success. After the revolution, audiences have been watching these films and relating their narratives to the events of the 2011 Revolution. Similarly, a few audience interested in independent films did not support their commercial success. However, these films were released on film channels, such as Rotana Cinema and ART, which exposed them to a wider public.

It is important to note that the films discussed in this chapter did not trigger the uprising; instead, they 'reveal quite plainly what was simmering beneath the surface of Egyptian society' (Tabishat, 2012, p. 395–6). Although there are no figures or statistics about film styles produced during this period, mainstream productions, led by young film stars, were popular for their comedy and action Hollywood style. However, a few films challenged the dominant political views and proved that they could be contested. It is fair to speak of these films as contributing to the public's awareness of the extreme poverty conditions and police brutality for example. They reinforced the popular discourses of the widespread corruption among Mubarak's regime and thus contributed to the political crisis. As Gramsci explains,

> In every country, the process [of conflict] is different, although the content is the same. And the content is the crisis of the ruling class's hegemony, which occurs either because the ruling class has failed in some major political undertaking for which it has requested, or forcibly extracted, the consent of the broad masses (war, for example), or because huge masses (especially of peasants and petty-bourgeois intellectuals) have passed suddenly from a state of political passivity to a certain activity, and put forward demands which taken together, albeit not organically formulated, add up to a revolution. A 'crisis of authority' is spoken of: this is precisely the crisis of hegemony, or crisis of the state as a whole. (Gramsci as cited in Forgacs, 2000, p. 218)

Although the films discussed in this chapter have not led to the revolution, in the form of a cause–effect model, they have promoted social change through revealing images of protests, marches and sit-ins against the government. Gaines's concept of political mimesis addresses the relationship between (documentary) films and bodies. Gaines explains, 'We still need to think the body in relation to films that make audience members want to kick and yell, films that make them want to do something because of the conditions in the world of the audience' (1999, p. 90). She emphasizes the use of images of revolt and struggle in films is not only to represent historical events but also 'because they want audiences to carry on the same struggle' (p. 91). Gaines suggests aesthetic realism in films 'align the viewer emotionally with a struggle that continues beyond the frame and into his or her real historical present' (p. 93). Egyptian high-budget dramas and independent films have constructed realistic representations, through engaging with sociopolitical issues and (sometimes) using distinctive aesthetics including improvisation and shooting in real locations, to connect emotionally with audiences. They have also used images of mass protests and marches as imagined consequences of police brutality and social injustice.

These films are also a form of, what Nichols (2001) calls, 'wish-fulfilment'. In contrast to documentaries, these fiction films have depicted contemporary sociopolitical matters, such as excessive poverty, political corruption and police brutality, and combined them with their imagined (and wished) consequences. According to Nichols:

> Documentaries of wish-fulfilment are what we would normally call fictions. These films give tangible expression to our wishes and dreams, our nightmares and dreads. They make the stuff of the imagination concrete – visible and audible. They give a sense of what we wish, or fear, reality itself might be or become. Such films convey truths if we decide they do. They are films whose truths, insights, and perspectives we may adopt as our own or reject. They offer worlds for us to

explore and contemplate, or we may simply revel in the pleasure of moving from the world around us to these other worlds of infinite possibility. (2001, p. 1)

The chapter divides the films into three main categories: popular dramas, political satire and independent films. In each of these categories, I analyse the role of films produced and released during 2006–10 in the uprising. With reference to academic analyses, the chapter examines the texts, reception and issues with censorship of the films. I argue pre-revolution films captured the public's sociopolitical and economic conditions that led to the uprising and imagined potential consequences (e.g. the overthrow of the regime). These different genres have produced a political affect through revealing images of protests and rebel in response to issues of poverty, political corruption and police brutality.

In contrast to the vast literature examining the relationship between social media and the Egyptian Revolution, few scholars have shed light on the role of film in the uprising. Tartoussieh (2012) considers the role of other media formats in 'voicing discontent', since 'digital activism alone cannot do justice to years of on-the-ground anti-neoliberal and pro-labour right activism' (p. 156). He focuses on 'Imarat Ya'qubiyan, a film based on a novel of the same name (written by the political activist 'Ala' al-Aswani) and one of the most expensive Egyptian productions at that time. The cast includes the 1980s and 1990s film stars such as 'Adil Imam, Nuwr al-Shirif and Yusra together with the younger stars such as Hind Sabri, Khalid al-Sawi and Khalid Salih. Also, the high-budget social melodramas of director Khalid Yusif are popular for their depictions of poverty and violence among lower classes. The following paragraphs will focus on 'Imarat Ya'qubiyan and Khalid Yusif's films as examples of popular films that dealt with issues of political bribery and poverty using high budgets and films stars. It provides a close textual analysis of scenes and sequences from these films that represented the public's discontent and were evident during the 2011 Revolution. The representations of anger in popular films demonstrate the role of film in reinforcing and spreading notions of resistance during the pre-revolution period.

Set in the 1990s, 'Imarat Ya'qubiyan reveals the substantial changes within Egyptian society since the 1952 Coup d'état. The film uses a building in downtown Cairo as a metaphor for contemporary Egyptian society and engages with issues of political corruption, poverty and radicalization through intertwining stories of the inhabitants of the building. Although, following Ahmad (1987), I disagree with Jameson's (1981) generalized view of all Third World texts as 'national allegories'; *'Imarat Ya'qubiyan* conforms to Jameson's description: 'the story of the private individual destiny is [...] an allegory of the embattled situation of the public third-world culture and society' (1981, p. 69). The film starts with a historical account of the building, which started with ministers, pashas, foreigners and Jewish inhabitants before the 1952 Coup d'état. The residents gradually changed according to the political and economic changes in Egypt, such as the 1956 War and Sadat's *infitāh*. The rooftop that accommodated the door attendant and storage rooms for each flat has now turned into a slum neighbourhood. The current building inhabitants come from different social backgrounds, such as Zaki al-Disuki, one of the oldest bourgeoisie inhabitants of the building (played by 'Adil Imam), and Busayna, a roof-dweller who accepts her boss sexual harassment for extra money to provide for her family. The film represents class struggle through the refusal of the Police Academy to accept Taha (the doorman's son), due to his father's job, which is deemed as a low-status job within Egyptian society. Consequently, Taha joins an Islamist radical group as a fighter leading to his torture and raping by the police. Among the other residents is Hajj 'Azzam, a rich businessman who becomes a member of the parliament.

Tabishat (2012) claims that pre-revolution films in Egypt created an 'imagined society' with elements of unity and fragmentation. He explains, 'In these works of art, unity is generally expressed in terms of the nation and the family, as well as in terms of an assumed collaboration among different classes. Disunity is generally portrayed as a consequence of injustice against low-income groups and women' (Tabishat, 2012, p. 377). *'Imarat Ya'qubiyan* portrays different social classes and forms of power and ideologies within a single society. It reveals the contemporary Egyptian social structure in relation to changes in political ideologies (such as Nasser's socialism and Sadat's *infitāh*) and rising corruption. The film uses a historical approach to visualize the political, cultural and social transformations that Egypt witnessed in the past few decades. Following the novel, *'Imarat Ya'qubiyan* uses parallel storylines to address issues of bribery, police brutality, poverty and radicalism. The contrast between the film's mise-en-scene, in particular, the settings of the bourgeoisie flats and rooftop, visually expresses Tabishat's (2012) theory of unity and fragmentation. Although the building unites both the elite and the rooftop dwellers, the settings and use of props expose the binary opposition of the social classes. The film is set in downtown Cairo, which portrays the social and cultural changes in Egypt. Commercial offices and stores have now seized the nineteenth-century French-style buildings, which were once the home of the elites.

The film reveals the political structure of Mubarak's Egypt including issues of political corruption and bribery involved in parliamentary elections. It confirms the domination of one political party (representing Mubarak's NDP) and the depletion of al-Ikhwan al-Muslimin's (the Muslim Brotherhood – the largest opposition group) representatives in the people's assembly in an undemocratic political system. When Hajj 'Azzam decides to join the parliament, he visits Kamal al-Fuwli (in reference to Kamal al-Shazli, a long-serving parliament member and representative of the state's corruption in the film) who asks for one million pounds in return. When Hajj 'Azzam requests to pay less, al-Fuwli replies, 'this amount is shared among several authorities … I already have enough'. He also tells 'Azzam that he is in competition with Abu Rihab, one of the Muslim Brotherhood members running for the parliamentary elections. Hajj 'Azzam discloses his expectations of losing against Abu Rihab, who is very popular among his district for his financial aids, but al-Fuwli states, 'anyone can run for the elections, this is a democracy, but who wins is our game. Not through fraudulence, but we have well studied the public's psyche'. The 2010 parliamentary elections, one of the main triggers of the revolution – where the NDP's representation increased by 21 per cent in an obvious vote rigging (Mumtaz, 2011), recalls the film's depiction of corruption and the domination of a single political party. This scene confirmed the political corruption during Mubarak's era and implicitly documented the NDP's domination within the narrated historical timeline of Egypt (from 1937 to the 1990s).

The film also engages with the policemen's brutal handling of protests and torture of detainees. One scene shows Islamists' mass protest originating from the University of Cairo, led by Taha chanting 'Islamic, Islamic … neither eastern nor western'. The attack of the central security forces (specialized in dealing with crowds and riots) against the protesters using batons is similar to shots of the uprising. Hamid emphasized the violent attack in this sequence, through using action film techniques of fast pace editing, wobbly camera movement and chaotic music that punctuates the action, to rationalize the violent response of radical Islamists. The scenes of Taha's torture and rape illustrate the excessive violence exerted against detainees during the pre-revolution period. The scenes reveal the state security officer hanging and slapping Taha blindfolded. The orchestral score by Khalid Hammad, together with low-key lighting in these scenes reinforces the sympathy with Taha's character and rationalize the Islamists' use of violence against the police to take revenge. The construction of Taha as a hero, in this storyline (who was rejected from joining the Police Academy due to his father's job), in relation to the state security officer as a villain, generates anger towards social injustice in Mubarak's Egypt.

As a popular film, *'Imarat Ya'qubiyan* uses drama genre conventions in narrating its stories. The film employs emotional soundtrack to sympathize with characters and represent them as victims. In addition, the construction of heroes versus villains and traditional narrative structure abide by generic conventions of popular drama films. Near the end of the film, Taha takes revenge by killing the police officer who tortured him, signalling an expected move of the oppressed against injustice. Optimistically, the film ends with Zaki (the elite) marrying the much younger Busayna (the roof-top girl), representing hope and a new beginning of congruity between different social classes. However, the film reinforces the notion of the indisputable power of the regime and detrimental consequences of engaging with politics. It does not accuse Mubarak's regime directly and links the economic deterioration and culture and social degradation to past political events (such as the 1952 Coup and Sadat's *infitāh*).

Although censorship has been strict with the taboo triad of politics, religion and sex, some productions have addressed issues of political corruption, social injustice, Islamism and homosexuality. The leniency of censorship towards these films has complicated the process of our understanding of the decision-making process of the censors. The elastic rules which the censors operate under, such as the protection of 'public morals' and 'public order', give them space to accept or reject scripts and films based on unclear criteria.[2] Although Mubarak's regime allowed some films, such as *'Imarat Ya'qubiyan* and *Hiyya Fawda*, as if to prove that freedom of expression exists, they underestimated the power of film in charging audiences emotionally and reinforcing the popular notions of the state's corruption and use of violence. Mubarak's regime was confident of their 'control' over the country. *'Imarat Ya'qubiyan* does not only reveal political corruption and engage with issues of social injustices and Islamism but represents homosexuality through one of the inhabitants of the buildings. Although censorship prohibits explicit sexual and homosexual scenes, they allowed the release of *'Imarat Ya'qubiyan* with a 'for adults only' classification to limit its viewership.

'Imarat Ya'qubiyan, as a blockbuster, garnered many local and international audiences and achieved mixed reviews from film critics and viewers. Members of the parliament, such as Mustafa Bakri and Hassan Hamdi (spokesman of the Muslim Brotherhood), condemned the film's portrayal of homosexuality that collides with 'morals and values of Egyptians'. On the other hand, some film-makers, such as Aytin Amin and Hala Lutfi, view *Imarat Ya'qubiyan* as a conservative film. Although the film does not directly accuse the regime of Mubarak of the transformation of the social structure, it depicts issues of

corruption, poverty and police brutality, which were among the main triggers of the 2011 Revolution. Reviews of the film considered its 'despairing view of Egyptian society, whether in its political injustice or sexual hypocrisy; the virus of corruption invades every level of the milieu, and its social divisions render it a breeding ground for terrorism' (Quinn, 2007). In a television interview, film critic Tari' al-Shinnawi recognized the film's bold analysis of religious radicalism and its link to the regime, state and political and social corruption. *'Imarat Ya'qubiyan* encouraged a few film-makers, such as Khalid Yusif, to represent poverty more openly in popular dramas.

Film director Khalid Yusif, one of the students of the internationally acclaimed director Yusif Shahin, is known for his sociopolitical concerns, liberal political views and support for the 2011 Revolution. The pre-revolution tragedy films of Khalid Yusif, such as *Hiyna Maysara* and *Dukkan Shihata*, are popular for their depictions of poverty and social injustice. Khalid Yusif's films are high-budget productions that cast stars. Although his films are successful at the box-office and receive some positive critical reviews, some spectators criticize his portrayal of Egypt in a negative light. They accuse him of spreading Egypt's 'dirty laundry' among international audiences. Film reviews criticize his films for its poor and 'naïve' cinematic language (such as the direct and obvious analogies) and 'superficial depiction of social problems' (al-Ghitani, 2015). Some film-makers, such as Hala Lutfi (2013), accuse him of commodifying issues of poverty. Being from the urban elite, Khalid Yusif and his cast represent these issues of poverty, stereotypically, from above. For example, the leading characters accept their deprived living conditions and work in drugs or sex trafficking. However, he still showed images of poverty and violence in popular films that attracted mass audiences.

Hiyna Maysara focuses on the marginalized and deprived slum dwellers and exposes their inhuman living conditions. At the time of its release, the film sparked controversy around its fierce portrayal of conditions of extreme poverty, which Yusif apologises for at the end of the film 'the reality is even crueller than to be presented on screen'. A few writers and journalists, such as 'Abd al-Latif al-Manawi (2012, p. 180), claimed the exposition of social injustice and political oppression in the film suggested an upcoming 'revolution of the hungry'.[3] The film triggered the anger of conservative viewers due to its portrayal of a homosexual relationship between two women. Islamic scholars, such as 'Abd al-Sabur Shahin, accused the film of promoting moral vandalism and called for an investigation of the director and actors. The film is produced by Albatrous (owned by Kamil abu 'Ali), which built a large set of the slum that was demolished by the police at the ending sequence of the film.

Hiyna Maysara begins in the 1990s and goes through to the early 2000s, and narrates the story of Nahid, a young working-class woman who escapes from her mother's house because of her sexual harassment by her stepfather. She gets into a sexual relationship with 'Adil Hashisha, a mechanic who lives with his mother and nine nephews in a cramped room, leading to her pregnancy. 'Adil refuses to marry Nahid, as he cannot provide for the family. After giving birth, Nahid fails to embrace her son and leaves him behind on a public bus. 'Adil turns into a drug dealer and hooligan moving around the neighbourhood with a penknife.[4]

The film represents the deprived living conditions of slum dwellers and acts as a warning alarm of the growing oppression and violence within slums. It notes how slums embrace terrorism, through an Islamist radical group and a weapons storage hidden in the neighbourhood. In order to arrest the group, the police must demolish the neighbourhood, which happens in the penultimate sequence. The film also tackles police brutality through scenes of torturing of 'Adil's family, who are suspected of knowing future terrorist incidents. Similar to *'Imarat Ya'qubiyan*, the film exposes humiliating torturing methods such as using electric shock and savage dogs to terrify the detainees, and disrobing the female members of the family.

In contrast to mainstream films, which usually limit its depiction of poverty to families living in popular neighbourhoods, Yusif intensely portrayed the impoverished lives of the slum inhabitants. The design of the slum neighbourhood rooms shows the families crammed into small units, leaving no space for privacy. The scene of sexual intercourse between 'Adil and Nahid takes place in 'Adil's room while his family is sleeping, with only a curtain separating them, conveying the dehumanized nature of their living standards. Fathi, 'Adil's neighbour, is living with his two wives in the same room. On the night of Fathi's second wedding, he asks his first wife to leave the room so he can have sex with his new wife. Scenes of stealing a sheep's head from a butcher, searching in the garbage for leftovers and a fight over a cloth banner (originally used to promote a parliamentary election candidate, but reused as an underwear) reinforce the conditions of absolute poverty. Saa'diyya, one of the girls living in the neighbourhood, sells her body to the young men of the neighbourhood for only five Egyptian pounds. The film expresses the marginalization and insignificance of the slum dwellers. In one scene Fathi tells 'Adil:

> Back then when you were young, a big quarrel happened. Tanks filled up the street and curfews were set, but your brother and I did not care. We took a walk in the street between the tanks. No one felt us or asked who we were ... can you imagine! Your brother asked, are we non-existent or invisible?

These lines explain the insignificance of the slum dwellers not only to the state but also to the society as a whole. However, the film dramatizes sequences using exaggerated performances by the actors. It does not engage with the inner complexities and contradictions of the characters. Many of the characters' motivations are unexplained, due to the film's priority of representing issues of violence, fundamentalism and poverty.

Despite its fragmented narrative, *Hiyna Maysara* is one of the first Egyptian films to explore slum neighbourhoods. Before this, films were set in a *hārah* or an alley to represent working-class neighbourhoods. When *'ashwa'iyat* or slums started growing in Cairo, films such as *Hiyna Maysara* raised awareness among the public regarding an obscured social class and living standards. The popular film garnered many audiences and some positive reviews for discussing the issue of slums intensely. Writer and television presenter Mahmud al-Wirwari defended the film and appraised its representation of slums. He described the film's title, *When Convenient,* as a 'symbol for the delayed hopes of those crushed people' and added, 'silence is no longer enough to hide the stagnant water' (al-Wirwari, 2008). The film's commercial success encouraged Yusif to engage with similar sociopolitical issues, including poverty and violence, in his next film – *Dukkan Shihata*.

Khalid Yusif's *Dukkan Shihata*, although a romantic drama, also engages with the sociopolitical changes and economic deterioration. The film projects comparable images to violence and security issues during the 2011 Revolution. Inspired by Kissat Yusuf (The story of Joseph), *Dukkan Shihata* recounts the story of Shihata's family, an indigent family from Upper Egypt living in Cairo. His father favours Shihata, which stimulates the jealousy of his half-brothers. After the death of their father, the brothers accuse Shihata of forgery leading to his imprisonment and one of the brothers marries Biysa, Shihata's fiancée (played by the Lebanese singer Haifaa' Wahbi).

In *Dukkan Shihata*, Yusif continued his political practice of situating his sociopolitical concerns along his narrative. The film starts with the release of Shihata from prison in 2013 and the credits highlight significant local and international news headlines in a reverse fashion until 1981, where the narrative begins with the birth of Shihata. The headlines include 'President Sadat assassinated', 'America launches a war in Iraq' and '283 demonstrators arrested in April 6 strike'. Since the film is a 2009 production, it anticipated future headlines such as 'Unemployment and food crises sweep over Egypt' in 2010, 'Obama discusses the withdrawal of American forces from Iraq' in 2012 and 'Humanity on the threshold of a multi-power world' in 2013.

The sequences of *Dukkan Shihata*, which represented the political crisis, include the projection of the deteriorating economic conditions in 2013. Yusif envisioned his concerns through the perspective of Shihata, who has been in prison for almost eight years. Inspired by the bread shortages in Egypt during 2008, the opening sequence of the film (set in 2013) reveals the dire need for bread (which was one of the main demands of the 2011 Revolution). After his release, Shihata encounters a group of young men intercepting a train carrying wheat. The families and dwellers of an impoverished area, where the train stops, raid the train and snatch the wheat bags. The film also includes scenes of long queues at children's public hospitals and people selling unfiltered water, due to the water shortage. Journalists such as Waliyd Badran (2009) confirmed that 'the film expects an explosion and more violence in Egypt soon'.

The film augments Khalid Yusif's suggestion of the growing violence among the lower classes, represented through the fights in long queues for bread, and 'everyday' fights between young men using blades. The film ends with a montage that envisages the rise of violence in the near future. The montage includes close-up shots of penknives and crossing blades foregrounding iconic symbols of Egypt, such as the pyramids and Cairo's tower. Shots of intimidating the public, people running in different directions, and installation of iron gates and door locks are almost identical predictions of what happened during the revolution. The montage also forecasts the rise of Islamists, through shots of a radical group (stereotypically portrayed with their white galabiya and beards) breaking down film theatres and forcing women to wear Hijab (veil) – some of the popular fears among Egyptians during the ruling period of the Muslim Brotherhood. The montage ends with the deployment of central security forces in the streets of Cairo and the disappearance of people and cars from Ramsis (Cairo's train station and a very populated area), indicating a new curfew setting and suggesting the overthrow of the regime.

This sequence demonstrates Yusif's anticipation of the public intimidation and chaos as a result of the growing oppression and poverty and hinted the fall of the regime in *Dukkan Shihata*. However, similar to *Hiyna Maysara*, the sequence is not relevant to the main storyline of the film – a traditional romantic story of a couple who confront obstacles set by a group of villains. The unconvincing insertion of these shots within a clichéd dramatic narrative supports the view that Yusif exploits issues of poverty and violence in films using stars for commercial success. Censorship delayed the permit to screen the film due to its ending sequence. 'Ali abu Shadi, head of censorship at the time, viewed the montage as advocating chaos, which is against the law of censorship of 'protecting the public order'. The deployment of security forces in the ending montage suggests the overthrow of Mubarak's regime. Abu Shadi did not approve the film until the Ministry of Interior and Ministry of Defence approved it (Ezzat, al-Haqq and Fazulla, 2014, p. 33–4).

However, the fact that social problems were not limited to independent productions (known for their freedom and openness in discussing the 'taboos') and started to appear intensely in popular films indicates the excessive corruption, poverty and growing public anger. The constant comparisons of colonial Egypt (in *'Imarat Ya'qubiyan*) and Nasser's Egypt (in *Hiyya Fawda* and *Dukkan Shihata*) to Mubarak's Egypt represent the decline in social and economic spheres due to changes in political ideologies and led by social injustice and increasing corruption. These films continued to urge the necessity of considering social justice, through projecting 'undesired' endings that involve violence. Khalid Yusif's films, in particular, included violent fights over power in the lower classes. His portrayal of the hooligan as a hero within his district became a popular theme in post-revolution films. These films exposed under-represented stories about lower social classes and their living standards as well as political corruption and torturing of detainees. As popular films, they raised awareness among mass audiences of middle and higher social classes who can afford going to film theatres. They acted as means of expressing discontent at the time of production and release, and currently stand as explanatory accounts of the underlying conditions leading to the 2011 Revolution.

Meanwhile, the films discussed in the previous paragraphs engage with issues of hunger and violence but they do not use what Rocha (1983) dubs as the aesthetics of hunger. Their use of popular genres, high budgets and film stars does not relate to the depicted issues of poverty and suggests the bourgeoisie film-makers' view of the narrative. These film-makers and stars tend to portray the deprived living conditions 'from above'. They sympathize with poverty issues and exploit them in exaggerated melodramas for commercial purposes. Film-makers interested in engaging in politics did not restrict themselves to the high-budget dramas. They also used political satire, to fit within the popular comedy films that have dominated Egyptian cinema since the late 1990s. Using comedy has also made it easier to achieve the approval of censorship as it was considered as 'soft critique'.

Film scholars have extended their examination of the relationship between pre-revolution films and the uprising to different genres and stylistic approaches. al-Zubidi (2011, p. 236) suggests that the themes of the revolution were not limited to 'serious and realistic films', but were also reflected in commercial and comedy films.⁵ He refers to *al-Diktatur*, a comedy film that narrates public anger towards the dictator of Bambuzia and his two sons, leading to their fall. In the following paragraphs, I examine political satire and comedy films that deal with themes of dictatorship and anticipate public revolts. These films include *al-Diktatur*, *Zaza* and *Rami al-I'tisami* (*Rami the Protester*, Sami Rafi', 2008). In order to circumvent censorship, some of the films are set in imagined countries, but make clear references to Egypt's historical, political and social contexts. These films used comedy, the prevalent genre of that time, to engage with sociopolitical issues of poverty and unemployment. They imagine situations where the public has revolted against the long-standing ruler. Comedy films, such as *Rami al-I'tisami*, have also supported anti-revolution stances through portraying protesters as unserious.

One of the main reasons leading up to the 2011 Revolution was the public's certainty of the plan of Mubarak to pass the presidency to Gamal, the younger of his two sons. In contrast to his older brother 'Ala' (a businessman not involved in politics), Gamal had a politically active role as the deputy secretary general of the dominating NDP. The basic narrative of *al-Diktatur* – a dictator (who claims to be democratic) called Shanan and his two sons, draws closely on the family of Mubarak. The older son of Shanan is an authoritarian (wearing the uniform of a military dictator) and obsessed with business. He continuously gives orders to sell parts of the state including institutions and rents the presidential palace to an Asian country. The second son of Shanan, 'Aziz, is a spoiled young man who enjoys his family's authority and flirts with women. The film emphasizes Shanan's dictatorship through the Nazi salutation of the ministers and the picture of Hitler hanging in the palace.

In order to get the censorship's acceptance of his script, the director chose to set the film in Bambuzia – an imagined republic. Bambuzia appears in mainly two contrasting sets: the luxurious presidential palace and a desert village, where the public lives. However, the obvious metaphors in the film create an impression that the film is representing Egypt. The opening scene introduces Bambuzia as an ancient country that contributed to human civilization. The introduction includes the martyrs of Bambuzia and people's resistance to the invaders throughout ages, due to its 'strategic location', which strengthens the link to the history of Egypt. On their visit to Egypt, the secretary of 'Aziz announces the 'strong ties' between both countries (Egypt and Bambuzia) in a press conference stating, 'any assault or prejudice against Egypt is considered an assault or prejudice against Bambuzia'. In another scene, the succession of Shanan to presidency appears after killing the ruling leader. The narrator dubs the scene stating, 'Bambuzia is a role model of interchanging authority'. The scene draws upon mythologies of how Egyptian presidents succeeded their predecessors. In addition, Shanan sarcastically considers his seventy-year-old ministers young, in reference to Mubarak's old ministers.

The film does not only represent an allegorical picture of Egypt's political scene but also visualizes a revolution.[6] The film exposes public anger, although superficially, through events which are similar to the 2011 Revolution. In the film, protests call for the fall of the leader due to the prevalent conditions of poverty. The few short scenes of protests correspond to the 28 January chaos, including vandalizing government buildings, the police attack on demonstrators, and looting of markets (the film shows a montage of people stealing bread and fruits). Moreover, the development of the events of the revolution in the narrative, such as the takeover of the military, is similar to the sequence of events following the 2011 Revolution.[7] Unlike Mubarak and his sons, who were set free of charges, the film shows Shanan and his son sentenced to death. In the film, Shanan and his son escape by the help of a psychic Bambuzian citizen, who tortures them at his remote cottage. Although the film presents the torture scenes in a comedic style, it reveals the citizen's pleasure in torturing and ridiculing Shanan and his son. The scene portrays the desire of taking cruel revenge of the long-standing injustice. The film ends with the dictator and his son back in power. They take revenge on the psychic citizen, through burning his cottage, which reminds the audience of the power of the ruler and the danger of rebelling against him.

Despite the employment of commercial elements in the film, such as comic actors including Hassan Husni and Khalid Sarhan, and female singer, Maya Nasri, it was not commercially successful. Film reviews criticized *al-Diktatur* for the poor development of its narrative. Mahmud al-Turki described the film's events as disjointed, distorted and failed to combine comedy and satire with critical criticism (al-Turki, 2009). The film focuses more on 'Aziz's flirtation scenes, rather than poverty in Bambuzia. The rationalization of the failure of the revolution and return of the dictator in leadership is not clear in the ending of the film. The film includes songs shot with a music-video style for commercial purposes, but with no dramatic reasoning. However, the film treats the issue of poverty and dictatorship with an imagined scenario of what happened years later. Film critics, such as 'Adli (2009), who criticized the film for its poor narrative structure, have also acknowledged the film's few political hints and reference to the presidency succession plans. Viewing the film after the 2011 Revolution does not only recall comparable images and events from the uprising but strengthens the different forms of expressing discontent and expectancy during the pre-revolution period. *al-Diktatur* was not the only Egyptian film to create an imagined country and criticize Mubarak's regime. *Zaza* is also set in a 'third-world' country to circumvent censorship.

Although *Zaza* uses made-up flags and police and army uniforms, the settings of the presidential palace, the working-class neighbourhood of Zaza and the police station are typically Egyptian. Inspired by the 2005 presidential elections – the first multi-candidate presidential election in Egypt – *Zaza* is a comedy film about a long-reigning autocratic leader forced to make democratic elections due to 'external pressure'. The film narrates the engagement of the government and media in the electoral fraud and supports the claim of foreign interest in taking control over Egypt.

The film depicts a live broadcast television show that uses Sa'id Zaza, a middle-class young man, to fake telephone calls to support the president in the elections. The Ministry of Interior kills the 'dangerous' contenders, which drives all the candidates away, leaving the president with no real opponents. The television anchor, working secretly with a foreign ambassador (apparently American), extorts Zaza to run for the presidency. The chief of presidential staff convinces the president that Zaza is infamous and will not achieve any votes. Zaza earns the support of the majority and wins the presidential elections after an emotional speech that he makes on television. Zaza takes a set of decisions as a president, such as sending brutal police officers to jail, accepting the resignation of the government and 'liberating the nation' through refusing foreign aid, which is usually exchanged for the subordination and indignity of the country. In 2006, the censorship department approved the popular comedy after cutting some scenes, such as the trial of the ministers, and adding a note that reads 'The film has nothing to do with the reality we are living at all … at all … at all' at the beginning of the film.

Zaza expands on the need to change the long-standing president and his ruling ideologies. The film proposes an imagined scenario of electing an ordinary citizen as a president. A citizen who feels the hunger and poverty of people, as Zaza declares. Thus, the film represents Zaza as an 'Egyptian Dream' of empowering the oppressed and regaining dignity and liberty. The long-awaited dream and its aspects of justice and freedom are pertaining to the spirit of the revolution supporters. In one scene a citizen reports 'Sa'id [Zaza] is the dream; if he dies the dream dies'. However, the film was unpopular upon its release. It was only watched by a few audience due to its release alongside films for more popular stars such as 'Adil Imam's *'Imarat Ya'qubiyan*, Karim 'Abd al-'Aziz's action film *Wahid min al-Nas* (*One of the People*, Ahmad Nadir Galal, 2006) and

Ahmad Hilmi's comedy *Ga'alatni Mugriman* (*She Made Me a Criminal*, 'Amr 'Arafa, 2006).

Similar to other political satire films of the time, *Zaza* acquits Mubarak of responsibility for poverty and police brutality. In the presidential debate scene, Zaza blames intermediaries between the president and the public for the economic deterioration, which reinforces the popular notion that Mubarak is 'an innocent man misled and manipulated by his advisors' (Snowdon, 2016, p. 270). Although the film might have endorsed this position for censorship purposes, it confirms the views of Mubarak's supporters and confines the demand for change by the public. The film also supports the anti-revolution beliefs of conspiracy theories. The involvement of the American ambassador and the 'infiltrator' anchor in choosing and supporting Zaza to become their subordinate supports counter-revolution arguments of the involvement of conspiracies in the revolution. *Rami al-I'tisami* also supported counter-revolution conspiracy theories of foreign funding for protesting.

The comedy film, *Rami al-I'tisami*, narrates the story of Rami – an irresponsible rich young man, trying to get the attention of Yara (an attractive girl obsessed with celebrities) through being popular. Rami creates a Facebook group to change the national anthem. The group gets popular and attracts the attention of the media. The government rejects the demand of the group and describes the anthem as 'one of the constants of the nation'. Inspired by a workers' strike (referring to al-Mahalla al-Kubra's strike on 6 April), Rami calls for a sit-in at the headquarter of the prime minister. Rami and his friends start the sit-in hoping that Yara will join them. Later on, Yara joins Rami's protest and turns it into a 'five-star' sit-in, including food catering, gym equipment, toilets and sleeping tents. The 'Change and Change Yourself' sit-in grows through American financial support as well as the participation of Islamists and a group of low-class citizens. The latter group joined the protest after police officers forced them to evacuate their slums as an investor has purchased the land.

The film's representation of the revolutionaries as spoiled youth instigated the anger of some political activists (Shabab 6 Ibril). Film critics, such as Rami 'Abd al-Razi', also commented on the film's 'superficial and naïve engagement with political issues' ('Abd al-Razi', 2008). The film, realizing its comedy genre, depends on a few and simplistic stereotypes to represent the characters of social or religious groups. The actors exaggerate the spoiled attitude of the wealthy sector, the conservative behaviour of the religious and the barbaric appearance of the lower classes. However, the film shows the three groups (high class, low class and religious) segregated in the sit-in area, with the same demands of changing the national anthem and the flag. The segregation (especially between Rami's group and the working-class group) emphasizes the wide gap between the social classes, which led to the 2011 Revolution.

Whereas the sit-in has much relevance to the 2011 Revolution, including the call through Facebook, Armbrust (2012) argues that *Rami al-I'tisami* anticipates the anti-revolutionary stance that took place during and after the revolution. He asserts the film depicts the main accusations held against the revolution such as unserious protesters, conspiracy theories and bribery. The film also prospects the varied social and political groups gathering in a sit-in. During the eighteen days of the 2011 Revolution, protesters from different social backgrounds and political ideologies occupied Tahrir square. Conglomerating the upper-class demonstrators with their luxurious lifestyle beside the lower class and the Islamists demonstrates the film's suggestion of an intersection point between different social and political ideologies. It supports Tabishat's (2012) theory of unity and fragmentation through contrasting three different categories of the Egyptian society grouped against the government. The film also realized the role of social media, specifically Facebook, as a potential tool for crowding youth against the government.

The film projects the participation of the Muslim Brotherhood in the uprising. In the film, they are the last group to join the sit-in and their leader seeks to represent the sit-in during negotiations with the government. The Muslim Brotherhood, through their strong presence in and support for the revolution, seized the uprising to achieve their plans of ruling the country. The film imagines the government's use of hostility between the three groups to break up the sit-in, similarly to what happened shortly after the revolution. The media called the alleged deal between the Muslim Brotherhood and the Supreme Council of the Armed Forces (SCAF) to support the March 2011 constitutional referendum as 'the first nail in the coffin of the revolution'.[8] Similar to other political satire films discussed in this chapter, *Rami al-I'tisami* did not radically engage with political issues or criticize the government. The film did not politicize viewers due to its unpopularity. However, the film represented the understanding of the film-makers of the social and political scene and recognized the potential of aggregating different social and political groups.

The rise of *mugat āl-āflām āl-kumidiya* (comedy film wave) by the end of the 1990s led to the remarkable popularity of comedy films in Egypt during the noughties. However, the growing expression of anger in 2005 influenced some comedy films to move towards political satire. These films sought to address political criticism through the genre of comedy, to appear as 'soft' and 'light' for the regime and ease the claim of censorship's approval. Like other comedies, the narratives of these films use a plot twist (in this case politically related) to stimulate laughter and possibly evoke feelings of oppression. Some of these films chose to set their narratives in vague or invented countries to bypass censorship, while others redirected their accusations to the advisors of the president and took an anti-revolutionary stance. They commonly engage with themes of poverty and (partially) dictatorship and intersect in their expectancy of rebellion against the ruler or the government. These films did not create a political affect due to their unpopularity and use of images of revolutions in a sarcastic context. However, they are a form of wish-fulfilment as they represented dreams of revolting against dictatorship and injustice.

These films imagined political scenarios (influenced by real events) to create humorous scenes. Many of these imagined scenarios were actualized years later during the 2011 Revolution. But these films, together with popular dramas, are rarely seen as forms of resistance. Independent film-makers usually view these films as a part of the mainstream commercial industry. Albeit representing political critiques, these films are preserving the status quo and conforming to the capitalist Hollywood star-system that Egyptian cinema adopted since its inception. In the meantime, technology has empowered a few film-makers to express themselves freely. These independent film-makers used inexpensive digital cameras and alternative aesthetics as a form of political and artistic resistance.

The development of digital technologies has meant that independent productions have proliferated since 2005. Film-makers have used digital cameras (as an inexpensive medium) to tell their personal stories and express their visions of society. Independent films include Ibrahim al-Battut's *Ithaki* (2005), which instigated the rise of other independent productions, such as *'In Shams, Basra, Hiliaupulis* and *al-Khurug min al-Qahira*.[9] Unlike other pre-revolution productions, 'independent films' did not capture revolutionary-like images, but they represented political and social oppression during the pre-revolution period. They consider the revolution, not only as a part of their texts but also as a part of their film form and aesthetics. Quite similar to the Third Cinema movement, film-makers sought to oppose the mainstream film industry through considering alternative means of production, distribution and exhibition. Technological developments helped them to make their films freely, without being subject to the choices of producers. With the support of inexpensive digital cameras, film-makers financed their own films using their personal savings, film institution funds and/or voluntary crews. Since most of these films are not commercially successful, they are released for a few weeks in a few film theatres. Film-makers who use this style aim at showing their films at international film festivals and local cultural centres.

These film-makers do not comply with the commercial market considerations usually through choosing simple narrative structures and casting new actors. The use of digital cameras (which produced sharp images) and natural lighting in many cases, as well as improvised scenes and shooting in real locations, emphasizes the 'realistic' depictions of the contemporary Egyptian society. These realistic approaches aimed to connect emotionally with audiences and leave them with a political feeling. Films such as *'In Shams*, *Basra*, and *Hiliaupulis* were shot using digital/HD cameras then transferred to 35 mm film for theatrical release.[10] By the end of 2010, Ahmad 'Abd Allah directed a film called *Mikrufun* (*Microphone*) about the underground art in Alexandria including music bands, graffiti artists and film-makers.[11] It is the first feature film shot on a 7D Canon camera and released in film theatres. These films incorporate documentary-like segments within them. They merge footage of protests or interviews blurring the distinction between fiction and reality. They persistently use hand-held and long-take shots to engage the audience in the struggles of the characters. These stylistic elements became an integral part of many 'independent films'. In fact, the use of digital cameras in the production of these films is in itself revolutionary.

In their discussion on the question of realism, Shohat and Stam (1994) explain that oppressed groups have used realism 'as a style or constellation of strategies aimed at producing an illusionistic "reality effect"' (p. 180) to contest the hegemonic representations of mainstream films. However, they argue, '"Reality" is not self-evidently given and "truth" is not immediately "seizable" by the camera' (p. 180). While many Egyptian independent film-makers aim at representing social realities, using a deconstructive and reflexive style, it is important to consider Shohat and Stam's question of the ideologies and discourses that construct these films. It is crucial to view these films 'as a delegation of voices' (1994, p. 180) rather than contrasting them to 'truth' or 'reality'. Independent productions in Egypt during the pre-revolution period relayed dissent discourses of class struggle and social injustices.

Films represented the growing dream of immigration among youth as a way out of oppression and poverty. Film-makers used digital mediums to represent voices as a practice of delegation rather than depiction (Gilroy, 1988, p. 44). These films, although only watched by a few (mainly international film festivals and the intelligentsia) audiences, were statements of resistance to the hegemonic ideologies. In 2010, Egyptian novelist Dr Khalid al-Khamissi was part of a discussion about independent cinema in Egypt in a television show. al-Khamissi asserted the relevance of independent films to the contemporary social and political crisis. He said:

> We are going through a difficult economic and political situation and youth are looking for a ground to lean on. In their search journey, they create. They are moving towards liberation. There are about 400,000 online bloggers writing daily, new music bands, a new style of journalism and online radio stations. Cinema is part of this movement. It is related to a specific social, economic and political situation. We are currently witnessing a significant cultural mobility that youth started in 2005. (al-Khamissi, 2010)

The development of digital technologies before the revolution, as a new form of self-expression, gave voice to individuals. It helped them to resist or bypass mainstream film-making and develop their own styles.

Although the narratives of these films seem traditional, their distinctive (usually simple) narrative structures differentiate them from mainstream films. They tend to heighten the struggle of people similar to cinemas of resistance, such as Third Cinema. For example, *In Shams* is about a young girl called Shams diagnosed with leukaemia. Ramadan, the father of Shams, is a taxi driver and a businessman's chauffeur. *Basra*, set in 2003, reveals the fears and concerns of a young photographer within the growing oppression and the Fall of Baghdad. The film integrates footage of anti-war protests in Egypt. *Hiliaupulis* is a set of interrelated stories taking place in one day and one neighbourhood – called *Hiliaupulis* (Heliopolis). During this day, none of the characters (frustrated and struggling young adults) accomplishes their goal(s) set for the day. *al-Khurug min al-Qahira* narrates a love story between Tari' and Amal in one of Cairo's poor neighbourhoods. Their marriage is restricted by their different religions (Muslim and Christian). Tari', unsatisfied with his job as a deliveryman and supermarket cashier, decides to immigrate to Europe. However, instead of committing to the traditional storytelling structure of context, conflict, climax and closure, these films attempt to evoke sympathetic feelings about, thoughts of and reflections on the story and the characters. These films, among other independent productions, narrate one day or a part of the life of the characters without a definite ending. The main characters are usually victims of social injustice.

Unlike mainstream films, which are usually centred on a leading character, independent films account the stories of multiple characters. The film-makers represent the characters in relation to the wider social and political issues. In some cases, the representation of characters takes place within the context of a specific area. *'In Shams* and *Hiliaupulis* are the names of popular districts in Cairo where the narratives take place. Both of these films recount the structural transformation of their areas (representing Egypt) throughout history. *'In Shams* reveals the neglect of the neighbourhood after being the capital of Egypt, and *Hiliaupulis* depicts the vanished grandeur of Cairo's cosmopolitan district. One of the scenes in *'In Shams* shows Ramadan (the chauffeur) retelling the great history of 'In Shams to the businessman while he is driving him home. The camera is following the car (sometimes taking the driver's subjective point-of-view) in one of the main streets of 'In Shams, revealing the poverty and inhuman living conditions such as garbage, pollution and overpopulation through the surroundings of their neighbourhoods.

The scene reinforces the representation of 'In Shams of Egypt through Ramadan's (apparently improvised) lines "In Shams is the centre of the world' referring to the geographical position of Egypt and 'It is floating on a sea of monuments'. *In Shams* compares inhuman living conditions and disseminating diseases in Egypt to the situation in Iraq during the post-war period, suggesting that Egypt is engaged in an unannounced war (the public vs the government). This suggestion is further reinforced by the footage of riots in Egypt, which the director blends within the narrative. Similarly, *al-Khurug min al-Qahira* emphasizes prevalent poverty through showing overcrowded flats, such as Tari's who is living with his mother and the family of his brother and Amal living with her mother, stepfather, sister and nephew.

'In Shams, Hiliaupulis and *al-Khurug min al-Qahira* share the 'immigration dream' theme through one or more of the characters of the films. Their urge to leave the country is originating from the frustration and oppression that the films show. They resort to immigration as a way out of their undesirable living conditions. Some narratives portray immigration as a dream, while others reveal the actual planning of immigration for a better job and life. In *'In Shams*, 'Amr, a young man representing working-class youth, seeks to work in Italy. The film allegorically links 'Amr to his aspiration of freedom, through showing him keeping and flying pigeons. In another scene, 'Amr helps Shams, who represents the younger generation, flying a kite in search of freedom.

In *Hiliaupulis*, one of the characters is planning to immigrate to Canada. His first appearance in the film is in the Canadian embassy while applying for a visa. Also Ingi, a receptionist in a motel, daydreams that she is in Paris enjoying the clean streets and 'people minding their own business'. The dream sequence is animated (heightening the dream theme) using shots of Ingi wandering through different layers of images of streets of Paris and the Eiffel Tower.

Tari', the lead character in *al-Khurug min al-Qahira*, is unsatisfied with his work as a deliveryman and supermarket cashier. After encountering cronyism when applying for jobs and undergoing aggressive humiliation by the police, Tari' plans to immigrate illegally to Europe through the Mediterranean Sea. He does not fear to take the risk of illegal immigration as he is 'drowning anyway'. In one scene, he admits travelling not only to seek a better job but also to take control of his rights. The film reveals the desire of other characters to travel, such as Amal (whose name literally means hope), the girlfriend of Tari', who gives up and decides to escape with him. Also, Rania, Amal's best friend, marries a man from the gulf and travels with him for a better life. The film's promotional poster shows Tari' and Amal facing the Mediterranean Sea emphasizing the aspiration of the characters to immigrate.

Casting new actors, using improvisation and shooting in real locations have added a sense of authenticity to these films. This has further helped viewers to relate emotionally to the characters and their struggles and left them with political feelings. Film director Aytin Amin describes her feelings towards this style,

> I feel that it was one of the apparent things that a revolution is about to happen, because something has started to change. This is what I feel; I felt that some sort of rebel started to happen artistically on many of the cinematic styles. Even censorial wise, because the short films were not subjected to censorship they were bolder than the other films. (A. Amin, interview, 30 December 2015)

These films address the social structure of the Egyptian society through contrasting different classes. However, in contrast to the generic conventions of drama and comedy, film-makers used the progressive realism style. They employed digital cameras, natural lighting, new actors and improvisation to portray themes of oppression and poverty and contrast different social classes in an authentic manner. These techniques were also affordable to their restricted, low budgets. These films represent the pre-revolution discourses of social injustice. For example, the transitions between the houses and neighbourhoods of the businessman and his chauffeur in *'In Shams* accentuate the wide gap between both classes. One of the film scenes depicts a candidate of the parliament who promises the inhabitants of *'In Shams* with the development of services (such as electricity and gas) for their votes. The scene reveals the outburst of Ramadan saying, 'Our problem is not electricity, we can use candles ... But all the food is filled with chemicals or pills' which has increased childhood cancer, including that of his daughter. The genuine performance of Ramadan and the emotional soundtrack by Amir Khalaf combined with close-up shots of

'In Shams inhabitants (not actors) stress the state of oppression they are living within and highlight the gap between social classes, as higher classes do not share similar concerns. *al-Khurug min al-Qahira* also contrasts social classes by showing Amal delivering food orders to luxurious houses (Figure 1). The camera takes the perspective of Amal sneaking into the spacious houses inviting viewers to align with her discontentment.

As a part of their rebellion against on the guardianship of the government, some independent films disregarded censorship. These films were secretly shot, due to the lack of censorship's approval and Ministry of Interior shooting permits. Ibrahim al-Battut refused to submit the script of *'In Shams* to the censorship department before shooting (as they require), due to his disapproval

Figure 1 Top: Amal delivering food to a luxurious house. Bottom: a hand-held shot of the house from her perspective (*al-Khurug min al-Qahira*, 2010)

of censorship as a concept. However, after shooting the film, censorship refused to release the film in theatres, as it did not obtain a shooting permit in the first place. 'Ali abu Shadi, head of censorship at the time, suggested releasing the film as a Moroccan production since the film received a fund from Morocco to transfer it on 35mm film. al-Battut rejected the offer, insisting that it is an Egyptian film. According to al-Battut, 'After a while, they suddenly agreed to release the film' accentuating the obscurity of the censorship's decision-making process (al-Battut, 2010). The film was printed with only five copies and was not popular in cinemas. It achieved multiple awards, such as best film in Taormina Film Festival in Italy and the Arab Film Festival in Rotterdam. Similarly, censorship rejected *al-Khurug min al-Qahira*, due to its depiction of a love story between a Muslim and a Christian. The Censorship of Artistic Works approved the film after requesting some changes including the name of the film, which changed from *al-Khurug min Masr* (*Egypt Exit*) to *al-Khurug min al-Qahira* (*Cairo Exit*).[12] The censorship department allows the release of these films (sometimes after negotiations), perhaps of their understanding of the unpopularity of these films among the mass audiences.

* * *

During the pre-revolution period, specifically during the fifth six-year term of Mubarak, films intensively represented the growing public anger. These representations overlapped among popular drama films, political satire and independent productions. Using these different film forms and genres, films revealed prevalent issues of poverty, corruption and police brutality. Whereas these films did not trigger the uprising, they contributed to the growing political activism during the pre-revolution period. They raised awareness or reinforced political discourses of extreme poverty and corruption among middle to higher-class audiences who can afford to watch these films in cinemas. While political satire depended on exaggerated performances and stereotypes, popular films and independent productions employed realistic styles to connect emotionally with viewers. The films visualized the conditions leading to the 2011 Revolution, and (sometimes) imagined a potential rebellion against the police, government or ruler. Before the revolution, these films represented the desires and wishes of audiences. Many of these rebel images and narratives are highly comparable to pictures and events from the 2011 uprising. The films varied in their production scales from high-budget blockbusters, such as *'Imarat Ya'qubiyan* and Khalid Yusif's films, to low-budget 'independent films'. The latter did not only represent social discontent within their texts but also acted as a form of a rebellion against the mainstream film-making styles. These films challenge the formulaic film genres through creative narrative structures and casting new actors. They use alternative funding (such as crowd-funding) distributing and exhibiting methods, as well as ignore the censorship body.

Some of the pre-revolution films have used common strategies to criticize the regime and depict the deterioration of the economy. One of the recurrent themes is the comparison to the past, where the film explicitly accounts the historical social change of Egypt, such as *'Imarat Ya'qubiyan* and *Dukkan Shihata*, or a specific area, such as *'In Shams* and *Hiliaupulis*. These films tackle the disappearance of the glorified history of Egypt and the urbanization of its population, which led to the growth of low-class neighbourhoods. Whereas the films relate the transition mainly to the 1952 Coup d'état,[13] they emphasize the constant social restructuring due to increasing poverty and political corruption. These films, among others, accentuate the growing gap between social strata through contrasting the high- and working classes within a single society. Some films have also compared the state of oppression in Egypt to other events taking place in the Arab World, such as the war in Iraq. *Basra* and *Hiyna Maysara* directly contrast the tensions and anxieties of their characters to the war in Iraq, while *'In Shams* compared the spread of cancer in Iraq after the 1991 War to the growing disease in Egypt. The films do not only situate their events within the context of the Middle East politics but also portray the situation in Egypt as involved in an unannounced war. The direct comparisons and exposition of similar consequences of a war (spreading disease and deteriorating economic conditions) imply an internal conflict between citizens and the government/military dictatorship that has been ruling Egypt since 1952.

Pre-revolution films expanded on one of the main 'triggers' of the revolution, police brutality, through exposing images of torture and abuse of Emergency Law. The films emphasize the prevalent police brutality and humiliation as one of the factors leading to the frustration of Egyptians, and the rise of violence as a consequence of police brutality, oppression and poverty. Popular films such as *'Imarat Ya'qubiyan*, *Hiyya Fawda* and *Dukkan Shihata* have ending sequences of taking revenge of policemen or a general growth of violence among the public. While the 2011 Revolution is characterized by its peaceful protests, demonstrations and marches, the depiction of attacks on police officers and public intimidation in the films was realized. After the revolution, portraying the hooligan as a hero became a popular theme in films. Furthermore, *'Imarat Ya'qubiyan* and *Hiyna Maysara* have also proposed the formation and development of terrorist groups based on issues of poverty and oppression. Although the uprising did not include any acts of terrorism, Egypt has witnessed several terrorist attacks after the removal of Muhammad Mursi.

The films also portrayed immigration as a dream or ambition among youth. Given the conditions of unemployment, oppression and poverty, the theme represented the desire of many suffering characters (usually young men) to escape from Egypt.[14] '*Asal Iswid*, a black comedy starring one of the most famous comedy actors Ahmad Hilmi, reveals the daily challenges faced by Egyptians through a returning expatriate. The name of the film literally translates to *Black Honey*, indicating the bittersweet feelings Egyptians have towards their country. The film attempts to balance the 'good versus bad' habits that Egyptians practice, reinforced by one of the song lines of the film 'It [Egypt] is everything and its opposite'. The film's penultimate scene at the airport reveals two Egyptians sitting around Masry, the main character, and describing to him the 'savagery' and 'evil spirits' of Egyptians. *Bintiyn min Masr*, a drama film tackling the issue of spinsterhood, narrates the social pressure on two single middle-class girls in their early thirties.[15] The film also reveals the abuse of the Emergency Law by police officers (one of the main reasons for anger leading up to the revolution) as well as it deals with problems of unemployment and illegal immigration. Amin pictures immigration as an Egyptian youth dream, because of political oppression. Indeed, these films signal feelings of frustration among many Egyptians during the pre-revolution period.

Some of these films used comedy, a genre on the upraise of that time, to circumvent censorship. They set their narratives in vague or made-up third world countries if they are depicting a rise against the president in person. Meanwhile, the leniency of the Censorship of Artistic Works towards high-budget productions is referred to their associations with internationally acclaimed and eminent film-makers. Although independent film-makers ignore the approval of the censorship's sanction of their scripts, in some cases the censorship body approves the release of the films after negotiations and perhaps for their understanding of the unpopularity of these films. Many of these films, with the exception of the popular ones, were not widely seen or commercially successful. Conservative viewers criticized the films for their depiction of homosexuality or portraying Egypt in a negative light. These criticisms were sometimes a factor of commercial success for films, such as *Hiyna Maysara*. Today, these films stand as an expression of the desire of the public that was realized a few years later.

Even after the revolution, films continue to narrate stories of corruption, poverty and police brutality during the era of Mubarak. In some cases, film-makers use the footage of the uprising as a 'happy ending' to their stories. Egyptian cinema maintains its tradition in criticizing past regimes. The role of film in representing 'social realities' and expressing political views was extended to the 2011 Revolution. Film-makers represented the revolution in documentary and fiction films. The post-revolution films that represented the revolution continue the narratives of the films discussed in this chapter. They follow-up the political narrative of the nation at a specific time of history with an emphasis on the revolutionary moment. While film stars and some film-makers used the revolution for international exposure, other film-makers narrated the revolution in fiction and documentary films. Some of them used innovative approaches in terms of style and distribution strategies, to articulate the revolutionary moment.

4

Constructing cultural memory: Fiction and documentary films that represent the revolution

During the eighteen days of the 2011 Revolution (25 January–11 February) many film-makers were in a dilemma whether to film the events or not.[1] While some chose to participate in the demonstrations and live the experience rather than shooting them, others used their personal digital cameras to document the revolution with an intention to utilize it in the future. Film-makers, protesters, journalists and witnesses shot hours of footage, many of which were deposited in the Tahrir media tent. These clips facilitated the production of short and feature narrative and documentary films within a few months of the revolution. For example, one of the earliest films, *Tamantashar Yuwm* (*Eighteen Days*, 2011), consists of ten short films directed by ten prominent film-makers including Shirif 'Arafa, Marwan Hamid, Yusri Nasrallah, Kamla abu Zikri and Ahmad 'Abd Allah. After announcing Egypt as the guest of honour of the 2011 Cannes Film Festival, these film-makers together with film stars (including Ahmad Hilmi, Mona Zaki, Hind Sabri and 'Amr Wakid) shot and edited the film and premiered it at the festival within three months. The short films represent various experiences of individuals during the eighteen days of the revolution, such as state security officers, a barber, thugs and a tea seller at Tahrir Square. While some films used a comedic tone in representing the struggles of the public during curfews and their excitement of seeing the army tanks in the streets, other films used allegories to represent the reflections of different ideologies in relation to the revolution. The film was not released in film theatres for unclear reasons. While Dr Khalid 'Abd al-Gilil, head of censorship, has announced that the film has not been submitted to the Censorship of Artistic Works for approval (al-Kashuti, 2017), film director Yusri Nasrallah claimed that the film has been banned as a part of the 'removal of anything related to the 25 January 2011

Revolution' (al-Husini, 2017). The film was anonymously uploaded on YouTube in July 2017. Film-makers including Hala Lutfi, Aytin Amin and Nadin Khan criticized films such as *Tamantashar Yuwm* to have abused the revolution. They consider such films to have used the revolution for publicity, as 'it was too early for anyone to have a story to tell' (H. Galal, interview, 30 December 2015). These film-makers believe that it was premature to make films about the revolution (directly after the revolution) especially that 'it wasn't over and it is not until now' (H. Galal, interview, 30 December 2015). Also, *Sarkhit Namla* (*The Cry of an Ant*, Samih 'Abd al-'Aziz, 2011), a comedy about the political corruption, was premiered at the same festival as the first feature narrative to depict the 2011 Egyptian Revolution.[2] Film critics and film-makers criticized Samih 'Abd al-'Aziz to have forced shots from the revolution to the ending sequence of the film. However, these films, among others, still document images and narratives from the revolution.

Films that document historical events play a significant role in creating visual memories of lived experiences. In *Surviving Images: Cinema, War, and Cultural Memory in the Middle East*, Kamran Rastegar (2015) argues that cinema has constructed a cultural memory of social conflicts (including wars) within the Middle East. He examines the colonial supremacy in films that were produced during the colonial age (such as *The Four Feathers*, 1929), and the representation of anticolonial ideologies during independence and post-colonial periods. Rastegar (2015) considers that films such as *al-Midan* (*The Square*, Jihan Nujaim, 2013) contribute to the cultural memory of the 2011 Egyptian Revolution. Similarly, Hedges (2015) demonstrates the role of film in contributing to struggles in countries such as Japan, Spain, Palestine and Cuba. However, Rastegar (2015) contends the development of new technologies (particularly digital media) took part of cinema's role in contributing to the visual cultural memory. While new technologies played a significant role in documenting the uprising,[3] several feature narrative and documentary films have represented the revolution.

This chapter focuses on these films and (following Rastegar and Hedges) argues that they construct an audio-visual cultural memory of the 2011 Revolution. They historicize specific moments, such as the opening of prisons on 28 January, Battle of the Camels on 2 February and the downfall of Mubarak on 11 February. They combine fiction and non-fiction elements, such as re-enactments of popular events, the use of non-actors, and interviews and footage of protests to narrate their stories. The chapter examines feature narrative films including *Ba'd al-Mawqi'a* (*After the Battle*, Yusri Nasrallah, 2012), which depicts the 'Battle of the Camels' event that took place during the revolution, on

2 February, where camel and horse riders attacked protesters in Tahrir Square. The film narrates one of the stories of the attackers after the battle, in an attempt to show two different sides of the society during the revolution. *al-Shitaa illy Fat* (*The Winter of Discontent*, Ibrahim al-Battut, 2012) focuses on three characters: a dissident, a secret police officer and a television announcer during the 2011 Revolution. The film engages with stories of police brutality and torture during Mubarak's era. Also, *Farsh wa-Ghata* (*Rags and Tatters*, Ahmad 'Abd Allah, 2013), set during the eighteen days of the revolution, narrates the story of a prison escapee. While *Farsh wa-Ghata* does not show images of protests and demonstrations from Tahrir Square (the main site of the revolutionary protests), it depicts popular events of the revolution, such as the escape of prisoners on 28 January and the widespread popular committees.[4] The chapter also analyses documentary features such as *Mawlud fi Khamsa wa-'Ishriyn Yanayir* (*Born on the 25th of January*, Ahmad Rashwan, 2011), which narrates the director's personal experience during the revolution (from 25 January to 27 May),[5] and *al-Tahrir 2011: al-Taiyyib, wa-l-Sharis, wa-l-Siyasi* (*Tahrir 2011: The Good, The Bad, and The Politician*, Tamir 'Izzat, Aytin Amin, and 'Amr Salama, 2011) the first Egyptian documentary released in film theatres since four decades. The film consists of three segments: the good (protesters), the bad (police officers) and the politician (Husni Mubarak). Also, *Crop* (Johanna Domke and Marwan 'Umara, 2013) reveals issues of photojournalism and censorship within the complex building of *al-Ahram* newspaper.

In an interview about film and popular memory, Foucault discussed how cinema was a mean of 'reprogramming' popular memory. Foucault suggested, 'Since memory is actually a very important factor in struggle (really, in fact, struggles develop in a kind of conscious moving forward of history), if one controls people's memory, one controls their dynamism. And one also controls their experience, their knowledge of previous struggles' (1975, p. 29). However, the different perspectives in which a historical event is covered or represented allow the construction of multiple stories of an event. The films discussed in this chapter, for example, contribute to the cultural memory, which according to Sturken (1997, p. 1) is 'a field of cultural negotiation through which different stories vie for a place in history'. These stories are enabled through the various representations provided by media and popular culture. Sturken also emphasized the significant role of camera images in constituting cultural memory. For Sturken, these images are 'central to the interpretation of the past' and cinematic representations 'have the capacity to entangle with personal and cultural memory' (1997, p. 11). Thus, films that represented the 2011 Revolution embody and mediate cultural memories of a historical moment, which the counter-revolution aims to distort.

Film is also a significant mode of documenting images of historical events. The films discussed in this chapter are a form of, what White (1988) calls, historiophoty – 'the representation of history and our thought about it in visual images and filmic discourse' (p. 1193). They use 'actual footage (or still photos, or artefacts) from a particular time and place to create a 'realistic' sense of the historical moment' (Rosenstone, 1988, p. 1180). Jarvie (1978) and Rosenstone (1988) remind us that these films do not show the events as witnessed, but rather select particular images to construct a story. White (1988) confirms Rosentone's claim of the accuracy of films in representing historical events. 'Film lets us see landscapes, hear sounds, witness strong emotions as they are expressed with body and face, or view physical conflict between individuals and groups' (Rosenstone, 1988, p. 1179). However, Jarvie and Rosentsone question the film's ability to convey the complex and critical dimensions of historical events. While some films discussed in this chapter recount the events of the revolution using a newsreel style, such as *Mawlud fi Khamsa wa-'Ishriyn Yanayir* (2011), other films take a critical approach to documenting the revolution, including *Ba'd al-Mawqi'a* (2012) and *al-Tahrir 2011: al-Taiyyib, wa-l-Sharis, wa-l-Siyasi* (2011). The latter films aim to represent the complexity of the revolution through integrating multiple perspectives – pro and anti-revolution.

The chapter uses Brunow's (2009) critical tools for analysing historical fiction and documentary films. Questions regarding the narrative devices employed and the aesthetic choices of integrating testimonial witnesses (pp. 47–9) provide an understanding of the construction of 'authentic' representations of the events. The degree to which films represent realities has been the interest of several film scholars. Bazin (2005b) negotiated the concept of reality in films as a constructed illusion. He argued that realism is an aesthetic choice, which is composed of conventions, but also inevitably produced since 'art can only exist when such choice is made' (p. 26). Nichols (1991, p. 10) emphasized the role of documentaries in constructing social realities. He considered the control of film-makers on texts as well as the sense of truthfulness produced about the narrated events. He argued that fiction and documentary produce realities differently,

> Where fiction achieves a 'reality effect' by sprinkling doses of authentic historical references across the realm of its creation – costumes, tools, vehicles, known places, or prominent figures – the same references within documentary serve as tangible evidence from the historical world in support of an argument. (Nichols, 2001, p. 28)

Film-makers have carefully selected 'real' footage of the 2011 Revolution that supports their arguments in both documentary and fiction films. In some instances, documentary film-makers used voiceover to address the audiences directly and comment on the events. Nichols (2001) identified several practices of documentaries that engage with political issues, including the construction of national identities, justifying and/or criticizing actions and the recurrent use of metaphors. He uses *Far from Poland* (Jill Godmilow, 1984) as an example where the director did not have access to archival footage of the rise of the Solidarity movement in Poland and decided to make a film about difficulties of representation. The use of metaphors, parallels and contrasts is also evident in *Crop*, which displays visuals of a working day at *al*-Ahram complex to narrate the 2011 Revolution. The representation of the revolution through the perspectives of its participants, as in *al-Shitaa illy Fat* and *al-Tahrir 2011: al-Taiyyib, wa-l-Sharis, wa-l-Siyasi*, evoked senses of nationalism. These films addressed Tahrir Square as a community that shares common values and beliefs through integrating narratives and testimonies of individuals who represent different political affiliations and socioeconomic statuses. Nichols (2001, p. 142) explains,

> Individuals enter into very different forms of relationships with one another. Whatever basic drives or needs are involved, they take a variety of concrete forms, and these forms seem, at least in modern times, susceptible to social construction. Be it a bill of rights or a five-year plan, a benign despotism or a competitive spirit, ideologies come into play to provide stories, images, and myths that promote one set of values over others. The sense of community always comes at the price of alternative values and beliefs deemed deviant, subversive, or illegal. The politics of documentary film production address the ways in which this work helps give tangible expression to the values and beliefs that build, or contest, specific forms of social belonging, or community, at a given time and place.

Both fiction and documentary films have borrowed stylistic elements from one another. They confirm Nichols's (1994) argument of 'history and memory intertwine; meaning and action, past and present, hinge on one another distinctively. Documentary and fiction, social actor and social other, knowledge and doubt, concept and experience share boundaries that inescapably blur' (p. 1). Fiction films included documentary-like segments through incorporating non-actors and/or footage of Tahrir Square to evoke a sense of authenticity to their narratives. They intertwined 'real' footage from the events of the revolution, together with re-enactments of the same events to situate their plots and characters within the historical period of change. In *Ba'd al-Mawqi'a*, Nasrallah cast inhabitants of Nazlit al-Simman – a neighbourhood in Giza where the camel and horse riders (convicted for the attack on protesters) live – to reveal their reflections on the revolution. Nasrallah also intertwined footage of the Battle of the Camel with re-enactments using the actors of the film. al-Battut used improvised scenes between the film actors in Tahrir Square during the eighteen days of the Revolution in *al-Shitaa illy Fat*. Ahmad 'Abd Allah integrated interviews with the inhabitants of poor districts in Cairo in *Farsh wa-Ghata*. Documentary films (mostly independent productions) also used fictional narratives or re-enactments to support their arguments. In *Mawlud fi Khamsa wa-'Ishriyn Yanayir*, Ahmad Rashwan re-enacts scenes of his engagement on social media and following scenes of the revolution on television with his children as a part of his personal experience during the revolution. The narrator of *Crop* is a fictional character who narrates his experience as a photojournalist at the state-owned newspaper, *al-Ahram*. Domke and 'Umara created the character based on nineteen interviews with photographers.

In their representation of the revolution, fiction and documentary films have addressed Egyptian society in the form of binary oppositions. They created their narratives around the conflicts between pro- and anti-revolution, such as in *Ba'd al-Mawqi'a* which reveals the hostility between the protesters and the Battle of the Camel attackers. The film also represents the political positions towards the revolution in relation to social classes (Mahmud the horse rider, comes from a lower socio-economic class, while Riym the revolutionary is more privileged). *al-Shitaa illy Fat* also represents the revolution through the perspectives of the revolutionaries versus the state (represented in security officers and the media). Documentary films, such as *al-Tahrir 2011: al-Taiyyib, wa-l-Sharis, wa-l-Siyasi* aimed to voice multiple perspectives: protesters, police officers and politicians. However, the film challenges the testimonies of police officers through images of police cars running over protesters. Similarly, *al-Midan* is an observational documentary that follows six characters throughout the revolution until 2013. These characters represent different socio-economic classes and political affiliations (such as members of the Muslim Brotherhood and non-partisan). *al-Midan* is the first Egyptian film nominated for an Academy Award. However, these documentaries have used traditional modes and styles to represent the revolution. For example, in *Mawlud fi Khamsa wa-'Ishriyn Yanayir*, Ahmad Rashwan uses the first person mode to expose the events of the revolution in a newsreel style.

While the majority of fiction and documentary films used images of Tahrir Square to represent the revolution, only a few films chose more creative approaches to their representations. These include fiction films such as *Farsh wa-Ghata* and documentary films including *Crop* and *Muwg* (*Waves*, Ahmad Nuwr, 2012) a personal account of the revolution with a specific focus on Suez – a city in Egypt. These films, among others, have narrated the revolution away from Tahrir Square, which was the centre of international and local media's attention. The directors of these films sought to contribute to the cultural memory of the revolution through constructing narratives of under-represented individuals, places and experiences. For instance, *Farsh wa-Ghata* takes place during the revolution but focuses on marginalized districts which, 'Abd Allah argues, were among the reasons for an uprising. The aesthetic choices of 'Abd Allah, such as the lack of dialogue, distinguish the film from other narratives about the revolution. Similarly, *Crop* does not show any images of protests. The documentary associates the fictional narrative told through the voiceover with observational images of employees in *al-Ahram* building. In *Muwg*, Ahmad Nuwr uses animation and interviews to tell stories from the past as well as makes allegorical representations of freedom and change through birds and the waves of the sea. These films reveal parts of the revolution not only through their texts but also through their innovative film language that resists the traditional fiction and documentary techniques.

The chapter argues that these fiction and documentary films have contributed to the audio-visual cultural memory of the revolution through borrowing stylistic elements from each other to support the arguments of the film-makers. They addressed the revolution in the form of binary oppositions and, in some cases, mutually reinforcing 'senses of nationality'. These films participated in international film festivals and received mixed reviews. Fiction films, and the documentary *al-Tahrir 2011: al-Taiyyib, wa-l-Sharis, wa-l-Siyasi*, were released for a few weeks in film theatres but were unpopular. The continuous projection of images of the revolution on television channels reduced the chances of the popularity of these films. With the rise of the Muslim Brotherhood in 2012 and the counter-revolutionary discourses, fewer film-makers have engaged with the topic. The Censorship of Artistic Works has also limited films that promote the revolution and notions of rebellion since the 2013 Coup d'état. The censorship body did not issue a screening permission for *al-Midan* for its depiction of the violent incidents by the Armed Forces after the revolution. Also, Tamir al-Sa'id's *Akhir Ayyam al-Madina* (*In the Last Days of the City*, 2016) was not screened for unclear reasons. The film narrates the story of a film-maker and his relationship with his city – Cairo, including his experience of the 2011 Revolution.

The production of documentary and fiction films in a fluctuating political context led film-makers to depend more on improvisation rather than scripts. Film-makers shot and incorporated events into their films as they happened. The production of the films discussed in this chapter within two years of the revolution (2011–13) has limited their representation to the uprising and its impact on the public. During these two years, the interest of film festivals and television channels in the so-called 'Arab Spring' fostered the production of fiction and documentaries about the revolution. These films were independently produced, due to their unpopularity in the commercial market. I draw on interviews with film-makers including Ahmad Rashwan, Aytin Amin and Marwan 'Umara to explain the production contexts of their films. Ahmad Rashwan shot most of the footage himself without the intention of producing a film. The chapter also examines Alisa Lebow's interactive meta-documentary *Filming Revolution* (2015), which documents and archives films and projects related to the revolution. The meta-documentary includes interviews with film-makers, artists, activists and archivists discussing their documentaries and independent films produced during the 2011 Revolution. The interactive platform is rich with experiences and projects of film-makers during the revolution, which will be useful for future research.

Although more documentary films were produced about the revolution, only a few narratives have shown images of, and intensely engaged with, the revolution. In the following paragraphs, I examine fiction films that engaged with the revolution as the centre of events. Film directors Yusri Nasrallah, Ibrahim al-Battut, and Ahmad 'Abd Allah are known for their support and participation in the revolution. Their experiences of different events during the revolution influenced their films *Ba'd al-Mawqi'a* and *al-Shitaa illy Fat* and *Farsh wa-Ghata*. These films historicize particular events such as the Battle of the Camels on 2 February and the opening of prisons on 28 January 2011. They represent the revolution through various perspectives including political positions (pro- and anti-revolution) and social classes (upper and lower classes). They also contribute to the cultural memory of the revolution through narrating stories of individuals and places that were under-represented by the media during the revolution. *Ba'd al-Mawqi'a* reveals the Battle of the Camels from the perspective of the attackers. *al-Shitaa illy Fat* focuses on political oppression as one of the main motivations for the uprising through intertwining stories of police torture from 2009 and 2011. It also depicts the popular features of the revolution, such as the state media's deception, insecurity and popular committees. Meanwhile, Ahmad 'Abd Allah's *Farsh wa-Ghata* takes the revolution away from

Tahrir Square to Cairo's marginalized districts. These films engage with specific events and represent them through integrating documentary-like sequences to evoke a sense of authenticity and validate their arguments.

On 1 February 2011, Mubarak gave an emotional speech saying that he wants to die on the lands of Egypt. The speech affected many Egyptians and turned them against protesters. The next morning people on horses and camels attacked protesters at Tahrir Square. The media reported the attack from one-side, which dehumanized the attackers and supported the protesters' description of them as 'thugs' (*Plotted battle*, 2011; and Tarek, 2011).[6] *Ba'd al-Mawqi'a* reveals the motivation of the attackers of the Battle of the camels in an attempt to construct an alternative memory of the event. Along documenting the experiences of protesting at Tahrir Square, Nasrallah narrates the event from the view of the attackers. The narrative takes place from March to October 2011. The film narrates the story of Mahmud a horse keeper living at Nazlit al-Simman – a neighbourhood close to the pyramids and very popular for touristic shops, and horses and camels rental/keeping. Mahmud participated in attacking protesters at Tahrir Square during *mawqi'at āl-gamal* (Battle of the Camels) on 2 February 2011. He is well known to have participated in the battle, as he appears clearly in the videos shot and uploaded to YouTube. As a result, Mahmud's neighbours humiliate him and describe him as illiterate and ignorant.[7] Early on in the film, members of the animal rights association look down on Mahmud (using the classic high/low angle) and refuse to give him food for his horse. In school, students discriminate and beat-up Mahmud's sons.

On the other hand, Riym, played by Minna Shalabi, is a separated privileged woman who works for an advertising agency and supports the 2011 Revolution. As the majority of the protesters, Riym views the attackers (camels and horse riders) as thugs. However, throughout the film, Riym meets and sympathize with Mahmud and his family.[8] She understands the attackers' motivation and observes the unfavourable impact of the revolution on their business (tourism). The film uncovers the two different worlds of Mahmud and Riym (low versus high socio-economic classes and anti- versus pro-revolution) after the revolution. It documents images of the Battle of the Camels as well as other significant post-revolution events such as the Maspiro Massacre (where the army and security forces attacked Christian demonstrations in October 2011). The film utilizes footage of these events together with re-enactments using the actors to evoke a sense of authenticity and support Nasrallah's version of the attack story. The film also documents features of the post-revolution Egyptian society including improvised scenes of political debates, hype of political parties and rise of Islamist groups.

The production started with only the main storyline, but without a written script. 'Umar Shama wrote the script together with Yusri Nasrallah (the director) along the shooting, due to the constant news updates and rapid changes taking place in Egypt. In many scenes, Nasrallah cast the inhabitants of Nazlit al-Simman for secondary roles. Actors improvised some scenes to address the different perspectives on issues discussed (such as the pros and cons of the revolution) in documentary-like sequences. These scenes augment the sense of reality of the overall narrative and support Nasrallah's argument of explaining the rationale of the attackers.

The film participated in the 2012 Cannes Film Festival after a long absence of participation of Egyptian films in the Palme d'Or competition of the festival. Some audiences, mainly supporters of the revolution, and a few critics, such as 'Isaam Zakaria, have criticized the film arguing that it almost took an anti-revolution position (al-Arabiya, 2012). As the first feature narrative that engages intensely with the 2011 Revolution, audiences expected the film to celebrate the revolution rather than defend the attackers. However, the director (known for his support for the revolution) claims the film does not defend the attackers; it is a humanitarian story about individuals. The film unfolds the impact of Mahmud's participation in the battle on his social life, family and work. In his interviews about the film, the director reinforced that the film shows how Mahmud 'retains his lost dignity' (a main demand of the revolution) among his neighbours and friends.[9] Whereas television and print media pictured the camel and horse riders as the symbol of counter-revolution, the film argues that they should not be solely convicted of the attack. In one scene, one of the inhabitants of Nazlit al-Simman explains that the attackers were told to go to Tahrir and support Mubarak for the resurrection of tourism.[10] The film gives voice to the attackers and rationalizes their action, which the media and protesters condemned.

In addition to the film's reflection on the Battle of the Camels, the film incorporates images from the event. The film starts with a stock shot of people on horses and camels breaking into Tahrir Square and beating up protesters. Later on, the film reveals more shots from the battle, where some protesters detained a horse rider and battered him. The film intertwines footage from the event with a re-enactment using Mahmud (played by Basim al-Samra). Nasrallah shot the re-enactment at the same location and using the same angle and mise-en-scène of the recorded footage to blur the distinction between the 'real' footage and his narrative.

Although the transition between the footage and the re-enactment is clear (the hand-held low-quality footage cuts to a tracking cinematic shot), the combination of both brings the film's characters and narrative closer to the real incident. The clear shot of protesters beating up Mahmud situates the character and the narrative more genuinely within the wider historical event. Similarly, the film combines images from the Maspiro Massacre in October 2011 together with a re-enactment using actors. These sequences develop the narrative as well as register events of the 2011 Revolution visually. The sense of authenticity induced by these scenes supports the reality that the narrative aims to construct. Nasrallah emphasized 'reality' as to validate his argument of viewing the attackers as humans.

Ba'd al-Mawqi'a also documents political practices during the post-revolution period where the narrative is set. For example, the film portrays the increasing interest of Egyptians in politics and news following. The television at Riym's home projects political news such as protests and incidents of violence during the post-revolution period. One of the scenes, shot in a real political party conference, shows Riym's interest in the growing political activities. The film also addresses the role of women in the revolution through the characters of Riym, Dina (Riym's friend) and Fatma (Mahmud's wife). These characters represent radical political actions of women during the revolution, which Elmarsafy (2015, p. 134) describes as:

> One possible reason why the women of Egypt's revolution proved so threatening to the authorities lies in the intelligence and skill with which they managed to do all of the things that moralising discourse desperately tries to undo: they incited, opened and enabled certain deeds, words and actions, not as part of an organised programme necessarily but as part of an opening onto something wholly new, something quite unlike what was there before.

One of the sequences reveals Fatma visiting Riym at Tahrir Square during a protest.[11] The sequence, shot during an actual protest in Tahrir Square, depicts the features of the 2011 Revolution protests and demonstrations. The documentary-like sequence includes shots of Fatma going to Tahrir through Asr al-Niyl Bridge, the square's security searching Fatma and hand-held shots of side discussions in the square. Fatma's appearance alongside Riym represents the different social and educational backgrounds of women who participated in the revolution, which Sorbera (2014) confirms, 'During the 2011 revolution, women writers and intellectuals, alongside students and working-class women, inundated the public space, the square, to assert their will, as Egyptian citizens, to remove the regime' (p. 67). The sequence shows the development of Fatma's character as she observes and learns more about the square. The protesters inspire Fatma; she starts uttering the chant 'bread, freedom, human dignity'. The subjective shots, of Fatma's perspective, wandering in the square while listening to chants such as 'the people demand the cleansing of the Interior (the Ministry of Interior)' document the experience as well as provide a simulation of being/protesting in Tahrir Square. The representation of protests in Tahrir Square from Fatma's point of view emphasizes the film's aim to reveal the revolution through the perspective of Nazlit al-Simman's inhabitants. Before visiting the square, Fatma supported the anti-revolution notions that were popular in Nazlit al-Simman.

The film does not only capture images of the revolution but also conveys the political environment during the post-revolution period. One of the earlier scenes in the film reveals a debate on the view of Egyptian society of the role of women after the revolution in relation to the rise of Islamist currents. Riym is involved in this debate, which appears to be improvised due to the sudden camera pans, frame/focus adjustments and overlapping lines. The scene builds part of the post-revolution environment, where debates were held in public and private spaces between different ideological stances (such as pro- versus anti-revolution or progressive versus conservative). The scene also historicizes, according to Hala Kamal (2015, p. 152), the 'new wave of Egyptian feminist movement' that emerged after the revolution. The National Council for Women appropriated this feminist movement 'under the pretext of guarding women's rights against the Islamists' continuous efforts to marginalise these rights' (Kamal, 2015, p. 155). Integrating these perspectives using improvisation and documentary aesthetics of shooting footage supported the film's aim in documenting the historical moment in an authentic sense. The scene (in the beginning of the film) situates the viewer within the context of the post-revolution period. They historicize the conflicting political positions during a moment of crisis.

In representing post-revolution Egypt, *Ba'd al-Mawqi'a* represents the social and political structures in the form of binary oppositions: pro- versus anti-revolution and higher versus lower socio-economic classes. The film addresses social concerns such as the refusal of a romantic relationship between Mahmud and Riym. In the film, Riym's friends have radically rejected such idea due to their different social classes.[12] The representation of the revolution supporters as discriminators and hypocrites confirms the view of the film as anti-revolutionary. In the film, the revolution supporters refer to the inhabitants of Nazlit al-Simman as 'those people', and disregard the agency of the attackers' through accepting that 'it is not the attackers' fault, it is the people who incited them'. The film shows Riym, representing the protesters, enlightening the inhabitants of Nazlit al-Simman. From a superior position, she explains the benefits of the revolution and their rights as citizens. Meanwhile, the film represented the inhabitants of Nazlit al-Simman, including the attackers, with agency. They insist to educate their kids and have their own ideologies. For example, one of the significant scenes in the film involves a confrontation between Riym and Mahmud. While she informs him that the revolution will bring him a better lifestyle and education for his sons, he holds the popular counter-revolution position that the revolution will break down the tourism-related businesses.

Although the film's conception of the post-revolution sociopolitical and economic transitions is premature, it captures the changing society and hints the rise of the Muslim Brotherhood. The instant reflection on/representation of the revolution was not limited to its events and post-revolution environment. Films were also interested in the motivations behind the uprising and the interaction of state institutions with the revolution.

In *al-Shitaa illy Fat*, Ibrahim al-Battut was concerned with documenting images of torture and oppression that led to the uprising as well as the events of the revolution. He used integrated interviews with non-actors and narrated stories of torture during Mubarak's era to construct an audio-visual memory of the reasons leading up to the revolution. The film is structured around three characters: 'Amr (played by 'Amr Wakid) – a dissident, Farah (played by Farah Yusif) – an official state television announcer and 'Adil (played by Salah al-Hanafi) – a state security officer. In 2009, 'Adil detained and tortured 'Amr, among other activists, for his participation in protests against the war in Gaza.[13] Following the severe torture of the state security forces to 'Amr, including dousing water and electrifying him naked and blindfolded, 'Adil releases him. Since then, 'Amr lives broken in solitude and isolation. On the first day of the revolution, 'Amr hesitates to leave his house. He watches videos on YouTube of protesters recounting their experience of the protests or previous encounters with state security. 'Amr also hears demonstrations passing by his house and follows news on television.

Meanwhile, Farah ('Amr's ex-fiancée) and Tamir present a night talk show on the state television. On the night of 25 January, Farah believes she should talk more about the protests, while Tamir insists that they should 'calm things down'. After the argument escalates between Farah and Tamir on 28 January, Farah leaves the programme and quits. She records a video regretting her deceitfulness and resorts to 'Amr to upload her video online (since 'Amr is one of the few people who have internet access through his telephone satellite after the state security disrupted communication). ʿAmr uploads the video and the state security detains him again. After they release him, for no clear reasons, ʿAmr visits Tahrir Square and celebrates the fall of Mubarak with Farah. Although al-Battut shows images from Tahrir Square only at the ending sequence, he addresses the issues of political oppression – freedom of speech – and violence (some of the main reasons behind the uprising) and the state media's scandalous depiction of the revolution throughout the film. In addition, images of popular committees and robbery, and sounds of demonstrations and the speeches of Mubarak in the film construct an audio-visual memory of the eighteen days of the revolution.

The film's production started on 10 February 2011 (one day before the step down of Mubarak), when al-Battut called ʿAmr and Farah (who were already protesting at Tahrir) and asked them if they want to participate in a film. They improvised two scenes on 10 and 11 February (the celebration of the fall of Mubarak) at Tahrir Square. At that time, they had no further idea of how or what they will use the footage for. About two months later, al-Battut decided to make the film and integrate the scenes they shot at Tahrir Square. As with his other films (such as *In Shams*, 2008), al-Battut improvised the scenes with the actors before shooting them for more authentic and spontaneous performances. He had the main storylines of the film, but no detailed script due to the volatile nature of events.[14] The director and some actors co-produced the film with production and post-production services companies such as Material House and AROMA. The film participated in several international film festivals, such as Venice Film Festival and Dubai Film Festival. International and local film critics praised the film for its sharp depiction of the rising anger. However, when the film was released in Egyptian cinemas, it did not achieve the desired commercial success. In their interviews, the film-makers emphasized that the film is not about the revolution, but it is about individuals within the revolutionary context. al-Battut claimed that the revolution is complex and films can only express or represent parts of it. In his interview on ON E (2013a), al-Battut expressed 'Films will live longer than us … the film documents the feelings of the 18 days so it can remind us where we were, in case we get lost in the future'. al-Battut's claim supports the argument that the film constructs the cultural memory of the 2011 Revolution through documenting images and sounds of the eighteen days.

The film introduces themes of oppression and violence through the videos ʿAmr watches on YouTube on 25 January 2011. One of the videos shows a reporter revealing his experience with the state security when he was detained in 1996 after covering the Bosnian war. al-Battut, known for his documentaries, integrated the interview with the reporter, a non-actor, who spontaneously expresses his emotions.¹⁵ The reporter reveals in detail:

> I was blindfolded and handcuffed for 15 days [...] you hear screaming, either yours or others, on a daily basis from midnight to sunrise. During the investigation, three officers keep asking you questions, then they use one of their methods, mine was electricity. You sit on the floor naked, with tied hands, the officer sits above you with a chair, another one holds your head and they keep asking and electrifying ... (cries).

The emotionally charged testimony registers the oppression that Egyptians felt, as well as reveals one of the motivations behind the uprising.¹⁶ The integration of the interview within the narrative blurs the distinction between documentary and fiction forms but also adds to the authenticity of the narrative. al-Battut emphasizes the portrayal of torture during the pre-revolution period. He represents 'Adil, the state security officer, as a firm character who tortures his detainees harshly. In one of the flashback scenes in 2009, 'Adil forces an Islamist leader to drink volumes of water with no access to a toilet. The flashback sequences of torturing 'Amr among other detainees also rationalize the feelings of frustration among Egyptians during the early days of the revolution. Such scenes complement other representations of the uprising (images of revolt) as well as construct a historical narrative of the revolution.

Along the documentary sequences and authentic representations of the revolution, supported with improvisations and incorporation of non-professional actors, al-Battut used allegories and symbols to refer to themes of isolation and frustration. In the opening scene of the film on 25 January, 'Amr is watering dead plants in his balcony in reference to the reviving of the spirit of the people. 'Amr is placed in confined spaces in al-Battut's frames to visualize his frustration and isolation. The apartment of 'Amr is represented by desaturated colours. His balcony is blocked by a high brick wall and surrounded by iron frames. The film's aesthetics, as well as the narrative, unfolds the prevailing discontent during the early days of the revolution. al-Battut, loyal to his style (discussed in the previous chapter), combines documentary-like sequences with allegories to narrate the story of the revolution.

al-Shitaa illy Fat historicizes the aura of the revolution through depicting popular features of the eighteen days of the revolution. The film stays away from showing images of protests and demonstrations (except for the penultimate sequence in Tahrir Square) but documents the chaotic environment and common experiences during the revolution. Scenes of 'Amr participating in the popular committee of his neighbourhood and criminals robbing Farah register the insecure settings of the revolution. In addition, one of the film scenes shows people intercepting Farah's car to help them transport a wounded protester to the emergency medical unit at the Egyptian Cultural Centre (as they will be arrested if they go to a hospital). The use of private cars and motorbikes as ambulances and cultural centres as makeshift hospitals pictures a part of the emergency status during the eighteen days of the revolution. The images of solidarity and cooperation within these communities construct a sense of nationalism that was evident during the uprising. As Nichols (2001, p. 141–2) explains,

> The construction of national identities invokes feelings of common purpose and mutual respect, of reciprocal relationships closer to family ties than contractual obligations. Shared values and beliefs are vital to a sense of community, whereas contractual relationships can be carried out despite differences of value and belief. A sense of community often seems like an 'organic' quality that binds people together when they share a tradition, culture, or common goal. As such it may seem far removed from issues of ideology, where competing beliefs struggle to win our hearts and minds.

The film recreates the atmosphere of the eighteen days through popular sounds heard in Egyptian streets and on the media. For example, al-Battut uses demonstration chants as the background sound of 'Amr's scene in the balcony. Farah hears the curfew announcement through her car radio. In representing Mubarak's three speeches, the film avoids showing any images of Mubarak. Instead, al-Battut associates images of people (the main characters of the film) watching the speech with Mubarak's voice. The film's avoidance of showing images of protests and demonstrations as well as Mubarak's speeches reassures the director's aim to document the images that were not represented by the media. The film shows the revolution's impact upon Egyptians as well as its spirit and surroundings. These sounds and images contribute to the audio-visual cultural memory of the 2011 Revolution.

al-Battut also sought to contribute narratives of detainees during the revolution. He visualizes their stories and experiences that were not represented by mainstream media. One of the sequences of the film reveals the state security's questioning of detainees during the revolution. The sequence includes a long take (tracking shot) showing the one-on-one investigation between officers and detainees. Some of the detainees are not actors but participated in the protests of the 2011 Revolution, including Dr Rafik William, who was killed during the Maspiro events on 9 October 2011. The shot represents the power of the detainees (of various ages, religions and political affiliations) over the officers. When asked about the reasons for protesting, the detainees reply boldly or sarcastically. For example, one of the detainees responds, 'My wife is pregnant and I want my son to respect me because I didn't respect my parents'. Other sarcastic replies include 'my relationship with politics is a sexual one. You bring me every two to three days, beat me up and send me home', indicating the violent abuse and physical engagement with politics. The shot also includes a detainee who was captured on his way to buy pizza, which represents the haphazard and random detainment during the uprising. The long take shows the detainees faces and the backs of the investigators to accentuate the film's aim to reveal the perspective and voices of the revolutionaries. While international and local media was interested more in covering the significant events and images from Tahrir Square, al-Battut constructs a visual memory of the investigations during the eighteen days.

The film's representation of the state media during the eighteen days, demonstrates al-Battut's view of media as a significant stakeholder in the narrative of the revolution. The Egyptian state-run channels were popular for their bias towards the police and denial of the revolution during the eighteen days.[17] The film depicts the media's disparagement of the revolution, through the talk show *Alb al-Balad* (*The Country's Heart*) presented by Farah and Tamir. Through clearly referencing *Masr al-Naharda* (*Egypt Today*) – a popular night talk show on the state-run channels – al-Battut blurs the distinction between facts and fiction. The talk show has a similar set and colours to those of *Masr al-Naharda*.[18] The actors retell similar lines that the presenters of *Masr al-Naharda* said on 25 January such as 'Today Egypt is celebrating the police day' and announcing the death and injuries mostly from the police side.

The film documents the state's use of its media, besides its use of state security, to repress the uprising. They address the media's ineptitude through revealing the fake calls that criticized the revolution.[19] The film also historicize the state of confusion felt by many Egyptians, due to the media's deception. Multiple scenes showed the contrast between images broadcasted on the state-run media outlets and non-Egyptian channels such as BBC Arabic. While the Egyptian channels broadcasted national songs, BBC Arabic showed footage of the police using water cannons to disperse protesters. In one scene, 'Amr's neighbour tells him 'I see demonstrations passing by, but nothing on television'. In another scene, Farah's parents ask her 'what's going on? We can't understand'. In *al-Shitaa illy Fat*, al-Battut constructs reality through the clear references to specific talk shows and lines. He uses facts and incidents witnessed by Egyptians to construct a narrative, blurring the distinctions between documentary and fiction forms.

As the film ends with the fall of Mubarak, *al-Shitaa illy Fat* narrates the success of the people's will over the repressive (security forces) and ideological (local media) state apparatuses. In contrast to al-Battut's direct engagement with events of the revolution, film-makers have also represented and narrated the uprising in more subtle ways. Ahmad 'Abd Allah's *Farsh wa-Ghata* shows the revolution in the background of the events of the film while focusing on the marginalized districts of Cairo.

While the previous films focused on events that are directly related to the revolution, *Farsh wa-Ghata* represents a broader view of the uprising that is not limited to protests and Tahrir Square. *Farsh wa-Ghata* is a near-silent film that depicts a prisoner who was set free during the eighteen days of the revolution. Instead of explicitly stating the film-maker's reflection on the revolution, the film invites viewers to participate in the creation of meaning. The lack of dialogue obscures parts of the narrative, such as the nature of the relationship of the lead character with his family members. The film, unconcerned by why or who opened the prisons, follows the protagonist through three different marginalized neighbourhoods in Cairo. The protagonist – an unnamed male character – observes the tragedies and struggles of the inhabitants of the neighbourhoods, while following the revolution news on television.

After the opening of prisons, a Christian injured escapee hides with the protagonist in a dark room and gives him a letter. On his way home (the second day), the protagonist witnesses the police randomly shooting and killing prisoners who have escaped. He overhears a discussion between two prisoners in a microbus stating their fear from the police and desert guards who are shooting guilty and innocent prisoners as well as burying a number of dead bodies in the desert. When the protagonist arrives home, his mother greets him, but his sister's husband (who lives with them at the same home) rejects his stay. He sleeps over the night at a mosque that embraces a makeshift clinic in one of its rooms. The protagonist talks to one of the makeshift clinic operators who then helps him to get an electrician job at Turab Bab al-Waziyr (Bab al-Waziyr graveyard). The protagonist delivers the letter of the Christian escapee to his family at Manshiyit Nasir – Hayy al-Zabbaliyn (a garbage collector's district). The protagonist learns of his associate prisoner's death and engages in a violent fight in the neighbourhood between Muslims and Christians.

The film's opening with a mobile shot of the opening of prisons expresses the narrative as a personal experience/perspective. The film also ends with the protagonist voice (from the video he recorded on his mobile) saying 'I made this video so people can know what happened'. The ending sentence represents 'Abd Allah's intention of revealing the ground of the revolution. The film integrates interviews with the inhabitants of the neighbourhoods that the protagonist visits. Although images of the revolution appear through television and scenes of popular committee, the film profoundly engages with issues of poverty and discrimination as the rationale of the revolution and represents the neighbourhoods as isolated areas during the upheaval.

The film refrains from showing images of the revolution intensely, but it depicts some features and events of the uprising to relate to the historical context. For example, the film starts with a mobile camera shot of the prisoners' escape, followed by a sequence of a re-enactment of the event. The sequence includes dark hand-held shots of the prisoners running off in all directions in the desert combined with sounds of police sirens and shotguns. Once again, the blending of the footage together with the hand-held dark re-enacted sequence boosts the sense of authenticity that the film aims to convey. When the protagonist arrives home at al-Saiyyda Ziynab, the neighbourhood's popular committee obstructs and detains him. He hears the calls for support for the popular committees through the mosque's megaphones. The protagonist also follows the news of the revolution in different scenes including major events, such as the Battle of the Camels. He switches between Al Jazeera, which shows images from Tahrir Square, and the Egyptian state-run television channels, which claims that Alexandria is almost empty of any protesters. However, 'Abd Allah insisted on placing less emphasis on the popular images of the revolution and portraying instead the revolution in a wider context.[20] The film represents Egypt during the revolution, which is not limited to Tahrir Square as the media conveys, but extends to Cairo's under-represented districts.

The film combines both documentary and fiction style through integrating the interviews seamlessly within the narrative. Along his journey, the protagonist encounters the interviewees (non-actors) in various places and situations who express their feelings in an improvised manner. For example, the protagonist overhears an injured protester's mother narrating how a police officer shot her son during the protests. This scene introduces the documentary aspect of the film, as the mother (not an actor) is telling her son's experience of the revolution in an interview style. The interviews also addressed the struggles of the inhabitants of the marginalized neighbourhoods, such as the low standards of living and human dignity. One of the interviews addresses the scarcity of water in Turab Bab al-Waziyr and the environmental conditions of the families living at the graveyard. Another interview with a garbage collector reveals the society's perspective towards his job as 'worthless'. The

Figure 2 Top: popular committees. Bottom: the revolution appearing in the background (*Farsh wa-Ghata*, 2013)

young man narrates a situation where a woman threw the garbage to his face and told him that her relative is a police officer. He adds, 'She sees that I don't have dignity.' 'Abd Allah used the interviews to give voice to the inhabitants of Cairo's marginalized districts, which were under-represented during the revolution. The interviews construct a reality of the lived experiences of poverty and discrimination, which the film aims to contribute to the cultural memory of the 2011 Revolution.

The film does not focus on documenting the revolution's events.[21] Rather than providing answers and facts, it raises questions related to the revolution. 'Abd Allah represents his questions through the unnamed protagonist, the absence of dialogue and the open frames (in many instances). These choices develop the theme of vagueness, where many questions related to the revolution are unanswered yet (such as why or who opened the prisons). The film also represents these questions through the protagonist's character. 'Abd Allah chose a prisoner who suddenly found himself free in a rapidly changing world to represent many Egyptians during the revolution. The film addresses the lack of change and continuity of sectarianism after the revolution. Although Tahrir Square produced images of love and tolerance between Muslims and Christians, the film represented the sectarian strife at Manshiyit Nasir in March 2011. The unconventional lack of dialogue and integration of interviews encourages the contemplation of the visuals and questions that 'Abd Allah raises. The director communicated the revolution through his relatively innovative cinematic language (in relation to Egyptian cinema).

Farsh wa-Ghata participated in internationally acclaimed film festivals, such as Toronto and London Film Festivals, and won the Golden Antigone at the International Mediterranean Film Festival of Montpellier in 2013. It was released for only one week in seven Egyptian film theatres, as film distributors and exhibitors considered the film as non-profitable (mainly due to the absence of dialogue). *Farsh wa-Ghata* is one of the significant films that constitute the independent (post-revolution) Egyptian cinema.

Fiction films that represented the revolution have documented some of the major events that took place during the eighteen days. While some films reassessed the revolution events, such as *Ba'd al-Mawqi'a*, most of them used the events to situate their narratives within the context of the revolution. These films construct an audio-visual memory of the revolution through combining individual stories and experiences with imagined scenarios. The directors of these films intertwined footage of the revolution events together with re-enactments to situate their narratives within the historical moment. They encouraged improvisation to integrate different point of views and produce a more authentic performance. The films addressed the role of media during the revolution (such as state media versus international media outlets) as well as digital media (such as YouTube). The films have also explored some of the motivations behind the revolution including poverty, discrimination and oppression. Film-makers were keen not only to document the major events but also to capture the spirit and the feeling of the eighteen days. They have focused on images from not only Tahrir Square, but also popular committees and makeshift hospitals, which were common during the eighteen days.

However, most of these pictures were not commercially successful, since television was saturated with images of and stories about the revolution. Film producers explained that the audiences were not interested in watching political films directly after the revolution. Some film-makers and audiences classified these films as *āflām mahragānāt* or 'Festival Films' since they participated in several film festivals. Mass audiences usually stay away from these films due to the complexity of their narratives. The representation of the revolution was not limited to fiction films, but also documentaries. As any other significant political event in history, the 2011 Revolution attracted many documentary film-makers. Using documentary modes and fiction narrative style, documentary films represented the reflection of multiple political positions on the revolution.

While only a few fiction films represented the revolution, many documentaries addressed it through the perspectives of the protesters, policemen and the media. The access to footage and the demand of news television channels and international film festivals on films about the revolution motivated film-makers to produce documentaries. Similar to fiction films that engaged with the revolution, documentaries such as *Mawlud fi Khamsa wa-'Ishriyn Yanayir* and *al-Tahrir 2011: al-Taiyyib, wa-l-Sharis, wa-l-Siyasi* participate in constructing the cultural memory of the 2011 Revolution. However, in contrast to fictions, these films aim to represent 'real' stories and experiences through their original characters. Using various documentary modes and styles, such as first person and participatory, film-makers engage with and reflect on the events of the revolution. They narrativized the events through using fictional storytelling techniques such as re-enactments and a linear unfolding of events (context, conflict, climax and closure). While film-makers such as Ahmad Rashwan and Aytin Amin incorporated digital footage of the protests to their films, Johanna Domke and Marwan 'Umara opted out of showing any images from Tahrir in *Crop* (2013). The following paragraphs examine the documentaries *Mawlud fi Khamsa wa-'Ishriyn Yanayir*, *al-Tahrir 2011* and *Crop*. The analysis of the films considers their style and engagement with the revolution as well as the process of their making (based on interviews with the film-makers). Although documentary film-makers have attempted to include conflicting political positions, their support for the revolution has dominated their voices. The films celebrate the revolution and construct national identities through integrating representatives of different political affiliations that constituted the crowd.

Mawlud fi Khamsa wa-'Ishriyn Yanayir is a first-person documentary that accounts the personal experience of the director during the revolution. The interview with the film's director, Ahmad Rashwan, revealed that he started shooting on 27 January 'just as a form of documentation to what's happening.'[22] However, after the stepping down of Mubarak, Rashwan thought of making a film out of his footage. While editing the material at hand, Rashwan carried on shooting the protests held each Friday after the stepping down of Mubarak. He stopped shooting on 27 May, where he decided to end the film. The film starts with a brief review of the director's personal events (such as the birth of his sons) and political activities starting in 2003 (such as protesting against United States' invasion of Iraq). Rashwan then narrates the development of the revolution through recounting his participation in the eighteen days. He uses a combination of re-enactments of scenes (such as watching the news on television and visiting his kids) together with his recorded footage of protests, newspaper archives and screenshots of Facebook statuses. Rashwan created a narrative about the development of his experience during the revolution through linking his footage

Figure 3 Top: a re-enactment of Rashwan and his kids following the news. Bottom: Rashwan filming the events while protesting (*Mawlud fi Khamsa wa-'Ishriyn Yanayir*, 2011)

with these re-enactments and voiceover. He contributes his subjective view of the events to construct an audio-visual memory of the revolution.

The film documents some of the main features of the eighteen days of the revolution including cheering, the use of tear gas by the police, injured protesters and martyrs, Mubarak's three speeches, protest signs about the media's deception, people's committees, the participation of kids and the celebration of Mubarak's fall. The film also captures some of the post-revolution movements (such as the fall of Mubarak's government, the constitutional amendment referendum and the Christian protest at Maspiro). Rashwan ends the film with *gum'it āl-munādāa bi-l-dawla āl-madaniya* (The Friday of Calling for a Civil State), which he considers a milestone in the revolution.²³ The film ends with a growing sense of the counter-revolution, and that 'the revolution is not over yet'. *Mawlud fi Khamsa wa-'Ishriyn Yanayir* premiered at Dubai International film festival and participated in other international and local film festivals.

While the film includes a few comments from the protesters, it mainly represents a subjective view of the revolution. Rashwan constructed the film from a single perspective and focused more on including the main events of the revolution as well as his reflection on them. He directly addresses viewers using his voiceover to comment on what he experienced or learned. Rashwan re-enacted scenes with his children, such as the moment of the step-down of Mubarak, to reinforce his version of the story. He used his personal footage as well as pictures of him shooting at Tahrir Square to narrate his participation and how he viewed the main events. For example, Rashwan did not participate in any marches on the 25th of January thinking, 'it's just another futile protest'. He integrates shots of the marches he participated in on 27 January, showing the clash with the police and obstacles, such as water cannons and tear gas, from the perspective of the protesters. Rashwan narrates his personal feelings to explain the visuals, 'we are changing the nation and history'. The film does not favour multiple points of view and Rashwan's commentary on the events does not allow different interpretations.

Mawlud fi Khamsa wa-Ishriyn Yanayir lacks any critical views of the revolution. Although Rashwan hints the counter-revolution by the end of the film, he ignores the complications such as the opening of prisons and spread of insecurity. Viola Shafik critiqued the film's chronological order of events and news-like style. She considered the film to be a reflection of only the director's 'basic feelings' rather than dealing with how the revolution changed individuals.²⁴ However, the film still constructs an audio-visual cultural memory of the revolution. As in the beginning of the film, Rashwan reveals that he keeps a visual record of all the events he experiences for memory; as a film-maker, every shot he captures is a part of his personal as well as the world's memory. The documentary also further articulates the relationship between film-making and the revolution. It represents Rashwan's passion for filming the events and participating in the protests simultaneously.²⁵ He also made *Giziyrat al-A'bat* (*The Christians Island*, 2013), which narrates the participation of Christians in the 2011 Revolution. Rashwan considers *Giziyrat al-A'bat* to be the second part of *Mawlud fi Khamsa wa-'Ishriyn Yanayir*.

In contrast to Rashwan's subjective perspective, *al-Tahrir 2011* covers three views of the revolution through three distinctive parts: The Good, The Bad and

The Politician. While the first part is quite similar to *Mawlud fi Khamsa wa-'Ishriyn Yanayir* in revealing the revolution from the perspective of the protesters, the second part unfolds the story through policemen's point of view. The film's third part provides a guide to becoming a dictator in ten steps comically with a predominant focus on Mubarak. The film's producer, Muhammad Hifzi, had the initial idea but started working on the project after the eighteen days of the uprising. Aytin Amin, the director of the second part – 'The Bad', shot some footage herself, such as the break into the state security building. They also had access, through Ahmad 'Abd Allah, to the Tahrir's media tent – which gathered the footage shot during the revolution. The relationship between the revolution and *al-Tahrir 2011* is not limited to the film's content but also extended to its distribution and exhibition. *al-Tahrir 2011* was the first Egyptian documentary released in film theatres after almost forty years of absence of Egyptian documentaries on commercial screens. Although no documentaries have been released commercially since *al-Tahrir 2011*, the film-makers attempted at creating a new space for different film forms in the commercial market. The film's producer considers the revolution itself one of the main reasons for the film's release in theatres (M.Hifzi, interview, 25 January 2015). The film participated in several international film festivals and won awards, such as the UNESCO award at the Venice Film Festival. In my interviews with Hifzi and Amin, they talked about the abundance of funds that were available for documentaries addressing the revolution.[26]

The first part of *al-Tahrir 2011* trilogy, titled 'The Good', intercuts between interviews with protesters narrating their experience during the eighteen days of the revolution. The interviewees include an activist, doctor, singer, photojournalist and a university student (a member of the Muslim Brotherhood organization) all of whom have participated in the revolution. Some of the interviews were set where the told narrative took place (such as streets leading to Tahrir Square and Asr al-Niyl Bridge). Tamir 'Izzat, the director of this part, supported the stories of the interviewees with footage (shot on mobile phones and digital cameras) and pictures from the revolution in a classic documentary style. The intercutting between the interviews with young men and women of different professions constructs a sense of community. The clear links and overlaps between their testimonies demonstrate their shared experiences. This part of the film constructs a sense of nationalism through representing a collective experience of the participants of the revolution.

The second part of the film, titled 'The Bad', reveals the 'other side' of the story through interviews with four police officers (two of them appear in a silhouette or with a blurred face). 'The Bad' provides insights into the police officers' view, which has been ignored by many of the films about the revolution. The officers tend to shift the blame to higher authorities. They criticize the state's use of security in social, economic and political conflicts. They also emphasize that their job is to execute orders and 'secure the city'. The officers recount the injuries on their side and describe the protesters' use of Molotov cocktails and stones. During my interview with Amin (director of 'The Bad'), she disclosed that her relationship with the interviewees changed from time to time. While she questions the police officers about their brutal acts during the revolution, she sympathizes with them at parts (such as the burning of police stations). In constructing a memory of the revolution, Amin's part is significant in revealing the 'other side' of the narrative that was under-represented in documentaries about the revolution.

In the third part, titled 'The Politician', the director 'Amr Salama interviews politicians, such as Dr Muhammad al-Barad'i and Dr Mustafa al-Fi'i (Mubarak's former advisor), writers, including 'Ala' al-Aswani and Bilal Fadl, Dr Ahmad 'Ukasha (professor of psychiatry), and Yusri Fuda (TV presenter). The interviewees provide stories and facts about Mubarak in the form of '10 steps to become a dictator', which Salama represents in a satirical voice. He uses classic infomercial style, including a commercial-like jingle and graphics and represents archival footage to support the facts of the interviewees. The ten steps address features of Mubarak and his regime, including dying his hair and retouching his pictures (to appear young), having his name and pictures everywhere (schools, streets and hospitals named after him), dominating the media, laws and security, and creating an imaginary enemy. Salama ends the film with a quick review of how the people overthrew the dictator.

al Tahrir 2011 constructs the revolution through revealing three sides of the same narrative. The film groups interviewees supporting different political affiliations, such as liberal protesters and Muslim Brotherhood members and pro and anti-revolution, into three broad categories: protesters, policemen and politicians. The film ignores the nuance of the positions of the interviewees and romanticizes the revolution. However, the film still documents experiences of different stakeholders and offers them a space to rationalize their actions. The first two parts, in particular, capture the fresh experiences of the two opposite sides, as the film imagines them, of the revolution. The instant documentation of these experiences is significant, especially after a severe counter-revolution has taken over. *al-Tahrir 2011* stands as an evidence of a historical moment that anyone can hardly deny. Nevertheless, the film-makers did not represent the different voices equally. In contrast to the sense of nationalism evoked in 'The Good', 'The Bad' challenges the interviewed officers rather than supporting their stories. It foregrounds the internal contradictions of the police officers. While some of them revealed their aspiration to overthrow the regime, the immediate success of the revolution has yielded their sense of failure. Amin used footage of police vans running over the protesters to contrast their claims of their 'weakness'. She ends her part with an unanswered question about the use of violence, which emphasizes the officers' uncertainty of their actions.

al-Tahrir 2011 is among the earliest films that openly criticized Mubarak. However, similar to other documentaries about the revolution, *al-Tahrir 2011* limits the revolution to Tahrir Square. Although it is almost impossible to tell a coherent story about the revolution, *al-Tahrir 2011* reinforces the boundaries of the revolution to Tahrir Square through marginalizing protests that took place elsewhere (such as Alexandria, Suez and Mansoura). Only a few documentaries, such as *Muwg* recognized the struggle of the people of Suez, where the first civilian was killed on 25 January 2011, and did not show any images from Tahrir Square. Also, the French Egyptian *Je Suis Le Peuple* (*I Am the People*, Anna Roussillon, 2014) follows Farraj who lives in the poor villages of southern Egypt and follows the revolution through television screens and newspaper. These films have attempted to shift the centralized focus away from Tahrir Square.

Crop is also another documentary about the revolution that does not show any images from Tahrir Square. The directors wrote the narration script based on research interviews they made with nineteen journalists and photographers. The film narrates a fiction story of a photojournalist at *al-Ahram* – Egypt's oldest state-run newspaper. The photojournalist, who was at the hospital during the revolution days, narrates the relationship between Egypt's presidents (Nasser, Sadat and Mubarak) and images. For example, in contrast to the personal pictures of Sadat with his family and shaving in the bathroom, Mubarak's published photos were only during official ceremonies. The photojournalist explains how his job as a photojournalist (during Mubarak's era) was to 'falsify reality' and show representative images of modernity. In addition to recognizing issues of corruption, poverty and unemployment as an Egyptian citizen, the photojournalist recounts the suppression of the protests since 2006. He describes the sounds of cheering and fire guns he heard at the hospital and ignorance of state-run media during the revolution. Next to him at the hospital, an injured protester shows him 'unfiltered' pictures and videos that he captured on his mobile phone. Although the photojournalist describes some of these photos in detail, Domke and 'Umara do not show these pictures. The film displays fixed shots inside *al-Ahram* complex (where the photojournalist used to work) during a normal working day. The shots include employees passing through security doors, signing in, using lifts, working in offices, as well as empty meeting rooms, corridors, cafeteria, health clinic and printer halls. Through these shots, we see (and sometimes hear) the employees interacting with one another.

For *Crop*, suppression is one of the main motivations leading up to the 2011 Revolution. The narrator explains how *al-Ahram* edited and framed images to suppress rising anger and appraise the government. The detailed description of the narrator and his monotonous voiceover encourages viewers to imagine the discussed pictures in their minds and link it to the images on the screen. The visuals (being all away from the centre of events) explain the photojournalist's absence from Tahrir as well as the state media's ignorance of the revolution. In addition, associating images of *al-Ahram*'s employees during a working day (shot in an observational documentary style) together with the description of the narrator's experience as a photojournalist adds to the authenticity of the fictional narrative and supports the film's argument of suppressing political dissent during Mubarak's period.

The self-reflexive film does not only communicate the power of images through voiceover but also through a poetic portrait of shots that reveal the filtration process of news and photos. The narrative shows *al-Ahram*'s complex with its bureaucratic employees who frame their news according to the ruling government's policies. The images are selected and juxtaposed in the order of publishing news (starts with the entry of employees to the building in the morning and ends with the distribution of the paper at night). The images show the security measures in the old-aged building including x-ray baggage scanners and security guards on each level. The visuals also emphasize the bureaucratic hierarchy of the organization through different gates, elevators and office spaces assigned to employees according to their ranks. The fictional narrative that explains the state's use of media and images to deceive people, supported with shots of a state-run institution that was responsible for the censoring process, reflect on the power of images in constructing 'realities'.

In *Crop*, Domke and 'Umara represent the significant role that technology played in documenting the revolution. The narrator discusses the protesters' use of their personal digital cameras and mobile phones to capture images and videos of protests. The film emphasizes the concept of citizen photojournalism, and historicises its use during the revolution, as an alternative to the misleading state media. The film does not only contribute to the memory of the revolution through its distinctive perspective and approach but also recognizes how people documented the revolution creatively. The film is self-reflexive in this sense as it uses a unique approach to documenting the revolution. In contrast to other documentaries about the 2011 Revolution, the film does not show any images of protests, marches or sit-ins and associates a fiction narrative with documentary-style visuals.

The process of documenting the film-making practices and activities during the revolution has also been an interest of the film scholar Alisa Lebow. She created *Filming Revolution* – an online interactive meta-documentary about independent film-making and documentaries in relation to the revolution. The website, www.filmingrevolution.org (launched in 2015), comprises interviews with thirty film-makers, activists and artists discussing their projects and innovative strategies during the revolution. The interviews are cut into clips according to themes and projects. The creative design of *Filming Revolution* does not limit the audience to a particular narrative or order. The website allows the users to engage with the interviewees according to the themes (such as identity, women/gender, distribution) or specific projects discussed during the interviews. The 'curated dialogues' that the website offers to serve as an archive of the film-makers' discussion of/reflection on film projects related to the revolution. In contrast to other revolutionary film movements, Lebow (2016, p. 285–7) argues the film-makers did not develop a specific method or aesthetic approach that could distinguish film-making in Egypt since the revolution. However, Lebow identifies some commonalities in narrating the revolution such as representing the events indirectly or using first-person film-making style (including films about personal identity, cultural identity and sexuality).

The films discussed in this chapter confirm Lebow's interpretation of indirect representations of the revolution, such as in *Crop*, and using first person style in *Mawlud fi Khamsa wa-'Ishriyn Yanayir*.[27] Documentaries such as *al-Tahrir 2011* and *al-Midan* engage with multiple activists and protesters that participated in the revolution. They are concerned with various narratives of the participants (including protesters, policemen and journalists). These documentaries represent personal experiences and memories of a historical moment. Although these participants represent some of the different political ideologies involved in the uprising (such as liberal protesters and members of the Muslim Brotherhood), they represent them as a community with common goals to evoke a sense of nationalism. Aytin Amin challenged her police officers interviewees through integrating shots that contradict their witnesses. Film-makers used interviews and personal footage to construct narratives of the revolution according to their own voices. They contribute some of the voices of their interviewees, as well as their own, to the cultural memory of the 2011 Revolution. These documentaries construct a cultural memory in support of the uprising. Although film-makers attempted to mediate multiple voices, their support for the revolution dominated their voices and shaped the perspectives of their films.

* * *

The ethical dilemma of whether to make a film about the revolution or not was prevalent among film-makers. Those who condemned using the revolution in films, criticize the 'revolution films' for being premature or view the revolution as bigger than what a film can embrace. In reference to *Tamantashar Yuwm*, Hala Galal explained, 'People who wanted to take the opportunity of Egypt's presence in the International film festivals were investors who had money and produced a film quickly that participated in Cannes and Berlin' (H. Galal, interview, 30 December 2015). These film-makers prefer alluding to the revolution implicitly in their films or through their film style. On the other hand, film-makers who represented the revolution in their films emphasized the importance of documenting the historical moment on a form that will live longer than those who witnessed it. These film-makers presumed the instant urge of recording these feelings and memories on film before the counter-revolution obliterates it. Many of the fiction films started production without a written script, due to the rapidly changing nature of events. They mostly depended on improvisation to emphasize the sense of authenticity of their narratives. The demand of international film festivals and television channels on films about the revolution has led to debates around the 'abuse' of film-makers of the revolution. However, the popular positions of many film-makers in supporting and participating in the revolution demonstrate their aim in documenting the historical moment.

Fiction and documentary films overlapped in their representation of the revolution. They construct an audio-visual memory of the revolution through intertwining stories and experiences with images and footage of the revolution. Fiction films created narratives that combine imagined scenarios together with archival footage, re-enactments and interviews. Film-makers also used improvisation and non-actors to evoke a sense of authenticity. These scenes have supported film-makers in their construction of reality of stories that were under-represented by media during the revolution. Film-makers integrated interviews within their narratives blurring the distinction between documentary and fiction styles. Documentary film-makers have also attempted to give voice to conflicting and competing political positions. They represented the political and social varieties of the crowd in Tahrir Square as a community that shares common goals to construct a sense of nationalism. They narrativized the events through employing fictional storytelling techniques, including re-enactments and fiction scripts. Fiction and documentary films constructed reality and history through their imaginative and (sometimes) subjective narratives.

While some commonalities group the films that represented the revolution, a number of variants distinguish them from one another. Almost all the films, thus far, were advocates of the revolution and its supporters, which could be traced back to the support of film-makers for the revolution. Film-makers who represented the revolution in their films disclosed that they do not provide an exhaustive chronicle of the revolution, but attempted to document and reflect on particular events that took place. While many film-makers based their films on personal experiences, others represented different views of the uprising. Whether it is the perspective of the protesters and activists, media and journalists, and/or the counter-revolution, the films attempted to narrate stories of the revolution's stakeholders. Fiction and documentary films have comprised characters representing higher and lower social classes and different political affiliations (including liberal protesters, policemen and Muslim Brotherhood supporters) in order to construct national identity and the revolution as a historical moment that involved the participation of people from all walks of life.

Like fictions, some documentaries used archival footage of protests and others took the revolution to a wider context beyond Tahrir Square. Those films shed a light on people, cities and issues that media have been overlooked by the focus on Tahrir Square. Fiction films have used documentary style through incorporating footage from the uprising, interviews and improvised scenes with the inhabitants of the locations of the films. *al-Shitaa illy Fat*, focused solely on the eighteen days (sometimes with a pre-revolution context), and some others depicted the post-revolution struggle with the military forces and Muslim Brotherhood, such as *Mawlud fi Khamsa wa-'Ishriyn Yanayir*. Some of these films that deal with the pre-revolution oppression (such as *al-Shitaa illy Fat* and *al-Tahrir 2011*) were inceptive in terms of openly criticizing Mubarak. However, these films confirm the continuity of Egyptian film history in criticizing leaders during the succeeding periods. The Censorship of Artistic Works continues to prevent films that criticize the president and the Armed Forces. Both fiction and documentary films have borrowed stylistic elements from one another to evoke a sense of authenticity or support the arguments of their narratives. They construct the revolution as a historical moment of the public's rebellion against the long-standing reign.

Other narrative films such as *Kharig al-Khidma* (*Out of Order*, Mahmud Kamil, 2014) and *Sukkar Murr* (*Bitter Sugar*, Hani Khalifa, 2015) are set during the eighteen days of the revolution but did not engage intensely with the revolution as a political event.[28] These films use the revolution as a backdrop in narrating their social or romantic stories. In addition, comedy films such as *Tak Tak Bum* (Ashraf Faiy', 2011) and *Hazz Sa'id* (*Sa'id's Luck*, Tari' 'Abd al-Mu'ti, 2012) among others depicted the revolution within their narratives. In both films, the revolution came to alter the plans of the protagonists (e.g. in *Tak Tak Bom*, the revolution happens on the protagonist's wedding day, which obligates him to participate in popular committees). Film critics, such as 'Adli (2012), condemned these comedies for their sarcastic depiction of the revolution and the 'shallow' portrayal of the ideologies of the protesters.

Also, significant documentaries include *al-Thawra Khabar* (*Reporting a Revolution*, Bassam Murtada, 2012), which follows six journalists and reveals the struggles they face while covering the revolution. Meanwhile, some film-makers chose to document the consequences of the revolution on individuals through focusing on the post-revolution period. For example, Tahani Rashid's *Nafas Tawiyl* (*A Deep Long Breath*, 2012) depicts the hope, political participation of youth and the rise of the Muslim Brotherhood. The film focuses on the members of one family during the first six months after the dismissal of Mubarak.

Recently, more films have been representing the revolution. *Nawwara* (Hala Khalil, 2015) narrates the story of a working-class girl, played by Minna Shalabi, who works as a housemaid at a former minister's villa. She suffers carrying heavy water containers every day to her place, where she and her grandmother do not have access to water. After the revolution, she believes the rumours spread through the media that Mubarak's billions will be distributed among the public. Nawwara and her husband dream to buy their own flat. The female-centred melodrama represents class struggle in Mubarak's pre-revolution Egypt. Minna Shalabi won the best actress award at Dubai Film Festival for her role in *Nawwara*. Also, *al-Giziyra 2* (*The Island 2*, Shirif 'Arafa, 2014) is a sequel to a blockbuster action film that takes place in Upper Egypt. *al-Giziyra 2* is set after the revolution and is loaded with political projections. The film narrates the power struggle over the Island, where the film takes place, among Islamists, drug and weapon dealers (who escaped during the opening of prisons on 28 January) and policemen who have been sent to jail after the revolution.

Documentary films also continue to discuss the post-revolution economic and political status. Marwan 'Umara revealed his future project is about youth moving to Sharm al-Sheikh (an Egyptian resort town by the Red Sea popular for its beaches and coral reefs). The film focuses on a group of young men, who were part of the revolution, and are now moving on to search for jobs in another city. The film captures the post-revolution economic deterioration and status of tourism, as well as the convergence of Eastern and Western cultures (due to the number of Western tourists visiting the city). Youth approach Sharm al-Sheikh as a local destination that offers job opportunities within a more Westernized culture. Sharm al-Sheikh was also a political icon during the past decade. Several peace conferences were held in the city. Mubarak has moved to Sharm al-Sheikh after his step-down in 2011. Such films do represent further aspects of the revolution although they do not apparently engage with its manifestations. After a few years of participating in the 2011 Revolution, these youth return to Sharm al-Sheikh with political despair.

The representation of resistance was not limited to films. Artists and protesters expressed their feelings towards Mubarak's regime during the eighteen days of the revolution using poems, graffiti, memes and music. However, the rise of the counter-revolution during the ruling periods of the Muslim Brotherhood in 2013 and al-Sisi's military regime since 2014 has limited the representation of the revolution and the promotion of notions of rebellion. Film-makers continued to use low budgets and develop the earlier styles of film-making. They self-funded their projects and depended on some other funds from film festivals and non-profit organizations. They continued to employ digital cameras and new actors and use non-traditional narrative structures to represent themes of frustration and hope. The development of digital technologies facilitated the production and distribution of short films among youth. However, in contrast to revolutions in history, which were usually followed by film movements that applied 'revolutionary aesthetics', independent films in Egypt lack a clear and consistent methodology of approaching aesthetics. They remediate traditional realistic styles and formats, while a few film-makers have been creative in representing the revolutionary struggle. Post-revolution films configure change differently according to the distinctive views of film-makers of the revolution and due to censorship pressures.

5

Technology and revolution: The continuity of 'independent' films

New film-making waves around the world were usually associated with revolutions. As discussed in Chapter 1, film movements and practices such as Third Cinema and Eisenstein, Pudovkin and Vertov's distinctive style emerged after the Cuban and Soviet revolutions respectively. These film movements and stylistic tendencies were associated with specific revolutions as they contributed to goals of revolutions of deconstructing dominant ideologies and constructing new ones. Similar to the concept of a revolution, new film-making practices, such as the use of distinctive aesthetics and experimental film modes, have represented the resistance of film-makers to mainstream film-making styles. What is popularly known as *āl-āflām āl-mustaqilla* (or independent films) in Egypt can be compared to such revolutionary film-making waves. Given the common attributes of new film-making practices, such as resisting the commercial mainstream and innovating new production methods as well as crafting distinctive aesthetics, 'independent films' in Egypt are comparable in some respects to revolutionary film movements. However, this film-making style has started in Egypt during the late 1990s (known as digital cinema at that time) and proliferated since 2005. After the 2011 Revolution, this independent film wave did not develop into a revolutionary film movement due to the lack of a consistent aesthetic framework. Film-makers develop earlier styles of 'independent films', which were produced before the revolution and engage with sociopolitical issues. They continue using similar techniques and styles such as using digital cameras, casting new actors and depending on improvisation, with some developments such as the use of slow rhythm in *al-khurug li-l-Nahar* (*Coming Forth by Day*, Hala Lutfi, 2012) and lack of dialogue in *Farsh wa-Ghata* (*Rags and Tatters*, Ahmad 'Abd Allah, 2013).

A number of film-makers in Egypt depend on alternative methods of production, distribution and exhibition to liberate themselves from censorship and commercial market constraints. Film critic Rami 'Abd al-Razi' (2014) considers Muhammad Mamduh's *The Democracy of a Medium: The Rise of Independent Cinema in Egypt* (2007) a turning point in the use of the term 'independent films'. Mamduh's study explained what the term embraces in terms of style and modes of production of short and feature films that were produced at that time such as *Ithaki* (Ibrahim al-Battut, 2006) – a fiction film that includes documentary segments about the influence of war on fifteen characters living in Cairo. 'Independent films' use alternative styles of storytelling and resort to low-budget techniques including inexpensive tools and unknown actors.[1] The emergence of digital cameras by the late 1990s facilitated the production of films using low budgets. Film-makers raise funds, offered by international film festivals and institutions that support art-house films, to produce their films without conforming to the commercial market considerations. The films participate in local and international film festivals and only a few film theatres release some of them, due to their unpopularity. Cultural centres in Egypt screen these films to a specific audience who are interested in alternative cinema.[2] These films do not aim to mobilize the audience, but they are radical in terms of resisting the dominant film-making style. Since its inception, mainstream film-making in Egypt was characterized by its Hollywood commercial film style. Film production and distribution depended on film stars and popular genres, such as comedy during the late 1990s. By 2008, the production of more low-budget films that use digital cameras and new actors led to their inclusion under the umbrella of independent cinema. The term included films such as Ahmad Rashwan's *Basra* (2008), which depicts the fears and concerns of a photographer amid the Fall of Baghdad in 2003, and *'In Shams* (*Eye of the Sun*, Ibrahim al-Battut, 2008), which portrays the deprivation of the district of 'In Shams, the capital of Egypt during the Pharaonic era.

These films engage with politics through their expression and subtle representations of oppositional political and social views. They are relevant to Wayne's (2001) description of political films which 'address unequal access to and distribution of material and cultural resources, and the hierarchies of legitimacy and status accorded to those differentials' (p. 1). Thus, films discussed in this chapter do engage with politics not only in its narrow sense (the president, the government, political parties and systems) but also in its broader sense which includes its influence on social and cultural realms. For example, the political engagements of films such as *'In Shams* and *Hiliaupulis* (*Heliopolis*, Ahmad 'Abd Allah, 2008) include the depiction of poverty and impoverishment of once grandeur districts in Cairo. Films discussed in this chapter also make clear references to political oppression and include political events, such as the invasion of Iraq, along with the struggles of their characters. The subtle engagement of these films with political issues (as well as the ones produced after the revolution), along with the existence of the censorship body, demonstrates their attempts of resistance. The use of low budgets and digital cameras represents the persistence of the film-makers to produce their films without the intervention of commercial film producers. However, in contrast to other 'revolutionary' film waves, film scholar Alisa Lebow (2016) and film critic Amir al-'Umari (2014) argue film-makers in Egypt did not develop a specific aesthetic framework that could distinguish their film style. Although independent film-makers apply similar models of production and distribution, such as the use of digital cameras, their individual innovations complicate the recognition of their films as a movement. al-'Umari (2014) describes independent film-making in Egypt as lacking vision and critical theory foundations. He also confirms Lebow's conclusion about the Egyptian independent cinema's lack of a clear and consistent methodology in dealing with images. Lebow justifies,

> The revolution in Egypt is neither over nor can it have been declared successful at the level of having radically reorganized and reimagined the ruling regime. Thus there has been no opportunity to craft a new approach to cinema in line with the new reigning ideology, nor to narrate the revolutionary struggle. Secondly, this revolution was not driven by a specific, explicit ideology. There was no leader, no party, and no elaborated platform much beyond the basic chants of bread, freedom and social justice. (2016, p. 279)

Nevertheless, these arguments do not deny the creative engagement of film-makers with the revolution. Lebow indicates a few innovative practices of film-makers such as Jasmina Mitwally and Philip Rizk's *Barra fi-l-Shari'* (*Out on the Streets*, 2015), where ten factory workers, who were involved in protests, re-enact stories and images of injustice and police brutality on a rooftop acting studio. Also, Mitwally and Rizk's *Remarking January 25 – A Series of Six* (2011) consists of six short videos about the participation of factory workers in the revolution. Lara Baladi's *Alone, Together ... in a Media Res* (2012) is a 40-minute, three-channel video installation that reflects on the revolution. The channels show videos from Tahrir Square, clips of McLuhan and Sartre as well as excerpts of music videos and films. Nadin Khan's *I Will Speak of the Revolution* (2011) criticizes the use of revolution in films while it is still taking place. The one-minute film follows an unidentified person from home to Tahrir Square focusing on their walking feet and using jumpcuts. Khan states her anger of 'contextualizing the revolution' using her voice-over. These creative practices are associated with their film-makers/artists but do not create a post-revolution film movement. Instead, these films collectively represent the revolutionary struggle using different styles and forms.

Contemporary scholarship tends to situate independent cinema in Egypt within studies about new cinemas in the Middle East, North Africa and/or the 'Arab world' (Schwartz, Kaye and Martini, 2013; Jarjoura, 2014; and Armes, 2015). These texts provide an account of the contemporary Arab film-makers and the new styles and modes of their films. Scholars describe the alternative film-making practices as well as their challenges with governments and states. Film critics, such as Rami 'Abd al-Razi' (2014), have attempted to provide a holistic characterization of independent cinema in Egypt. He highlighted the use of new actors, digital cameras and non-traditional narrative structures as the main characteristics of independent cinema. Film-makers sought alternative means of production and distribution for their texts, which shed light on 'social realities'. These films include *Basra*, *'In Shams*, *Hiliaupulis, al-khurug li-l-Nahar* and *Akhir Ayyam al-Madina* (*In Last Days of the City*, Tamir al-Sa'id, 2016). Film director Ahmad 'Abd Allah explains the commonalities between these films that led to their grouping under the same category, which includes the use of video/digital cameras, natural lightings, real locations and new actors. Some of these films, such as *Basra* and *'In Shams*, have integrated documentary sequences within their narratives (A. 'Abd Allah, interview, 31 January 2015). Almost all these films, among other independent ones, engage with themes of gender power and/or class struggle within the context of oppression, minorities and marginalized groups.

Independent productions aim for 'realistic' representations of the contemporary Egyptian society. To achieve such reality effect, they resist mainstream formulaic genres and avoid casting film stars. They do not use traditional narrative structures of beginning, middle and end. Instead, they reveal a set of interrelated stories that narrate a specific theme, such as ambition and hope in *'Asham* (Maggi Murgan, 2013). They also construct reality through casting new actors who would provide fresh performances. These non-star actors do not mind to play smaller roles or to appear without make-up in scenes, which film stars would usually refuse. They also accept trying non-traditional acting techniques, such as improvisation, which in many cases film-makers depend on to give a sense of spontaneity. Film-makers shoot in real locations, instead of film sets, and depend on natural lighting to reinforce the sense of authenticity. They use long takes to convey a seemingly real-time action. Sound, including a few dialogue lines and long moments of silence, has also been a major element in creating an authentic ambience. These strategies were associated with independent cinema of the past decade – since Ibrahim al-Battut's *Ithaki* (2006) to Muhammad Hammad's *Akhdar Yabis* (*Withered Green*, 2016), a fiction about a young woman who, after the death of her father, tries to convince her uncles to attend her sister's marriage agreement. These films address a niche audience who are interested in alternative styles of cinema.

This chapter attempts to explain what the term independent cinema refers to in Egypt through providing a brief history and describing its position in relation to the mainstream film industry. Many film producers choose not to be involved in independent projects due to their limited revenues in comparison to blockbusters that feature film stars, such as Ahmad al-Sa'a and Ahmad Hilmi. I provide an analysis of independent feature films that were released after the revolution. These films include *al-Khurug li-l-Nahar*, which narrates the story of a daughter who, along with her mother, looks after her bedridden father. *'Asham* addresses themes of ambition and hope through a set of interrelated stories about six couples of different ages and social class in Cairo. *Harag wa-Marag* (*Chaos, Disorder*, Nadin Khan, 2013) reveals the stories of Zaki and Muniyr who live in an isolated society and love the same girl, Manal. The analysis focuses on the production methods, techniques (such as the use of improvisation and new actors) and themes of marginalization and frustration that characterize independent films. These films have not developed a particular aesthetic framework that constitutes a film movement, but they resist mainstream productions through using similar techniques and styles of independent films that were produced before the revolution. They address Egyptian society mostly through characters of middle to lower social classes who are marginalized and isolated, as in *Harag wa-Marag*. They emphasize on the dreams and hopes of their characters (as in *'Asham*) or their frustration (*al-Khurug li-l-Nahar*) within a sociopolitical context. These films have depicted the oppression of women not only within their texts but also through their differentiated cinematic language and depiction of reality, as Johnston (1973, p. 29) suggests in her notes on women's cinema. The women directors have foregrounded the feminine voice in these films, although they are set within a patriarchal society (Suter, 1988). In films such as *al-Khurug li-l-Nahar* and *'Asham* women are represented as the main characters, leading the narratives and forwarding the stories. Towards the end of the films, *'Asham* and *al-Khurug li-l-Nahar* have conveyed senses of hope.

The chapter engages with debates around the classification of films and the misuse of the term independent. Mainstream producers and distributors have used the term independent to marginalize film-makers and their projects. The different approaches to production (such as the involvement of production companies) and casting well-known actors in some cases have obscured what the term independent means. Film-makers associated with this term, such as Hala Lutfi, resist the label due to its connotations of complex narratives and elitist films.

The chapter draws on interviews conducted with independent film producers and directors who have contributed to the contemporary independent film-making wave. Film producers-directors such as Hala Lutfi, Hala Galal as well as film directors Ahmad Rashwan and Ahmad 'Abd Allah are among the earliest participants in the independent wave. In addition, film producers Muhammad Samir, Muhammad Hifzi, Shirif Mandur have supported independent films, albeit their engagement with commercial film production. Film directors Aytin Amin and Marwan 'Umara have raised funds for their short, feature fiction and documentary films independently. I conducted these interviews in Cairo in December 2014, January 2015 and January 2016. Since then, censorship on films has been increasing. The Censorship of Artistic Works has refused to issue screening permissions for films such as *Akhir Ayyam al-Madina*. The feature film narrates the struggles of a documentary film-maker living in Cairo.

The development of film-making technologies in the last decade offered more production and distribution opportunities. The introduction of DSLR cameras and smartphones together with the growth of online platforms encouraged young film-makers to produce and distribute short films. Some of these films engaged with the 2011 Revolution such as *Biy'ulu* (*They Say*, Ahmad Ghazal, 2011), which depicts the use of social media and spreading rumours during the uprising, and *al-Burtrai* (The *Portrait*, Ahmad Magdi, 2012), which is about an artist who draws a portrait for a protester as he gets killed in one of the protests. Also, *al-Asansiyr* (*The Elevator*, Hassan Rida, 2013) draws on the political conflicts during the Muslim Brotherhood period symbolically through an Islamist, a communist and a liberal trapped in an elevator. Short film festivals such as Tropfest Arabia and Cinemobile Film Festival have also encouraged the production of these films.

These films constitute a part of what Kraidy (2006) calls hypermedia space. Kraidy and Mourad (2010) use hypermedia space to refer to the development of communications technologies such as mobile phones, digital cameras and online platforms (such as Facebook, YouTube and Twitter) which have created a more fluid communicative and participatory environment. According to Kraidy and Mourad,

> Since communication processes flow in several directions, and since the roles of producer and receiver of information have been scrambled, and since more people are now theoretically able to shape a message, then we can expect a multiplicity of discourses to arise in public culture. (2010, p. 3)

The evolution of new film technologies, such as digital cameras, nonlinear editing software and video-sharing websites, has offered spaces for young film-makers to express themselves. Amateur and young film-makers who aspire to make feature films now produce short films, which were limited to film students and a few film-makers. The technological evolutions in conjunction with the revolution have encouraged the production of short films that engage with political issues. However, these films did not present a radically different film-making style from traditional short films that were produced before the revolution. In contrast to Kraidy's (2006) description of hypermedia space as 'a less controllable and therefore potentially subversive space created by various interacting media and information technologies', young film-makers have produced traditional short films through digital and online technologies.

The third section of this chapter discusses the expansion of independent practices after the revolution. Although the revolution did not create the independent movement, it stimulated the production of independent films, music and graffiti as forms of self-expression. The chapter sheds light on a few production companies and individuals that started initiatives to produce and/or screen alternative films and independent productions since the revolution. These initiatives include Misr International Films' Zawya, Hala Lutfi's Hassala, Tamir al-Sa'id and Khalid 'Abd Allah's Cimatheque and Wagih al-Laqani's sinima fi kul makan (Cinema Everywhere). Recently, a form of indirect censorship has challenged these independent practices for their link with the revolution. The state has been creative in banning films to avoid local and international discussions about freedom of speech in Egypt.

In order to understand the influence of the revolution and technology on independent productions, it is necessary to provide the context of producing independent films before the uprising. In the following paragraphs, I provide a brief background of independent cinema in Egypt. I attempt to define what this term refers to through differentiating it from mainstream productions. Some examples of independent productions that were released since the revolution include *al-Khurug li-l-Nahar*, *'Asham* and *Harag wa-Marag*. These films used low budgets, new actors and improvisation techniques. Film-makers self-funded their films and sometimes depended on other funding sources such as independent initiatives and crowdfunding. However, the association of independent film-makers with different film-making styles (sometimes including known actors and production companies) has obscured the term independent cinema.

By the late 1990s, a few directors used digital cameras to shoot their films. The first feature shot using a digital camera was Yusri Nasrallah's *al-Madina* (*The City*, 1999) – a fiction about 'Ali who travels to Paris following his dream to become an actor.[3] The film was co-produced by Humbert Balsan and Marian and Gabi Khuwri. Muhammad Khan also shot *Klifti* (2004) on a digital camera. However, *Klifti* required a lower budget, which Khan himself provided. The film narrates the story of a swindler who falls into a complicated romantic relationship. Nasrallah and Khan cast Basim al-Samra – a relatively new actor at the time – for the leading role in their films.

During the same period, independent artists and cultural entrepreneurs started venues and spaces for art and cultural events. For example, Muhammad al-Sawi established Sa'iyat al-Sawi (*al-Sawi Culture Wheel*) in 2003 to host musical performances, workshops and seminars. A film-makers collective initiated SEMAT (Abbr. *āl-sīnimā'yun āl-mustaqillun li-l-intāg wa-l-tawzi'* – Independent Film-makers for Production and Distribution) in 2001 to support independent film-makers. SEMAT issued a magazine called *Nazrah* and produced short films such as *Muraba' Daiyr* (*Rotating Square*, Ahmad Hassuna, 2002), which depicts the involvement of a young man and woman in a murder for jewellery and cash. SEMAT continues to organize several film-making workshops and screenings until today.

These initiatives encouraged the creation of a non-conformist independent film-making stream that parallels the mainstream film-making industry. Film director-producer Hala Lutfi comments,

> The fact about this film [*Muraba' Daiyr*] is that it was not produced by the National Centre for Cinema or the Higher Cinema Institute, which was a great opportunity to everyone because films were only produced through institutions or big production companies. No one could offer to rent a digital beta-camera, which used to cost 1,500 EGP a day. (H. Lutfi, interview, 17 January 2015)

By 2005, Ibrahim al-Battut wrote, produced, shot and directed his first feature narrative *Ithaki*.[4] The film inspired many film-makers, including Hala Lutfi, and reinforced the notion of producing a 'free' film with no regard to the commercial market restrictions.

The term independent film-making, globally referring to films made out of the studio system, is not accurate in the case of Egypt. Many of Egypt's film production companies, such as Film Clinic, al-Subki and New Century, are independent as they are non-governmental. However, these companies liaise with governmental authorities, such as security services and censorship. In the Egyptian context, the term 'independent' refers to texts that do not follow the regular process of production and distribution. Ahmad Hassuna and Muhammad al-Asiuwti have published a book in Arabic titled *al-Sinima al-mustaqilla fi Masr* (*Independent Cinema in Egypt*) in 2009 to shed light on and celebrate the growing achievements of the independent wave.

Producer-director Hala Galal identifies independent film-makers in Egypt as 'necessarily younger, and most of them used the new technology and did not coordinate with security services or the censorship or the sovereign systems or the big money that want to close their capital cycles to recover their money from the market' (H. Galal, interview, 30 December 2015). Independent film producers and directors Hala Lutfi and Muhammad Samir agreed that independent film-making is about the freedom of the film-maker. Independent film-making eliminates the market restrictions placed on film-makers, such as using certain genres, engaging with specific topics and/or casting particular actors. According to Hala Lutfi,

> Independent cinema for me means that you are the main decision maker in your film. No one tells you which actors to choose or not to. You can choose a star because you like his acting, not to depend on their names to sell the film. Similarly, the subjects you address, the aesthetics and visuals you use for framing and your narrative style [...] we try to tell our day-to-day life stories, which are 'real' not false or canned. (H. Lutfi, interview, 17 January 2015)

The availability of digital cameras has encouraged these film-makers to resist the mainstream film-making styles and produce their own films. However, the convergence of film modes and styles has blurred the distinction between popular and independent films. Film-makers defined 'independent film-making' according to their experiences, disregarding that the term covers a broad range of artistic products. After the 2011 Revolution, film-makers continued to use similar production modes and develop earlier styles.

Since the revolution, several independent films have meditated on marginalized communities. Film-makers have not only produced films about marginalized people but also used innovative production techniques to distinguish themselves from mainstream film-making. Through their use of alternative aesthetics, film-makers have 'reflexively addressed their own position vis-à-vis the people they aspire to represent' (Shohat and Stam, 1994, p. 279). Some of these films include *al-Khurug li-l-Nahar*, *'Asham* and *Harag wa-Marag*.[5] These three films, directed by women film-makers and released after the revolution, are considered among the 'radical cultural movement' in which women played a central role (Mostafa, 2015, p. 23). These feature films avoid using mainstream clichés of representing slums. Instead of shooting in film studios, casting film stars (who usually provide a stereotypical performance of working-class characters) and reusing classic wardrobe aesthetics, some of them challenge the conventional representations through shooting in real locations and casting new actors with 'fresh' performances. In constructing realities, they do not conform to mainstream Hollywood film-making style. Independent films narrate basic 'everyday' plots, without exaggerated dramatic events or plot twists. However, these films are not a result of the 2011 Revolution. Their meditations on issues of poverty, marginalization and engagement with themes of frustration and hope are indifferent to films that were produced prior to the revolution. They develop the independent film style and techniques that started before the revolution, without conforming to a consistent aesthetic approach or addressing revolutionary values. Hala Lutfi's *al-Khurug li-l-Nahar*, for example, started before the revolution but financial struggles delayed the release of the film to 2012.

al-Khurug li-l-Nahar reveals a day in the life of Su'ad, a middle-class woman in her thirties played by Dunia Mahir. Su'ad and her mother, who works as a nurse, look after the bedridden father. Set in a flat at one of Cairo's urban slums, the first half of the film shows the daily routine of Su'ad and the mother. The camera follows them in the flat as they wash the dishes, feed the father and change bed sheets. On her way to meet her boyfriend, who she did not see in five months, Su'ad meets a talkative girl on a microbus. The girl asks Su'ad if she is Christian, since she is not wearing a headscarf, and complains about being unmarried while approaching her thirties. Su'ad does not meet her boyfriend who avoids meeting her. She ends up going to her mother who took the father to the hospital. The film ends with Su'ad asking where they will bury the father when he is dead, while the mother is fixing his mattress.

The film depicts Su'ad and her mother in a state of frustration and depression. Su'ad does not work and fails to maintain a romantic relationship. She worries about being labelled as a maiden and is surrounded by deprived living conditions. The long takes and few dialogue lines suggest the monotonous life of the family. The impassive performances of the mother and the daughter express their despair. The film's use of its spatiotemporal elements invites the audience to examine unspoken feelings and emotions of the characters. Bordwell and Thompson suggest, 'Our time-bound process of scanning involves not only looking to and fro across the screen but also, in a sense, looking "into" its depth' (2001, p. 183). The lack of dialogue in most instances combined with static long-take shots emphasizes the slow and quiet moments the characters are living. The camera stands at a distance observing the actions and movements of the characters. The lack of dialogue explains the inability of the characters to communicate their internal conflicts and struggles. The low-key lighting created through the high contrast between the exterior (natural) and interior sources of light in the flat accentuates the frustration of the characters. Lutfi used a multi-layered soundtrack to indicate a broader world that takes place out of her frame, which the characters are confined within. We constantly hear sounds of roosters, cars, children and hawkers (depending on the time of the day) coming through the windows. Apart from Umm Kalthum's and 'Abd al-Wahab's songs that we hear on the cassette player, the film does not use any music to direct the audiences towards a specific reading. The songs, and lyrics in particular, are used to express the unspoken feelings of the characters. For example, Umm Kalthum's song about lost romance and hope, *Zalamna al-Hub* (meaning 'we oppressed love'), is used as a background for shots of the father and the mother.

The film's themes of disability (represented through the father's stroke), deprivation (the family's socio-economic and Su'ad's emotional deprivation), as well as the inability of the characters to communicate to one another can also be read in relation to Egypt's economic and political crises. The project, which started in 2008, addresses Egyptian society through its characters who are impelled to accept their living conditions. Su'ad, imprisoned in a dim-lighted flat, seems to accept her inescapable living conditions. The predominant theme of frustration signifies the lost hope in any (political) change. In the film, the father's stroke paralyses the family and lingers their movement and action. The film does not include any monologues where the main characters express or describe their feelings and emotions. The suppression of the feelings of the characters within themselves is a further representation of political oppression. Among the few changes that the revolution inspired is the title of the film. Lutfi changed the title of the film from *Galta* (meaning stroke) to *al-Khurug li-l-Nahar* (*Coming Forth by Day*) which evokes feelings of hope.

The film's crewmembers produced the film using their savings and some grants from *al-Mawrid al-Thakafi* (The Cultural Resource), screened it in several film festivals, such as Berlinale and Abu Dhabi Film Festival, and achieved many awards. The Dubai Film Festival chose the film as one of the top 100 Arabic films. Film critics praised the film for its differentiation in storytelling and aesthetics. Samir Farid (2014) described it as 'one of the Egyptian and world cinema's masterpieces'. Shawki (2013) explained Lutfi's self-financing the film as to 'free her creativity of all production and distribution restrictions'. Instead of committing to the traditional storytelling structure – context, conflict, climax and closure – the film narrates a usual day in the family's life. Similar to other independent films, distributors released the film in a few film theatres due to its 'unpopularity', using new actors and 'complexity' of narratives. Other films have followed a similar narrative structure that depicts the lives of the characters but through an ensemble cast such as in 'Asham.

'Asham is a set of interrelated stories about six couples of various ages, religions and social classes. The stories intersect in their representation of frustration, ambition and hope. All the characters in the film aspire to a better life through searching for jobs and/or stable relationships. The characters encounter 'Asham, a street hawker, in different situations. 'Asham is also an Arabic word that Armes (2015, p. 207) translates into 'fragile hope'. The film does not only focus on marginalized populations, as it depicts couples from middle and higher socio-economic classes, but it considers the struggles of impoverished couples such as Rida – a bathroom attendant – and her boyfriend Mustafa – a shopping mall security guard. In her television interview on ON E (2013b), Murgan explained that she was interested in exploring the lives of the people we see on a daily basis.

In accordance with the style of independent films, 'Asham disregards the classic dramatic structures of narratives. It exposes the characters, their struggles and aspirations without amplifying the narrative's action and climax.[6]

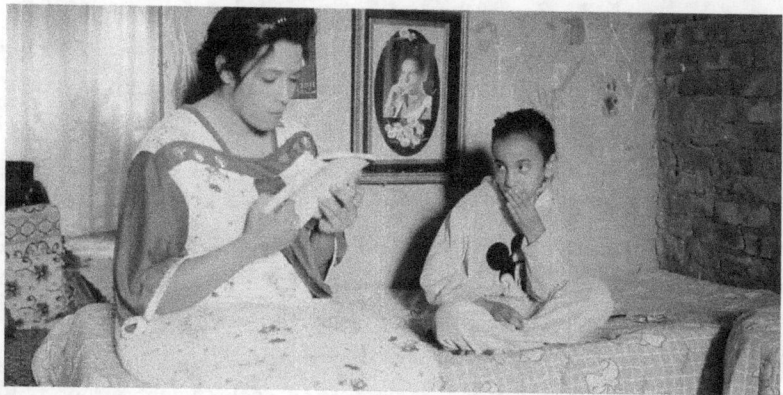

Figure 4 Underprivileged life and working conditions of characters in '*Asham* (2013)

The film's style is similar to other independent films that were produced and released before the revolution, in particular, Ibrahim al-Battut's *Ithaki* (2006) and Ahmad 'Abd Allah's *Hiliaupulis*, which narrate sets of interrelated stories. Murgan also used a limited budget to produce *'Asham*. She shot the film on a digital camera in real locations in Cairo and Alexandria. Murgan cast new actors and used improvisation in many scenes to approach a more authentic representation of the stories as in earlier films of the same style. Film critics, such as Farid (2012) and 'Abd al-Razi' (2014), have classified *'Asham* as an independent film for its low budget and 'high artistic value' along *al-Khurug li-l-Nahar* and *Harag wa-Marag*.

Nadin Khan's *Harag wa-Marag* is set in an isolated poor neighbourhood and loaded with sociopolitical allegories of Mubarak's Egypt. The film narrates the story of Zaki and Munir who love the same girl, Manal. Zaki and Munir decide to play a soccer match where the winner marries Manal. In contrast to popular dramas, which represent slums and poor living conditions sympathetically, *Harag wa-Marag* experiments the use of fantasy in its depiction of 'social realities'. The film shows trucks supplying water, gas and food (including meat, vegetables and even sweets and juice) on a daily basis, without unfolding the source of these trucks. The neighbourhood's central radio, a loudspeaker, plays songs, gives advice and highlights the major events of the day. The design of the set, where the film was shot, characterizes the enclosed neighbourhood through fences and walls. Khan used long shots to establish the setting and reassure the marginalization of the community. The cheerful piano music used in transition between the sequences, which contrasts the misery images of the neighbourhood, supports the social fantasy style that the film aims to create.

Although Khan obliterates the plot's space-time, she uses props and art direction details, such as dust and rubbish piles, to depict the contemporary Egyptian low-class neighbourhoods. The long queues and fights over the supplies refer to issues of poverty and suffering from a scarcity of resources. The dominance of Hajj Saiyyd, a rich shop owner, over the neighbourhood represents the struggle of the ruling capitalist class and the working class in Egypt. He invests in soccer matches between the neighbourhood's young men to meet his paramour. Hajj Saiyyd's exploitation of the neighbourhood's high interest in soccer games alludes to the popular discourse of Mubarak regime's use of entertainment and soccer to shift the public's attention away from politics and corruption. The Censorship of Artistic Works refused *Harag wa-Marag*'s script before the revolution. However, Khan submitted the same script after the revolution and obtained a shooting permission.

The film's reference to the sociopolitical condition of Egyptian society is clear. The use of fantasy to engage with political issues continues a trend that was popular during the 1980s. For example, Ra'fat al-Mihi – one of the film directors known for that style – used fantasy to criticize Sadat's economic policy (*infitāḥ*) in *al-Avukatu* (*The Lawyer*, 1984). The film narrates the story of 'Adil Sabanikh, a lawyer, who makes connections in jail after the court imprisons him. *Harag wa-Marag* is among the independent films that were produced after the revolution and do not conform to the conventional mainstream film-making style that uses traditional narrative structures and film stars. However, these films develop film styles that started before the revolution. Their different approaches to production raise question regarding their independence. In contrast to other films of the same style, the isolated neighbourhood in *Harag wa-Marag* was a built set. The film included a few well-known actors such as Aytin 'Amir who played Manal. Wika Production and Distribution, owned by film editor Dina Faru', produced the film. The different styles and approaches to the production of independent films challenge their recognition as a post-revolution film movement.

Moreover, a few socially progressive films have also represented religious, gender and political affiliation discrimination since the revolution. Examples include *Lamu'akhza* (*Excuse My French*, 'Amr Salama, 2011) and *Fatat al-Masna'* (*The Factory Girl*, Muhammad Khan, 2013). In *Lamu'akhza*, Hani 'Abd Allah – a middle-class Christian boy – is sent to a public school because his mother cannot afford his private school fees after his father's death. In his new predominantly Muslim school, Hani is mistakenly identified as a Muslim, which he exploits to avoid discrimination. However, Hani is alienated from his peers due to his privileged lifestyle, which is apparent in his dressing style and decent behaviour. Alongside the religious discrimination, the film tackles social discrimination and the deteriorated education system through satirical scenes. Muhammad Khan's romantic film *Fatat al-Masna'* depicts discrimination against women. The film narrates a story of a 21-year-old middle-class girl who asserts her independence from the societal pressures and accepts all the false accusations of her sexual relationship with her manager. Whether intentionally or unintentionally, these films refer to the pre-revolution intolerance and inequality among gender, social and religious groups and advocate a progressive stance towards these issues.

Similarly, *Ishtibak* (*Clash*, Muhammad Diab, 2016) addresses the post-revolution political divisions. The film, shot entirely in the back of a police van, shows the diversity of the detainees' social and political backgrounds during one of the protests held after the removal of Mursi in 2013. Although these films required relatively smaller budgets, the involvement of production companies or prominent directors (such as Muhammad Khan in *Fatat al-Masnaʿ*) complicated their classification as independent or commercial. These films engage with political issues, but they do not contribute to a new cinematic style. They reproduce popular styles of Egyptian cinema using generic conventions of comedy, romance and drama.

The continuity of these films to earlier film styles does not distinguish them as a post-revolution film movement. They develop a style that was started before the revolution through individual innovations and disparate attributes. Mainstream film-makers effortlessly label these films as independent, due to their low budgets and nonconformity to the dominant film-making style and storytelling techniques. However, the diversity of film styles and production modes raised questions regarding what constitutes an independent film. A few film producers have funded some independent films, such as *Harag wa-Marag*, *Farsh wa-Ghata* and *Villa 69* (Aytin Amin, 2013). These films required comparatively higher budgets for their use of relatively popular actors and (sometimes) construction of film sets, which does not perfectly comply with the characteristics of other independent films (such as Hala Lutfi's *al-Khurug li-l-Nahar* and Tamir al-Saʿid's *Akhir Ayyam al-Madina*). The involvement of film producers in a late phase of a self-financed project, such as Muhammad Hifzi's support for *'Asham* and *Akhdar Yabis*, has further complicated the issue. Categorizing films into two main categories – commercial and independent – is simplistic. It does not consider the complexities of film funding and attracting audiences.

Independent film-makers are not subject to the decision of producers of giving the green light to a film. They develop their own projects and self-finance it or collect funds to produce it. The internet has helped independent film-makers to allocate funds for their projects through local and international organizations, including governmental and non-governmental funds. These organizations support films according to their artistic values, rather than their commercial merits. Some examples include Dubai Film Festival's Enjaz – a post-production fund for projects led by Arab film-makers – Abu Dhabi Film Festival's SANAD and The Arab Funds for Arts and Culture (AFAC). These funds have supported producing films such as *al-Khurug li-l-Nahar*, *Fatat al-Masnaʿ* and *Villa 69*. The major involvements of Gulf funds to complete these films have raised questions of nationalities of the films and their 'independence'. Recently, young film-makers have also used crowd-funding websites to collect funds for their independent projects. For example, film director ʿAida al-Kashif used Indiegogo, a popular crowd-funding website, to collect funds for her documentary *The Day I Ate the*

Fish (in production).⁷ In some cases such as *Farsh wa-Ghata* and *Akhdar Yabis* the directors, directors of photography and main actors/actresses have shared in producing the films using their wages.

Along the technological developments and the growth of independent film-making in the past decade, film-makers have noticed the imprecise use of the term independent. Film producer-director Hala Lutfi expressed her concern about the misuse of the term by dominant film producers and distributors. She explains that producers have claimed to work under the independent umbrella to cut down some of the wages of crewmembers, while they profit from selling these films to satellite channels. Lutfi also notes that producers and distributors have consistently used the term independent to refer to films as *aflām mahragānāt* or festival films – which consist of complex narratives and artistic representations to approach international film festivals rather than the mass audience. Meanwhile, Lutfi, among other independent film-makers, disclaimed that their aim is not to be on the margin (H. Lutfi, interview, 17 January 2015). Instead, they aim to integrate their work as a part of the mainstream film-making. Thus, Lutfi encourages using the term 'new cinema' to 'independent cinema'.⁸

Film producer Muhammad Samir confirms the impreciseness of the term independent cinema and prefers calling it 'free production', referring to the freedom of the commercial production restrictions. He explains, 'They are not independent because they want an audience, a cinema, a distributor, and a profit. One might want to make a free production film using a very well-known star. They might want to use the same tools, but deal with them in a more free way.' He adds, 'Free production is where a group of friends choose to get a camera and shoot a simple script in one location then put it on YouTube, they are free. Capital forces you to take specific actions, but I will call this type of production a free production' (M. Samir, interview, 27 January 2015).

Film-makers and critics have engaged in extended discussions about what constitutes independent cinema in Egypt. They have been involved in debates around whether the term independent refers to the independence of the content they present or the independence of the production's format. Identifying different forms of film-making as independent has further complicated what this category comprises. Commonly confused with cinéma d'auteur, many director-led or artistic films are labelled independent. Several directors classified as independent film-makers have been involved in high-budget productions featuring film stars. For example, Ahmad 'Abd Allah directed the high-budget *Dikaur* (*Décor*) in 2014, following his independent production *Farsh wa-Ghata* in 2013. The producer of *Dikaur* is New Century, one of the major film production companies in Egypt since the revolution. The film featured stars such as Magid al-Kidwani, Khalid abu al-Naga and Huriyya Farghali. 'Abd Allah, who resists labelling films as commercial or independent, comments,

> I believe that both are means of expression, at the end, I deal with it as a film. In my opinion, the only way you can classify films is according to their format, as in short/long feature, documentary, docudrama, animation, or video art. But you cannot further classify short films as commercial or not. My latest film, *Dikaur*, is targeted towards a wider portion of the audience because they prefer these types of films. While *Farsh wa-Ghata* was known that it will be hardly understood by many people, and it will be appreciated by a fewer audience. (A. 'Abd Allah, interview, 31 January 2015)

However, 'Abd Allah has approached *Dikaur* using distinctive aesthetics and artistic style. *Dikaur* is a melodrama about Maha, a set designer, who imagines living in a completely different persona. 'Abd Allah has symbolically represented the high contrast between Maha's real and imagined characters through colouring the film in black and white. Independent film directors, such as Aytin Amin and Marwan 'Umara, have also confirmed that the frames defining independent and commercial film-making are obscure. Amin explained that film directors Kamla abu Zikri and Muhammad Yassin produce highly artistic films, yet work within the commercial production standards (Aytin Amin, interview, 30 December 2015). Film producer Muhammad Samir also refuses to classify his first feature, *Fatat al-Masna'*, as an independent film, despite the veteran director's association to the new cinema wave in the 1980s. Samir explains,

> I was aware and intended to integrate the merits of the art cinema and director's film, which was translated into the choice of new actors, and shooting in real locations with a young team – my generation. In addition to considering the commercial aspects such as the film's length, 90 minutes for theatrical release and promotion plan to return the invested money. (M. Samir, interview, 27 January 2015)

A few film-makers, such as Ahmad 'Abd Allah and Muhammad Samir, have challenged the classification of films as independent or commercial. These film-makers, among others such as 'Amr Salama, have integrated elements of mainstream and artistic films. Their films achieved commercial and critical success. However, these films extend the debate of what can be defined as an independent film among film curators, critics, film-makers, distributors and audience. In practice, the evolution of film-making technologies has increased the convergence of amateur and professional film-making and blurred the distinctions between film-making styles.

Since recent technological developments offered low price and high quality mobility, and user-friendly operating systems, the process of making a film became less complicated. During the revolution, protesters, witnesses, journalists and film-makers shot and uploaded footage of events instantly. The internet has served as an archival backup and, in some cases, an alternative distribution and screening option to circumvent censorship. The demand for learning film-making encouraged initiatives, such as SEMAT, to organize workshops. Young film-makers shot, edited and uploaded short films online. Although some of these films represent the revolution or engage with political issues such as social, religious and gender discrimination, they did not develop radical form or style of film-making. Instead, they remediated traditional short film styles online.

Film-making, since its inception, has always been associated with technology. One of the fundamental aspects that facilitated the production of independent films in Egypt is the evolution of technology, specifically digital cameras, during the past decade. The development of film-making tools including digital and mobile phone cameras, nonlinear editing software and enhanced sound recording microphones granted more opportunities for film-making. The good image quality that these tools offered and their availability at affordable prices widened the opportunities for making a film. These technologies did not only facilitate independent productions, but they also influenced film texts in some instances. Film director Hala Lutfi narrates,

> Since 2005, which I think was a turning point, appeared the small digital camera 3ccd, which was a great invention. I saw this camera for the first time when I was directing a film named 'An al-shu'ur bi-l-Buruda (*About Feeling Cold*) produced by the National Centre for Cinema. The film's topic was slightly sensitive; I interviewed girls about their past relationships, and how they were brought up, so I decided to use this camera rather than the big digital beta-camera. I did not want the girls to fear the camera size, lighting, technicians, etc. I borrowed the camera from a friend of mine, who bought this camera, and it was amazing. The way they told the stories was very different. We did not have to use a tripod. It was user-friendly. This gave the material I shot by myself more freedom and spontaneity just like the girls' lives. (H. Lutfi, interview, 17 January 2015)

Digital technologies also allowed Lutfi to shoot long takes in *al-Khurug li-l-Nahar*. With some shots running up to nine minutes long, Lutfi's technical strategies would have been impossible with film reels.

During the interviews, film-makers also emphasized the role of technological developments in documenting revolutionary moments and expanding independent productions. Film director Ahmad Rashwan discussed how digital cameras allowed the people to document events of the revolution and upload them online as they witness them. Citizen journalism has served as a genuine and trusted source of information during the revolution against the deceitful state media. Kraidy and Mourad (2010, p. 3) argue, 'When a context is rife with social and political tensions, and when social agents are willing and able to use hypermedia space with the objective of inducing change in the social or political status quo, then the availability of hypermedia space can play a crucial role in the performance of contention communication in public discourse.' The abundance of digital and mobile phone cameras together with multiple video platforms online, which constitute a hypermedia space according to Kraidy and Mourad, facilitated the documentation and archival of footage of the revolution. This footage has been a significant resource for films about the revolution.

Several initiatives aimed for archiving this footage such as Vox Populi (tahrirarchives.com) and 18 Days in Egypt (beta.18daysinegypt.com) which invited people to share their videos, photographs and stories from the revolution to compile web-based archives. The American University in Cairo (AUC) has also initiated a project called University on the Square: Documenting Egypt's 21st Century Revolution. The project included a recording of testimonials and experiences of participants, a website to gather the digital photos and videos as well as the collection of memorable tangibles such as banners and tear gas canisters (Urgola, 2014). Film initiatives, such as SEMAT, organized film-making workshops after the revolution to help produce films out of the available footage. Hala Galal narrates,

> One of our experiences during the first two years, 2011 and 2012, we received hundreds of hours of footage from tens of youth directors. They shot everything that happened and wanted to make films out of it. We then organised many workshops, because some of them did not even know how to make films – how to edit and shoot. (H. Galal, interview, 30 December 2015)

The internet has served as an alternative form of screening through several platforms, such as YouTube, Vimeo and Facebook. Some film-makers have used this hypermedia space to show their short films and contribute to social and political discourses as well as reach a wider audience. The internet facilitated the links and connections between film-makers and international film festivals and organizations, where they apply for funds and participate in international film festivals through online facilities. It allowed individuals to self-learn film-making as an alternative to the Higher Cinema Institute, which accepts only eight students per department each year. Online streaming services facilitated watching films from different parts of the world. The internet and other technological tools also supported film-makers in circumventing local censorship. For example, film producer Shirif Mandur narrates,

> A clear model is in December 2010. I produced a film called *al-Khurug min al-Qahira* [*Cairo Exit*] and it is one of the films that said we [Egyptians] have reached our limits. Therefore, censorship rejected the film. But I decided to do it and after I produced it we smuggled it to Dubai Film Festival where we took an award. They went crazy here, how did we get away with the film! I told them that through technology now I could take the film on a small hard disk in my pocket and leave. (S. Mandur, interview, 25 January, 2015).

Marwan 'Umara, Nadia Munir and Islam Kamal uploaded their documentary film *al-Ziyaara* (*The Visit*, 2015) online and made available to the public during the Cairo Cinema Days Festival. The Censorship of Artistic Works did not grant a screening approval for the film, which was part of the festival's programme. Although other film festivals in Egypt have shown the film, the censorship board did not give clear reasons why they refused to permit the screening in Cairo Cinema Days. The film reveals the mainstream media's construction of stereotypical images of Egypt's countryside. In two days, the online film views increased by 500, which exceeds the capacity of the film theatre, where the festival planned to show the film at (*Mada Masr*, 2017).

Digital cameras and video-sharing websites also facilitated film production and distribution among youth. Since film-making is centralized in Cairo, young film-makers have shot films using mobile phones and cameras and uploaded them online to reach a wider audience. Film director Hala Lutfi highlights the decentralization of film-making as one of the advantages of the recent technological developments. She explains,

> Filmmaking was very centralised in Egypt, specifically Cairo. The fact that filmmaking now is decentralised, people in Alexandria are making feature films, or teenagers producing films in Upper Egypt, or even participating in the mobile phones film festivals, is a revolution in my opinion. This art is now democratic; it is not related to geographic distance or economic abilities anymore. (H. Lutfi, interview, 17 January 2015)

One of the examples is a five minutes film that I made in 2011 called *Biy'ulu* (*They Say*) about the rumours spread through social media during the revolution. I shot the film using a zero cost budget in Alexandria, with natural lighting, my 5D Canon camera and my friends as actors. After participating in Tropfest Arabia (a short film festival in Abu Dhabi), the film was uploaded on YouTube and offered to the public. Also, films such as *al-Burtrai* and *al-Asansiyr* were produced using

Figure 5 A screenshot of *Biy'ulu* (2011)

minimal budgets and uploaded online. Although these amateur films, among many others, depict the revolution as part of their narratives, they did not represent radical film-making style. Instead, they represented traditional short film styles, such as the use of allegories. In *al-Burtrai*, the artist spills red-colour paint on the portrait of the killed protester and in *al-Asansiyr*, three characters representing liberals, communists and Islamists are stuck in an elevator that was taking them to the same floor.

Hala Lutfi assumes that the pervasiveness of film-making tools, in particular, the 'democratic medium', will lead to new film topics and characters based on their settings. For example, films from al-Si'id or Upper Egypt will depict characters talking and dressing differently than those we see in Cairo or Alexandria. She contends that these films will expose various subcultures within Egypt, which mainstream films and media have been portraying as the 'other'. Even before the revolution, Kraidy and Khalil (2008, p. 339) have discussed the role of new media in encouraging indigenous cultural productions which challenge the dominant (westernized) television channels. Kraidy and Khalil have emphasized the personalized and interactive nature of new media, which contribute to the construction of youth identities. However, the short films produced in Egypt thus far are mainly limited to cities such as Cairo, Alexandria and Suez. Only a few attempts have engaged with under-represented locations and languages, such as Nubia in *Jaridi* (Muhammad Hisham, 2015). The short film is about a young boy who overcomes his fear of reaching a rock in the middle of the Nile. The film's director, Muhammad Hisham (originally from Cairo but lives in Dubai), shot the film in Nubia and using Nubian language.

The production of these online short films is not only a result of technological developments. The internet and digital cameras facilitated their production and distribution. In addition, the 2011 Revolution encouraged young film-makers to express themselves visually. Film director Ahmad 'Abd Allah explains,

> For the first time, you can see the youth carrying their cameras and shooting, even if they are not filmmakers, and search for online footage to edit a clip. [...] it is a type of filmmaking where a one's vision or point of view is visually developed. If there is a change, it is that many people now think that they can express themselves through this medium. This wave [...] slightly broke the idea that you have to graduate from the Higher Institute of Cinema or learn filmmaking, to become a filmmaker. [...] This concept has brought a new industry that broke the 'priesthood', which dominated the filmmaking industry, such as the filmmaking syndicate or the Higher Cinema Institute. I believe that this has a strong relation to the philosophy of the 2011 Revolution. (A. 'Abd Allah, interview, 31 January 2015)

The notions of political resistance of the revolution in conjunction with technological developments encouraged young artists to express themselves visually.

The revolution prompted 'independent' forms of self-expression. Protesters have used various types of arts, including poems, songs, graffiti and films as a form of self-expression and resistance during the revolution. The growing interest of some audiences in these forms encouraged the inception of several initiatives that support producing and screening independent films. Recently, the state has been indirectly banning films for their engagement with the revolution.

The independent wave is not a result of the 2011 Revolution. In fact, independent productions were part of the activism that took place before the revolution. Film director Aytin Amin notes that the pre-revolution independent art was an indication of rebellion (A. Amin, interview, 30 December 2015). *Mikrufun* (*Microphone*, Ahmad Abd Allah, 2010), which profiles independent music bands in Alexandria, was symbolically released on 25 January 2011.[9] Amin also claims that almost all independent film-makers participated in the revolution. Film producer-director Hala Galal believes the radical practices of artists and intellectuals during the mid-to-late 1990s had a role in the intensive political activism in the 2000s. She describes cultural institutions such as Townhouse, Sa'iyat al-Sawi and the one she manages (SEMAT) as "harbingers" of the revolution (H. Galal, interview, 30 December 2015). These institutions, among others, aimed to spread alternative types of art. They organized workshops to teach the use of digital cameras, which led to a wave of video art productions.

Galal also notes the evolution of communication forms, such as mobile phones and pagers, as well as the emergence of satellite channels during this period has urged a need for creativity among the audiences. She explains that security systems have recently understood the impact of these cultural institutions on audiences' awareness, and thus they shut down some of them.[10]

However, the revolution proliferated independent productions and influenced the use of different forms of self-expression. For example, people have used films, songs, video blogs and graffiti as popular media forms to represent themselves and/or their ideologies. Independent musicians, such as Rami 'Issam, became popular for their reappearances and performances on Tahrir's stage. Lara Baladi and Khalid Abd Allah started Tahrir Cinema during the sit-in of July 2011.[11] Using a screen, a projector, a laptop and speakers, they showed raw footage that the Tahrir media tent gathered from protesters. *Kazibuwn* (literally 'liars') – a series of public screenings of footage revealing the military's and Muslim Brotherhood's violence during their ruling periods – has developed the concept of public cinema. A memes culture also pervaded social media networks. Activists used stills from popular films to comment sarcastically on political actions and social trends. More than 14 million users follow 'Asa7be Sarcasm Society' – a Facebook page popular for its memes that started in 2012. A number of scholars have been studying the political representation of visuals and images of the revolution (Mehrez, 2012; Gröndahl, 2013; Dal, 2013; Khatib, 2013; Weibel, 2015 and Mehrez and Abaza, 2017). For example, Khatib (2013) examines public spaces and the image of Mubarak before the revolution (including the use of images in protests as a tool of resistance), in contrast to images of the revolution and Tahrir Square. She argues the protesters use of public spaces to display graffiti and murals during the revolution was not only a symbol of 'reclaiming the notion of agency' but also a medium to send political messages (Khatib, 2013, p. 154–5). Lucia Sorbera (2014) also examines the representation and participation of women in the production of graffiti. In December 2011, a 30-year-old woman told Sorbera, 'I make street art to represent my identity and express myself and to express solidarity with people protesting in Tahrir Square and everywhere in Egypt nowadays. I started doing it during the 8th July sit-in, after 25th January then. I am expressing myself through messages' (Sorbera, 2014, p. 67).

The various creative means of expression used by protesters during the Arab uprisings have been an interest of Marwan Kraidy. For example, Kraidy's book *The Naked Blogger of Cairo: Creative Insurgency in the Arab World* (2016a) examines the role of human bodies as the source of such creative insurgencies.

He discusses several examples of political humour including puppetry, graffiti and political jokes that protesters used to attack rulers. He argues, 'Creative insurgency gives voice and shape to revolutionary claims as much as it prods insurgents to always reassess their aspirations and identities' (Kraidy, 2016a, p. 16). Also Kraidy's chapter on revolutionary creative labour in *Precarious Creativity: Global Media, Local Labour* (2016b) has distinguished the differences between industrial and revolutionary creative labour. The differences include the latter's 'radical rejectionist expression' (Kraidy, 2016b, p. 234) and working underground, with no managerial constraints or paid wages. Kraidy's (2016b) discussion of the revolutionary creative labours refers to the artistic modes of expression during the revolution including the example of Basim Yusif's show, which started on YouTube during the early days of the revolution and turned into the most popular television show a few years later.

People feared to produce such art forms, although the tools required were available before the revolution.[12] The revolution gave people an instant feeling of liberation that did not last for long. This feeling was partially expressed through using public spaces. Film director Ahmad 'Abd Allah explains that after the revolution, 'people reacquired their rights in the streets and places [...] which led to the feeling that they own the country'. 'Abd Allah confirms Lewis Sanders's conception of street art as 'an aesthetic product of resistance [...] providing a new understanding of the city as rightfully belonging to the people' (2012, p. 143). 'Abd Allah recalls his experience in casting graffiti artists while shooting *Mikrufun* in 2010, 'Only 4 people in Egypt drew graffiti, although it did not require any technological tools. Now it is widely known and used, for self-expression and even for promotional purposes' (A. 'Abd Allah, interview, 31 January 2015). Hala Galal confirms that the revolution had a role in liberating film-makers, 'it gave them legitimacy or power that did not exist before the revolution' (H. Galal, interview, 30 December 2015). Groups of youth holding cameras and making films became phenomenal.

In conjunction with the technological developments, the revolution allowed more space for expressing one's identity or voicing an individual's perspective on issues. Film-makers have emphasized that the revolution 'broke' the boundaries of criticizing a certain idea or person (M. 'Umara, interview, 14 January 2015). The revolution's notion of rising up against the ruler has encouraged a few creative productions as a form of resistance to the mainstream type of arts. Both the revolution and technology have encouraged the idea that film-making, among other types of art, is feasible and not limited to a specific group of people. However, many of these productions have developed and remediated earlier styles of independent or 'realistic' films. They did not produce radical film-making styles or conformed to a consistent aesthetic approach. The rise of the Muslim Brotherhood and the military along with a strong counter-revolution discourse in mainstream media challenged the production of these films.

On the other hand, the revolution has arguably influenced the audience's perception of new types of art. During my interviews, film-makers noted that a growing audience is now more receptive to independent productions. Similar to the impact of the technological development on film-makers, the internet has helped to introduce different types of art and media formats to Egyptian audiences. In practice, film-makers have been recognizing the growing audience awareness of and interest in the non-mainstream type of art. Film director Ahmad Rashwan explains,

> Proportionally, if we say that the awareness has grown since the revolution, then the interest on these [independent] films has grown. Zawya, for example, shows independent films, and narrative and documentary feature films and from different countries. No one could have imagined that a Korean or a Tunisian or Jordanian film like *Theeb* would have a turnout … there is awareness and different tastes to accommodate non-mainstream films and non-mainstream books or any non-mainstream form of art. (A. Rashwan, interview, 5 January 2016)

Similar to concepts of produser and prosumer, the conjunction of the revolution and technological developments has facilitated film production and distribution among amateurs as well as influenced behaviours of some of the audiences in considering new types of art. According to film producer Muhammad Samir, 'People value cinema differently now because they feel they are affiliated with it. They know they can make films […] and the filmmakers do not monopolise cinema' (M. Samir, interview, 27 January 2015). Samir argues that mainstream cinema is separate from the audience, in contrast to independent films, which aims to represent the under-represented social lives of its audience authentically. The increasing interest in producing and watching independent films fostered the creation of independent initiatives to support their production and distribution.

Among the political film practices since the revolution is the establishment of initiatives that supports producing, screening and discussing independent films. Hassala (meaning moneybox), found by Hala Lutfi and her film crewmembers, is an independent production house that supports film-makers with their first features away from the commercial market pressures. Hala and her crewmembers decided to establish Hassala as a collective to share the experience they gained in producing *al-Khurug li-l-Nahar*. Hassala aims to facilitate the production process through offering information about locations, cameras, actors and crewmembers who are willing to work for low wages. In addition, Hassala offers sound recording equipment, editing suites and a limited stock of props and costumes. Lutfi has also been involved in forming an independent film workers' syndicate (*Nikabat al-'Amilyn bi-l-sinima*) to defend the technicians' rights, such as working hours limit and minimum wages, which the state-sanctioned syndicate does not claim.[13] The independent syndicate gives wider access to film-makers, where the state-sanctioned syndicate only allows Higher Institute of Cinema graduates to be its members and limits the shooting permissions to its members. Tamir al-Sa'id and Khalid 'Abd Allah started Cimatheque, an alternative film centre that provides a shared space between film critics, audience and film-makers. Cimatheque screens and discusses films, as well as organizes specialized workshops.[14]

A few production and distribution companies, as well as individuals, have offered screening opportunities to promote independent and alternative films. Misr International Films launched Zawya in March 2014, an art-house cinema that screens alternative films from different parts of the world. Zawya hosts special events, such as the European Film Panorama, and organizes a short film festival to encourage and promote local film-makers' work. Although Zawya focuses on a specific target audience, mostly young with a special interest in alternative cinema, they get large turnouts. Wagih al-Laqani started sinima fi kul makan (Cinema Everywhere) in 2013 to screen independent and experimental films in public spaces such as cafes, clubs, schools, non-governmental organizations and streets. Similar to the Mobile film projection units that followed the Iranian and Chinese revolutions, sinima fi kul makan aims to introduce new and alternative types of cinema to a wider audience, many of which do not have access to film theatres (such as Nubian and rural villages). These initiatives, along with others, have encouraged expanding the independent productions. The revolution did not instigate these initiatives; however, it stimulated their inception and facilitated their regulatory establishments. In order for these initiatives to develop into a wider film movement, they require a network that would connect them to one another. These initiatives strive to show independent films, which the state considers some of them as unpleasant for their criticisms of the current regime. To avoid international condemnation, the state has repressed these films surreptitiously.

The participation of independent film-makers in protests and the political engagement of their films have created strong ties between them and the revolution. While a counter-revolutionary rhetoric has been dominating mainstream media outlets, different forms of censorship have been limiting independent practices. Cairo International Film Festival pulled out *Akhir Ayyam al-Madina* from its programme schedule a few weeks before its start. The festival's director claimed that the film has participated in other international film festivals, which infringes Cairo Festival's policy. The film's director appeared on the popular talk show *Huna al-'Asima* on CBC and claimed that other films participating in the festival have been shown in other international festivals too (CBC, 2016). The independent film narrates a film-maker's struggle in making a film about Cairo. Film critics, such as Jay Weissberg (2016), appraised the film that won the Caligari Film Award at the 2016 Berlin International Film Festival. Sharm al-Sheikh Arabic and the European Film Festival also excluded the film due to the lack of censorship permit to show the film. Tamir al-Sa'id, the film's director, has rejected several invitations to show the film in Arab film festivals, such as the prestigious Dubai Film Festival, as his dream was to show the film in Cairo (the film's main subject). The consistent resistance to showing the film and postponement of issuing the censorship permit mean that the film is not in the state's interest. However, rather than directly preventing the film, which will instigate public and media discussions over freedom of expression, state authorities choose to oppress such films obliquely.

Other examples include the withdrawal of the distributor of the political film *Ishtibak* two days before its release. The internationally acclaimed film was the opening film for the Un Certain Regard competition at the 2016 Cannes Film Festival. The film's director claimed that rather than banning the film in Egypt, state authorities combat the film furtively.[15] One of the Egyptian national television channels broadcasted a report about the film's director implying his betrayal to the country. The report included biographical facts about Diab such as his previous work for a foreign bank and role as a funded political activist. The three minutes report describes Diab's films as portraying the Egyptian society in negative ways, such as his previous film *678* (2010), which discusses sexual harassment. The suggested reason behind the attack on the film is the 'neutrality' of the plot in addressing the conflict between the Muslim Brotherhood and the Armed Forces. The state authorities have been implicitly oppressing cultural icons and representations of the revolution in the process of imposing a counter-revolutionary narrative.

* * *

The 2011 Revolution did not instigate independent films in Egypt. This wave started before the revolution when a few directors decided to use low budgets and digital cameras to produce their own films. These films resisted mainstream film-making styles, which were limited to producing popular genres such as comedy and action and casting film stars. After the revolution, film-makers continued the independent film-making style through casting new actors, using improvisation and developing non-traditional narrative structures. Film-makers self-fund their films and depend on grants from film festivals or cultural institutions. Similar to independent films that were produced and released before the revolution, films such as *al-Khurug li-l-Nahar*, *'Asham* and *Harag wa-Marag* represented issues of marginalization and poverty and emphasized on themes of frustration, ambition and hope. These films did not engage directly with the revolution or develop a particular aesthetic framework that constitutes a post-revolution film movement. But they represented struggle through various creative and realist approaches. On the other hand, popular film-makers have used the term independent to marginalize these attempts and contend that they are produced for an elitist, rather than a mass audience. After the revolution, a few film producers have claimed to produce independent films to pay fewer wages for the crewmembers. However, the term 'independent' is vague as these films vary in their production methods and stylistic tendencies.

Film-makers and critics consider independent films and their production and screening initiatives as individual trials and experiments. In order to recognize these practices and activities as a movement, al-'Umari (2014) recommends the formation of a common aesthetic approach and production form. Film-makers also suggest a network grouping independent film-makers and initiatives or an organization with a clear agenda should support this type of film-making. Debates around classifying films and film-makers as independent or not continue to take place, particularly within the convergence of production and distribution models. Independent film-makers, such as Ahmad 'Abd Allah and Aytin Amin, have cast well-known actors in their films and released them in many film theatres. The major involvement of Arab film festivals and organizations, such as the Dubai Film Festival, in funding Egyptian films has raised questions about the 'independence' and nationality of these films.

The developing film-making technologies have slightly blurred the distinctions between professional and amateur films. Mobile cameras and video-sharing websites have facilitated the documentation, circulation and archival of footage during the revolution. In a few cases, the internet has also served as an alternative screening form to circumvent censorship. Young film-makers have used digital cameras to produce short films and upload them online. Whether these films include the revolution in their narratives or discuss issues such as sexual harassment and oppression of women, they have not produced radical film-making styles. They reuse short film styles including allegories and symbols. Only a few attempts have engaged innovatively with the revolution and contributed to the development of the independent wave. These include *Alone, Together … in a Media Res* (2012), the 40-minute, three-channel video installation that reflects on the revolution, and Nadin Khan's one-minute film *I Will Speak of the Revolution* (2011). These projects have expressed the resistance of their makers to the conventional representations of the revolution.

The revolution has encouraged independent productions. Artists used various forms of self-expression including film, music, graffiti and poems. Film companies such as Misr International Films and individuals including Hala Lutfi, Tamir al-Sa'id and Khalid 'Abd Allah started a number of production and screening initiatives to support independent productions. The favourable reception of audiences to independent art has also encouraged their growth; however, the state continues to challenge film-makers through indirect censorship and limiting shooting permissions. Leftist and independent film-makers also continue to portray themes of struggle and frustration to express their feelings during the post-revolution period.

Conclusion

This book has identified the relationship between cinema and revolution through four different, but interrelated, notions of 'revolutionary cinema'. These notions consider cinema both as an artistic form of self-expression and as an industrial sector that adapts to sociopolitical, economic and technological factors. The four perspectives are a result of studying the scholarship that focuses on particular cases of cinemas during revolutionary periods as well as the broader literature of film and politics throughout history. The first conception of 'revolutionary films' is the role of pre-revolution films in raising awareness and mobilizing audiences. These are socio-political conscious films that contribute to the practices of political activism. The second aspect is the role of film in documenting revolutions as a historical moment. These films are a form of 'historiophoty' (White, 1988) that develops the visual memory of their respective revolutions. The third perspective is the impact of revolutions on film industries, which influence the type of films produced during the post-revolution periods. The fourth dimension is the influence of revolutions on film content and styles. Revolutions have been usually associated with new film waves and movements that aim to apply the revolution's ideologies and philosophies. These films use alternative production and narrative styles to communicate the values of their revolutions and resist mainstream film-making modes.

By focusing on the case of Egyptian cinema and the 2011 Revolution, I examined the continuities and discontinuities in the relationship between cinema and revolution. The continuities include the use of film as a form of political expression and documentation of the events of the revolution, while the discontinuities comprise the support for film by post-revolution governments and a post-revolution film movement that uses a particular aesthetic approach to represent struggle. The examination process included an in-depth textual and contextual analysis of pre- and post-revolution films. These analyses included the content, style and production formats of these films. It also included personal interviews with key 'mainstream' and 'independent' producers and directors to understand the dynamics of the film industry during a period of crisis and transformation. The interviews were significant as the academic literature lacks any discussion on the 'Egyptian Film Industry Crisis', which accentuated the industry since the 2011 Revolution.

The scholarship articulating the relationship between film and politics has shown interest in film industries as economic and cultural instruments. The level of support of governments for film industries has influenced the film texts according to the dominant political ideologies. Government support also contributes to the economic power and value of film industries. Wheeler (2006) demonstrated the support of American governments, such as the reform of the tax system, in transforming Hollywood from an industry to a global business. In the cases studied in Chapter 1, governments understood the power of film in celebrating the revolutionary ideologies and thus, supported film industries. The support came in financial and regulatory forms such as financial subsidies and nationalization of film industries. The nationalization or support of post-revolution governments in Egypt (post-1952), the Soviet Union, Cuba and China has encouraged the production of socially conscious films.

However, the case of the 2011 Egyptian Revolution had a different impact on the film industry. The revolution exacerbated the decline in film production that started after the 2008 global financial crisis. Chapter 2 examined post-revolution issues of extended piracy, recurring curfews, insecurity and unexpected censorship practices among the factors that increased the risk of producing films. In addition, an oligopoly of production and distribution since the late 1990s has limited the scope of film-making to a few production companies. The expansion of what film-makers addressed as a 'crisis' after the revolution led to the production of low-budget films and the migration of most film-makers to the production of television series. The interviews with film producers and directors revealed that the state is currently unconcerned with the film industry's crisis. The state's intervention is limited to censorial practices and an inconsistent (and insufficient) funding system.

Unlike Nasser's plan to develop film-making through nationalizing the film industry after the 1952 Coup, post-2011 Revolution governments did not respond to the industry's problems seriously. Despite the several calls of film-makers for state support in television shows, al-Sisi gives minor consideration to the film industry. Film-makers re-emphasized the state's significant role in supporting the film industry financially and through reconsidering the legal framework, which regulates film-making matters. Meanwhile, al-Sisi's priorities during his first term in office were directed towards security and economic development. Although a governmental committee was set-up to discuss the industry's issues, film-makers found that no further actions were taken. The state has been encouraging the extended piracy on television channels through delaying the required legal amendments and broadcasting public service announcements on 'piracy channels'. On the other hand, the crisis in producing mainstream films has allowed more space for the production and reception of independent films.

The cases studied in Chapter 1 have also demonstrated the use of film as a form of political activism before revolutions. Film-makers such as Fernando Solanas and Octavio Getino (1970) and Sanjines (1970) have emphasized the role of revolutionary films in mobilizing people and calling for action. Film movements have encouraged the production of socio-political conscious films to raise awareness in countries such as Argentina, Bolivia and Senegal without revolutions (Gabriel, 1982). Moreover, a Chinese left-wing film movement started to engage with political issues in 1930 before the revolution (Pang, 2002). Although Egyptian films have always criticized preceding rulers, film-makers have denounced Mubarak's regime since the 1990s. Films such as *al-Irhab wa-l-Kabab* (*Terrorism and Kebab*, Shirif 'Arafa, 1992) and *Isharat Maurur* (*Traffic Light*, Khairi Bishara, 1995) were critical of Mubarak's government. They represented the public's growing anger towards issues of social injustice and corruption (Tabishat, 2012). Along the public dissent that came with Mubarak's re-election for a fifth presidential term in 2005, films started to contribute to political activism in Egypt.

I argued that since 2006, film-makers have used different genres and production modes to voice discontent. Chapter 3 examined popular high-budget dramas such as *'Imarat Ya'qubiyan* (*The Yacoubian Building*, Marwan Hamid, 2006) and Khalid Yusif's films – *Hiyna Maysara* (*When Convenient*, 2007) and *Dukkan Shihata* (*Shihata's Shop*, 2009). These films used high budgets and film stars to depict issues of corruption, poverty and radicalization in contemporary Egypt. I also analysed comedy films such as *al-Diktatur* (*The Dictator*, Ihab Lam'i, 2009), *Zaza* ('Ali 'Abd al-Khalik, 2006) and *Rami al-I'tisami* (*Rami the Protester*, Sami Rafi', 2008), which used political satire to depict themes of dictatorship and rebellion. The high-budget dramas and comedy films anticipated the 2011 Revolution with scenes and sequences of revolution-like images and public revolts. The rise of independent films within the same time period was also a significant manifestation of rebellion. Films such as *'In Shams* (*Eye of the Sun*, Ibrahim al-Battut, 2008), *Basra* (Ahmad Rashwan, 2008), *Hiliaupulis* (*Heliopolis*, Ahmad 'Abd Allah, 2009) and *al-Khurug min al-*

Qahira (*Cairo Exit*, Hisham Issawi, 2010) used creative production formats to resist the dominant film-making style including digital cameras, new actors and innovative storytelling techniques to express 'social realities'. While mainstream high-budget films depended on the connections that film stars and film-makers have with the Censorship of Artistic Works to release their films, some comedy films such as *al-Diktatur* and *Zaza*, set their plots in imagined countries. In many cases, independent film-makers ignored censorship in their film-making processes. These films do not fit perfectly in Sanjines (1970) category of 'revolutionary films' as they did not aim to mobilize audiences. However, these films participated in raising the public's awareness or reinforced discourses of political and social corruption.

Film also continues to serve as a significant form of documenting revolutions. Egyptian films have a long tradition of engaging with historical events such as the 1952 Coup, the Six Day War and the 1973 War. Sharaf al-Din (1992), Gaffney (1987) and Gordon (2001) discussed how films glorified the revolution and victory or criticize Nasser's policies as the reason behind the defeat in 1968. Films such as *Darb al-Mahabiyl* (*Path of Fools*, Tawfi' Salih, 1955), *Sira' fi-l-Wadi* (*Struggle in the Valley*, Yusif Shahin, 1955) and *al-Mutamarridun* (*The Mutineers*, Tawfi' Salih, 1966) documented historical moments within a wider social context. In a different context, Naficy (2012a) explained how film-makers used the footage shot on 16 mm and Super 8 cameras to assemble 'compilation films' of the 1979 Iranian Revolution. The technological evolution of digital cameras and online video sites provided hours of footage of the 2011 Egyptian Revolution. People have used their digital and mobile phone cameras to shoot and upload events of the revolution. Film-makers used the available footage, as well as other footage that they personally shot, to produce short and feature narratives and documentary films about the revolution.

Chapter 4 examined fiction and documentary films that represented the revolution. The chapter focused on *Ba'd al-Mawqi'a* (*After the Battle*, Yusri Nasrallah, 2012), *al-Shitaa illy Fat* (*The Winter of Discontent*, Ibrahim al-Battut, 2012), *Farsh wa-Ghata* (*Rags and Tatters*, Ahmad 'Abd Allah, 2013), as fiction films that were set during the revolution. I also analysed documentaries such as *Mawlud fi Khamsa wa-'Ishriyn Yanayir* (*Born on the 25th of January*, Ahmad Rashwan, 2011) and *al-Tahrir 2011: al-Taiyyib, wa-l-Sharis, wa-l-Siyasi* (*Tahrir 2011: The Good, The Bad, and The Politician*, Tamir 'Izzat, Aytin Amin, and 'Amr Salama, 2011). Following White (1988) and Rastegar (2015), I argued that these films are a form of historiophoty and that they contributed to the cultural audio-visual memory of the collective struggle experienced during the

2011 Revolution. They documented specific moments of the revolution and used fiction and narrative elements to construct their arguments. For example, *Baʿd al-Mawqiʿa* (*After the Battle*, Yusri Nasrallah, 2012) focused on the Battle of the Camels event that took place on 2 February 2011 as the centre of the film's plot. Nasrallah combined footage from the Battle of the Camels with re-enacted scenes using the lead actor. This technique has provided a sense of authenticity to the narratives.

Documentary films also used re-enactments and fictional narratives to support their arguments. Both fiction and documentary films attempted to voice multiple perspectives through addressing Egyptian society in the form of binary oppositions (pro- vs. anti-revolution, upper- vs. lower classes and police vs. protesters). They represented the different political affiliations and social backgrounds in Tahrir Square as a community that shares the same values to construct a sense of nationalism. *Mawlud fi Khamsa wa-ʿIshriyn Yanayir* and *al-Tahrir 2011* used traditional documentary styles and revealed the subjective perspectives of their directors. A few fiction and documentary films represented the revolution away from Tahrir Square. They used unconventional styles, such as the lack of dialogue in *Farsh wa-Ghata* and the absence of images of the revolution in *Crop*.

The literature on the relationship between films and revolutions has mostly focused on post-revolution films and film movements as representations and expressions of liberation. Chapter 1 explored post-revolution film movements such as Third Cinema, which reconsidered film content and style, and production modes to resist mainstream film-making in Latin America. Film directors such as Solanas and Getino and Sanjines contributed to the framing of Third Cinema as a movement that aims to deconstruct the pre-revolution dominant ideologies and construct new revolutionary values. Their manifestos encouraged the production of liberated films that raise awareness through exposing the 'truth' and 'living realities' (Solanas and Getino, 1970; and Sanjines 1970). Egyptian cinema has witnessed multiple 'new film waves' throughout its history. After the 1952 Coup, Nasser's support for cinema supported the start of *sīnimā āl-wakiʿ* (Realism Cinema). In contrast to the colonial cinema, film directors Salah abu Siyf, Tawfiʾ Salih, and Yusif Shahin shaped *sīnimā āl-wakiʿ* through engaging with socio-political issues. Another 'new realistic cinema' wave started in the 1980s by film-makers, including ʿAtif al-Taiyyb, Muhammad Khan and Khairi Bishara, to resist the dominance of commercial films at that time. These directors employed artistic aesthetics to engage with issues of opportunism and alienation (Malkmus, 1988).

A few independent productions started in the late 1990s in Egypt. The introduction of digital cameras helped to generate several independent films before the 2011 Revolution. Films such as *Ithaki* (Ibrahim al-Battut, 2005), *Basra* (Ahmad Rashwan, 2008), *'In Shams* (*Eye of the Sun*, Ibrahim al-Battut, 2008), and *Hiliaupulis* (*Heliopolis*, Ahmad 'Abd Allah, 2009) signalled a wave of new film-making style in Egypt. Their use of digital cameras, new actors, real locations, natural lighting and improvisation helped their distinction from mainstream film-making. In addition, their disregard of commercial considerations and censorship grouped them under the umbrella of 'independent film-making'. After the 2011 Revolution, independent films have continued to use similar techniques and approaches to production. Although these films share a few commonalities with post-revolution film movements, such as opposing mainstream film-making, the lack of a common aesthetic approach hinders their recognition as a movement and association with the 2011 Revolution. Film-makers have used their own individual styles and creative approaches to represent struggle. Film scholar Alisa Lebow (2016) explains that the revolution has not been successful in radically changing the ruling regime. She also notes that the lack of a particular ideology, leader or a party to represent the revolution complicates the formation of a post-revolution film movement. In contrast to the support of post-revolution governments for new cinemas in other cases, the current Egyptian government used indirect methods to limit the production and screening of political films to avoid public debates on freedom of expression.

Chapter 5 also discussed the expansion of independent productions in relation to the developments in film-making and screening technologies coupled with the revolution. The availability of transnational funding sources, digital cameras, nonlinear editing software and video sharing websites facilitated film production among youth. The revolution has also allowed space for self-expression in its first years. Young film-makers shot, edited and uploaded their films online. Despite a few innovative engagements with the revolution, such as Jasmina Mitwally's and Philip Rizk's *Barra fi-l-Shari'* (*Out on the Streets*, 2015) and Lara Baladi's *Alone, Together ... in a Media Res* (2012), many online short films have represented the revolution in traditional styles (such as using allegories). The chapter also considered independent film initiatives that demonstrate the continuity of film activities after revolutions. For example, Tamir al-Sa'id and Khalid 'Abd Allah's Cimatheque, which screens and discusses alternative films is very similar to 'Cinematheque', which started to show and discuss classic and contemporary films in Cuba after the revolution. Waguih al-Laqany's *sinima fi kul makan* (Cinema Everywhere), which shows independent films in cafes, clubs, schools and NGOs in rural villages is very much the same idea as the mobile projection units that supported the screening of films in Cuba's and China's countrysides (Hernandez, 1974; and Balaisis, 2010). Although these are only individual attempts by Egyptian film-makers and curators, they demonstrate the continuity of film culture development after revolutions.

This book has developed my understanding of film as a mode of documentation and resistance during a period of crisis. Egyptian films that were produced before the revolution are currently significant resources in terms of revealing the excessive political corruption and social injustice during Mubarak's period. They also demonstrate the role of popular and independent films in resisting dominant ideologies and contributing to the public's anger. Films that represented the revolution, despite the critiques of their perspectives and traditional styles exposed in this book, are chronicles of a historical moment. These films stand against the counter-revolutionary claims of the 'conspiracy' of the revolution and show that it was a 'revolution from below'.

I realized the growth of independent films after the revolution when I first started working on this project in 2013. I expected these films to form a post-revolution movement since they resist mainstream film-making styles and use quite similar production modes. However, this project has informed me that struggle has been represented using diverse styles, especially during the dominance of a counter-revolutionary rhetoric in mainstream media and state institutions, including the censorship department. Mainstream media frame the current economic deterioration and terrorist attacks as repercussions of the 2011 Revolution, which prompted the denunciation of the events among wide segments of the public. The dominant discourse of the 'conspiracy' of the revolution diminishes the chances of producing films that celebrate it. The Censorship of Artistic Works adopts the same view and approves or rejects films based on vague criteria and without giving clear reasons. Future studies may examine the decision-making process within this department, and its transformation along the political history of Egypt. Future studies can also provide a closer examination of the state's use of indirect forms of censorship to repress political discontent.

Mainstream media have also reduced film production in the last decade to al-Subki's films and discussed the 'negative' effect of these texts on the behaviour and taste of audiences. Television commentators, such as Usama Kamal and Wa'il al-'Ibrashi, have suggested the production of serious films that reveal heroic stories of police and military officers. In one of his public speeches in 2015, al-Sisi addressed film actors Ahmad al-Sa'a and Yusra in the audience asking them to 'give people hope for tomorrow and enhance our values and ethics' (Sada al-Balad, 2015). Despite the lack of support for the film industry, the current military regime realizes the significance of cinema since it has prevented the screening of a few films that criticize military or police officers. Recently, some films have started to propagate the ideologies of al-Sisi's regime in response to the state's and the media's demands. For example, *al-Khaliyya* (*The Cell*, Tari' al-'Irian, 2017) emphasized the struggles of policemen in confronting terrorism. *Gawab I'ti'al* (*An Arrest Letter*, Muhammad Sami, 2017) criminalized Islamists and portrayed them as terrorists. Future studies regarding Egyptian cinema and the 2011 Revolution might consider some of these recent films as a form of propaganda. They support mainstream media channels in constructing Egypt's 'war against terrorism'.

However, the state did not prevent piracy channels that threaten the box-office, which became a major source of film revenue after the retreat of Rotana and ART. Film producers have thus avoided taking risks of producing in an insecure marketplace. Despite a few high-budget film productions, television series are still dominating the mediascape and a few film producers continue to release low-budget action and comedy films during the high seasons of *'id al-Fiṭr* and *'id al-Aḍḥā*. Nevertheless, the current economic crisis will reshape media industries in the Middle East, and in particular Egypt. The increase in the costs of *musalsalāt ramaḍān* has led Egyptian private television channels to set a price limit to the series they will purchase for 2018 (Al Tawy, 2017). This will eventually lead filmmakers to produce more films, but they will still have to confront the challenges of piracy and inconsistent state intervention. The domination of the traditional ruling class means that filmmakers will continue to produce high-budget action and comedy films, in which some have recently garnered mass audiences such as *Hurub Idtirary* (*Forced Escape*, Ahmad Khalid, 2017). Some film-makers will continue to challenge the current regime through producing socio-politically conscious films. They will continue their struggle against the censorship department through subtle representations or using alternative means of distribution and exhibition such as the internet.

The relationship between Egyptian cinema and revolution in particular remains distinctive due to the prevalence of digital technologies, which added a new force to the relationship of film and revolution. The ways in which young film-makers used digital technologies to produce and circulate films that express them (their identities and perspectives) during the revolution inform us of their activism and empowerment. Digital and mobile cameras and online platforms have served as an alternative means of documentation to film, but they have also facilitated the production and distribution of films. They offered a wide database of footage that film-makers could select from to produce their narratives. The continuous development of film-making technologies and the persistence of film-makers to express their political views will develop the struggle between film-makers and governments.

Many Egyptians speak of the 'failure of the 2011 Revolution'. Supporters of the uprising justify that the Muslim Brotherhood and the Armed Forces have overridden the revolution. Scholars, such as Achcar (2013), have criticized using the term 'revolution' yet, as the 2011 uprisings toppled a dictator, but did not lead to a radical change in the regime or the social structure of Egypt. The continuous deterioration in education, health and economy (marked by a recent dramatic inflation) means that the revolution has not achieved its fundamental objectives – bread, freedom and social justice. The recurrent arrests, detentions and forced disappearances of the 2011 Revolution supporters demonstrate the state's hostile attitude towards the revolution. Although the current constitution acknowledges the events of January and February 2011 as a revolution, the state (dominated by a military government that opposes the revolution and favours the ancient regime) does not demonstrate its support to the revolution or its values. The current practices of political repression have created a general mood among youth that gravitates towards immigration in search of a better income and lifestyle. However, a few are optimistic about Egypt's future and raise the slogan that the revolution is not over yet. They believe that the current affairs are only episodes during a longer revolutionary process. The further influence of these issues and debates on the film industry's crisis and film content is significant in Egypt's film history. Future studies can also take a wider approach and explore Arab revolutions in relation to film to enrich the understanding of the relationship between cinema in the Middle East and contemporary revolutions. Researching the Syrian and Tunisian films and film industries during times of revolution will support framing the relationship within the context of the Arab world and developing technologies. Although the post-2011 Revolution period did not witness the formation of a film movement, Egyptian films and film industry have demonstrated a reciprocal relationship with the revolution. The impact of the uprising on the industry and films and the engagement of films with politics have revealed the continuities and discontinuities in the relationship between cinema and revolutions.

Notes

Introduction

1. The Ministry of Information disrupted the internet and telephone services on the night of 27 January, in an attempt to cease the protests. They restored the internet services on 2 February.
2. Hala Lutfi started shooting *al-Khurug li-l-Nahar* before 2011, but she notes that the revolution provided an emotional support for the crew to finish the film.

Chapter 1

1. Naficy (2012a) argues that the post-revolution regime implemented an Islamicate culture rather than an Islamic one. The Islamicate is based on not only Islam but also traditions of Persia.
2. 'Independent' here does not refer to the financial independence, as some of these films were funded by the state, but to the independence of thinking and challenging the traditional film styles. Pre- and post-revolution regimes were upset with the results of these films, as they did not reinforce their dominant ideologies.
3. The post-revolution independent movement did not start until 1984 (five years after the revolution).

Chapter 2

1. Film-makers who use this film style have concerns with classifying their films as 'independent', since the connotations associated with these films are usually complex narratives that target film festivals rather than mass audience.
2. Film directors Hala Lutfi and Ahmad Rashwan have also criticized the involvement of film producers as a part of the Cinematic Syndicate together with other film-making professions. They discussed how this results in a conflict of interest and recommended that producers should have a separate syndicate.
3. Ramadan is the popular month for radio and television shows, as well as advertisements, to cater gatherings of families and friends.
4. Turkey's prime minister, Recep Tayyep Erdogan, supported the Muslim Brotherhood president Muhammad Mursi.

5   al-Sisi had made a phone call in one of the show's earlier live episodes.
6   Film producers, such as Gabi Khuwri, have also been complaining about the growing number of crewmembers, sometimes counting up to 200, on a set. Producers argue that many of these crewmembers, such as the six or seven assistants per actor/actress, are unnecessary. Consequently, the extensive number of crewmembers increases the production's budget (CBC Egypt, 2013b).
7   These prices are according to the date of the interview in 2015. Recent inflation in prices has led to an increase in film ticket prices.
8   These channels also offer inexpensive advertising spaces on their screens. According to film producer Muhammad al-'Adl, they charge 40 to 80 Egyptian pounds per minute, while the average cost of advertising is 12,000 to 14,000 Egyptian pounds on other channels, such as CBC. This has led to advertisements of 'quacks, charlatans, and fake medicine' (M. al-'Adl, interview, 27 January 2015).
9   In a recent television interview, Muhammad Hefzy has declared that issue is resolved. The transfer of ownership of films now requires an official certificate from the Chamber of Film Industry (DMC, 2017).
10   Muhammad al-'Adl was referring to Dr 'Abd al-Sattar Fathi, the chairman of the censorship body at the time of the interview. The current chairman is Dr Khalid 'Abd al-Gilil.
11   The censorship department is currently applying the age rating system. However, it still rejects films that criticize the military or police officers.
12   The events and main characters of both films, in addition to the other Subki's productions, are usually located at Cairo's popular districts and neighbourhoods.
13   Both films have grossed significant profits and created a wide fan base for the now film star Muhammad Ramadan among young audience.
14   Many people associated this film with al-Subki as it incorporates similar features of the hero as a 'thug' (fighting with blades), the belly dancer and the popular song.
15   Recently, films such as *Hepta* have invested in social media campaigns to encourage audiences to watch the film in theatres. They show photos and videos from behind the scenes and start contests to build audiences for the films before their release.

Chapter 3

1   In 2001, *Gawaz bi-Qarar Gumhuri* (*A Marriage with a Presidential Decree*, Khalid Yusif) also depicted Mubarak himself attending a wedding in a popular neighbourhood based on an invitation from the middle-class couple. They give him all the neighbourhood's complaints, which the parliament representatives have ignored.
2   Censorship must permit a film script before shooting and they require watching the final version of the film before release.

3   The term refers to a revolution instigated by poor people (rather than political activists) against the ruling regime due to the continuous increase in prices and difficulties in coping with the inflation.
4   Many of the thugs who appeared after the revolution were claimed to be slum dwellers, which recalls the film's portrayal of slum dwellers as hooligans.
5   Abdallah F. Hassan holds a similar argument in his book *Media, Revolution and Politics in Egypt: The Story of an Uprising*. He discusses comedy films and theatrical plays that portrayed the 'realities' of the regime through parody.
6   Referred to as a coup d'état in the film. However, the film shows that the military has moved upon multiple demonstrations by the public.
7   The similarities include a dark-skinned person (look-alike Marshal Hisiyn Tantawi) playing the role of the minister of Defence. The military's take-over speech in the film is similar to the 2011 announcement including 'the military will keep a rein on the country, until the rule is stable through a fair democratic election'.
8   At the time of the constitutional referendum (a few weeks after Mubarak stepped down), no parties were ready for the people's assembly elections yet. The support of the referendum meant a possible return of the NDP and/or having a parliament that did not represent the public.
9   Even Hala Lutfi's *al-khurug li-l-Nahar* (*Coming Forth by Day*, 2012)[10] and Tamir al-Sa'id's *Akhir Ayyam al-Madina* (*In the Last Days of the City*, 2016) are among this wave. They started their projects in 2008, but production matters delayed their release.
10 The transfer process is not needed anymore, since screening technologies have turned digital.
11 The film was released in theatres on the 25 of January 2011, which remarkably affected the film's revenues.
12 While the English title on the poster of the film is *Cairo Exit*, the Arabic is *al-Khurug* (*The Exit*).
13 Except for *Dukkan Shihata*, which compares Nasser's Egypt to Mubarak's Egypt.
14 By the end of 2010, two popular films '*Asal Iswid* (*Molasses*, Khalid Mar'i) and *Bintiyn min Masr* (*Two Girls from Egypt*, Muhammad Amin) have ending scenes set at the airport representing the state of unbearable pressure and desire to leave the country.
15 Nearly before the revolution, films also started to raise awareness regarding social issues such as sexual harassment in *678* (Muhammad Diab, 2010). Film critics praised the film for its deep focus on the omnipresent issue in Egypt. Although the film does not directly relate the widespread verbal and physical sexual harassment to political or social reasons, it still revolves around the theme of repression.

Chapter 4

1   Many protesters considered the step-down of Mubarak on 11 February the end of the revolution. For others, the date marked a milestone in the journey of the

revolution. However, the '18 days of the revolution' refers to the period between the start of protests and sit-in Tahrir Square until the overthrow of Mubarak.

2. Samih 'Abd al-'Aziz started shooting *Sarkhit Namla* before the revolution, but he changed the ending to include images of protests and demonstrations from Tahrir Square. Similarly, 'Issam al-Shama' changed *al-Fagumi*'s (2011) ending to include images from the revolution.
3. Protesters, journalists and witnesses constantly uploaded footage from their mobile phones and digital cameras online.
4. During the revolution, young men formed committees to fill in the security absence and protect their neighbourhoods after the withdrawal of the police.
5. Rashwan's last day of shooting was 27 May – *gum'it āl-munādāa bi-l-dawla āl-madaniya* (Calling for a Civil State Protest).
6. YouTube videos described the attackers as thugs in their titles, description or through the witnesses of the protesters (Mursi, 2011; and Yusif, 2011).
7. The director has witnessed a similar situation, where the inhabitants of Nazlit al-Simman humiliate one of the participants of the battle.
8. The development of Riym's character is similar to the transformation of the director's perspective on the event. Nasrallah believed that the attackers are thugs, but changed his opinion after a discussion with the actor Basim al-Samra (the film's lead) and several visits to Nazlit al-Simman (ON E, 2012).
9. Nasrallah clarified his view in multiple television interviews. His interview on ON E (2012) includes a comprehensive explanation of his perspective and production matters.
10. The film does not clearly say who incited the horse and camel riders, but Hajj 'Abd Allah – a rich Islamist character (played by Salah 'Abd Allah) owns shops and homes at Nazlit al-Simman and appears to be anti-revolution. Hajj 'Abd Allah dominates the neighbourhood and owns a weapons store. Nasrallah suggests, through the figure of Hajj 'Abd Allah, that Islamists adverse the revolution using violence and implicitly implies their support for the Battle of the Camels.
11. The protest followed a clash between protesters and police officers in June 2011 during a celebration related to the revolution.
12. The film represents societal pressure also through a schoolteacher who escapes to the rooftop for a smoke. She indicates that, as a woman, she cannot smoke in front of anyone even her husband.
13. Protests called for the opening of the Rafah border to allow the entry of Palestinians and the delivery of medicine and food.
14. The film was shot from 13 April 2011 (when Mubarak and his sons were sent to jail) to 23 June 2011.
15. In their interview on CBC Egypt (2013a) the film-makers declared that the interviewee is the director's brother.

16 'Amr predicts the revolution after he watches the video. In anticipation of chaos and curfews, 'Amr orders the doorman to shop groceries for him.
17 The Egyptian television channels broadcasted a live image of an empty bridge (next to Maspiro – the television's building) to falsify the protests during the eighteen days.
18 Even the presenter's name, Tamir, refers to Tamir Amin the presenter of *Masr al-Naharda*.
19 Many calls on Egyptian television programmes were clearly fake. The callers claimed they are at Tahrir Square with a silent surrounding. The callers usually testify that protests at the square are insignificant.
20 In one of the scenes, the protagonist watches a protester talking to his neighbours about the revolution and encouraging them to participate. We can barely hear the protester as the sound of a motorbike's engine (appears beside the protagonist) overlays his voice.
21 The film does not provide any dates of its start or end. 'Abd Allah compressed some of the revolution events into the three days, where the narrative takes place.
22 On 27 January, Rashwan started by shooting the meeting of the artists held at the Theatrical Professions Syndicate.
23 The Muslim Brotherhood refused to participate in the protests that were held on that Friday. The protests involved criticism of the Military Council too.
24 Shafik criticized the film during her interview in the meta-documentary *Filming Revolution* published in 2015. This part is accessible on http://filmingrevolution.org/clip/351/the_issue_of_the_%22i%22_in_recent_egyptian_documentaries
25 During the interview, the director revealed that he cheered and carried protest signs while recording the events.
26 Amin reveals that foreign producers suggested she includes the revolution as part of her feature's (*Villa 69*) plot.
27 *Crop* is one of the projects discussed on *Filming Revolution*. Marwan 'Umara, one of the film's directors, discloses that the revolution is bigger than what a film can embrace.
28 In *Kharig al-Khidma*, we see the revolution through news coverage on television at the protagonist's home.

Chapter 5

1 Henceforward, I will be using the term 'independent' without quotation marks. However, I will argue the ambiguities of the term and the resistance of film-makers to their labelling as independent.

2   In this context, alternative cinema is referring to the non-mainstream Egyptian and foreign (mostly non-American) films. These films are usually screened in cultural centres and a few screens such as Zawya, which hosts the European Film Festival. I used this term as a more comprehensive term that includes independent cinema – which in Egypt refers to a more non-governmental, self-financed and low-budget films that usually cast non-actors. Although the term 'independent' is widely used among audiences and mainstream film-makers in Egypt, I argue the ambiguity of the term and what it includes later on in this chapter.
3   *al-Madina* was transformed on to 35 mm negative for release in film theatres.
4   al-Battut had directed several documentaries about wars and revolutions around the world, such as *The War in Kosovo* (1999) and *Baghdad* (2004).
5   Also '*Ali Mi'za wa-Ibrahim* ('*Ali, the Goat and Ibrahim,* Shirif al-Bindari, 2016) is about two young men who refuse the dominant beliefs and standards of society. One of them loves Nada, a goat, and treats her as his fiancée.
6   The film also pays homage to the new Egyptian cinema of the 1980s, through casting Muhammad Khan (one of the leading directors of the 1980s film movement) in one of the roles. Khan's support for the film reassures the continuation of independent productions to the new Egyptian cinema movements that opposed mainstream films.
7   al-Kashif's documentary interviews women in prison convicted of murdering their husbands. The film has also received production and post-production funds from international film festivals.
8   Other challenges facing independent film-makers include shooting permissions in public spaces. The Ministry of Interior issues these permissions only for members of the Cinematic Syndicate – which only allows the few graduates of the Higher Cinema Institute to be its members. Independent film-makers resort to secretly shooting their outdoor scenes.
9   *Mikrufun* is the first feature shot with a canon 7D and released in film theatres.
10 Officials from the state censorship bureau, tax authority and national security had raided Townhouse Gallery, a non-profit art space, and shut it down two days before my interview with Hala Galal (Mada Masr, 2015). The space was reopened two months later.
11 Lara Baladi had also planned to start Radio Tahrir during the early eighteen days of the revolution; however, it was established as online radio after the revolution.
12 In order to use a professional camera in the street, you must have shooting permissions from the required authorities.
13 Dickinson (2012) compares film worker's wages and rights in Egypt and Syria. He argues how these discrepancies subsequently influence and politicize films.

14 Other independent production and distribution initiatives include Rahala and Seen Films. Also, Fig Leaf is a studio that provides film and sound production services in Alexandria.
15 Although the Censorship of Artistic Works has approved the release of the film, it added a sentence in the beginning that reads, 'After the 30 June Revolution, the Muslim Brotherhood led bloody clashes to prevent the peaceful transfer of authority.'

Filmography

Abu 'Ali, K. (Prod.), Yusif, K. (Dir.) (2007). *Hiyna Maysara (When Convenient)* [DVD]. Egypt: Albatros for Film Production and Distribution.

Abu 'Ali, K. (Prod.), Yusif, K. (Dir.) (2009). *Dukkan Shihata (Shihata's Shop)* [DVD]. Egypt: Misr Cinema.

Adib, 'I. (Prod.), Hamid, M. (Dir.) (2006). *'Imarat Ya'qubiyan (The Yacoubian Building)* [DVD]. Egypt: Good News Production.

al-'Agami, S. (Prod.), Rafi', S. (Dir.) (2008). *Rami al-I'tisami (Rami the Protestor)* [DVD]. Egypt: Image for Media Production.

al-Hanafi, S., Wakid, 'A. and al-Battut, I. (Prod.), al-Battut, I. (Dir.) (2012). *al-Shitaa illy Fat (The Winter of Discontent)*. [DVD]. Egypt: ZAD Communication and Production, Aroma Film Labs, Ein Shams Productions, and Material House Film Production.

al-Kurdi, W. (Prod.), Nasrallah, Y. (Dir.) (2012). *Ba'd al-Mawqi'a (After the Battle)* [DVD]. Egypt and France: New Century and Dollar Films, Siecle Productions, Studio 37, and France 3 Cinema.

Domke, J. and 'Umara, M. (Dir.) (2013). *Crop* [DVD]. Egypt: Danish Arts Council.

Faru', D. (Prod.). Khan, N. (Dir.) (2013). *Harag wa-Marag (Chaos, Disorder)* [Shahid.net]. Egypt: WIKA Production and Distribution.

Fawzi, H. G. (Prod.), 'Abd al-Khali', 'A. (Dir.) (2006). *Zaza* [DVD]. Egypt: HGF Film Production.

Hifzi, M. (Prod.), 'Izzat, T., Amin, A., and Salama, 'A. (Dir.) (2011). *al-Tahrir 2011: al-Taiyyib, wa-l-Sharis, wa-l-Siyasi (Tahrir 2011: The Good, The Bad, and The Politician)* [YouTube]. Egypt: Film Clinic and Amana Creative.

Hifzi, M. (Prod.), Murgan, M. (Dir.) (2013). *'Asham* [Television]. Egypt: Film Clinic.

Hifzi, M., and Shama, O. (Prod.), 'Abd Allah, A. (Dir.) (2013). *Farsh wa-Ghata (Rags and Tatters)* [DVD]. Egypt: Film Clinic and Mashroua.

Lutfi, H. (Prod. and Dir.) (2012). *al-Khurug li-l-Nahar (Coming Forth by Day)* [Shahid.net]. Egypt: Hassala Films.

Mandur, S. (Prod.), 'Abd Allah, A. (Dir.) (2009). *Hiliaupulis (Heliopolis)* [Television]. Egypt: Material House Production.

Mandur, S. (Prod.), al-Battut, I. (Dir.) (2008). *'In Shams (Eye of the Sun)* [DVD]. Egypt: Material House Film Production.

Mandur, S. (Prod.), 'Issawi, H. (Dir.) (2010). *al-khurug min al-Qahira (Cairo Exit)* [Television]. Egypt: Material House Production.

Rashwan, A. (Prod. and Dir.) (2008). *Basra* [Vimeo.com]. Egypt. Dream Production.

Rashwan, A. (Prod. and Dir.) (2011). *Mawlud fi Khamsa wa-'Ishriyn Yanayir* (*Born on the 25th of January*) [Vimeo]. Egypt: Dream Production.

Sarhan, K. (Prod.), Lam'i, I. (Dir.) (2009). *al-Diktatur* (*The Dictator*) [DVD]. Egypt: Soteer Productions.

Bibliography

'Abd al-Min'im, A. (2013, October 19). Baltagiyat 'al-Subki' wa-baltagat ma ba'd 25 Yanayir (al-Subki's thugs and post-25 January bullying). *al-Yuwm al-Sabi'*. Retrieved from http://www.youm7.com/story/2013/10/19/بطلجة-السبكي-وبلطجة-ام-بعد-٢٥-يناير

'Abd al-Razi', R. (2008, December 8). '*Rami al-I'tisami*' ... Kalam fi-l-siyasa min bab 'al-tahriyg' ('*Rami al-I'tisami*' ... A jesting approach to political talk). *al-Masri al-Yuwm*. Retrieved from http://today.almasryalyoum.com/article2.aspx?ArticleID=189480

'Abd al-Razi', R. (2014, February 3). al-Sinima al-mustaqilla fi Masr: Nihayat mustallah wa-bidayat tayyar (Independent cinema in Egypt: The end of the idiom and the beginning of the wave). *Eye on Cinema*. Retrieved from http://www.eyeoncinema.net/Details.aspx?secid=56&nwsId=1605

S'Abd al-hakur, M. (2015, August 7). Nisf zabit wa-nisf baltagi yuhaqiq qanunuh al-khass fi '*Shadd Agza*" (Half policeman half thug works out his own rules in 'Shad Agza"). *al-Arab*. Retrieved from http://www.alarab.co.uk/?id=58819

Achcar, G. (2016). *Morbid Symptoms: Relapse in the Arab Uprising*. California: Stanford University Press.

Achcar, G. (2013). *The People Want: A Radical Exploration of the Arab Uprising* (G. Goshgarian, Trans.). Berkley; Los Angeles; London: University of California Press.

'Adli, N. (2009, October 10). *al-Diktatur* ... komidiya 'ala al-tariqa al-bambuziya (*al-Diktatur* ... a Bambuzian comedy). *Masress*. Retrieved from https://www.masress.com/soutelomma/3070

'Adli, N. (2012, April 20). Hazz Sa'id ... ru'ya murtabika li-thawrat yanaiyr! (*Hazz Sa'id* ... a confused vision about January's revolution!). *al-Ahram*. Retrieved from http://www.ahram.org.eg/archive/Cinema/News/144480.aspx

Ahmad, A. (1987). Jameson's Rhetoric of Otherness and the 'National Allegory'. *Social Text*, 17(Autumn), 3–25.

al-Arabiya (Producer). (2012, October 10). *Ba'd al-Mawqi'a*. al-mukhrig Yusri Nasrallah wa-l-naqid 'Isaam Zakaria (*After the Battle*. the director Yusri Nasrallah and film critic 'Isaam Zakaria). In *al-Hadath al-Masry*. Cairo: al-Arabiya. Retrieved from https://www.youtube.com/watch?v=UJstMVu-ctE

al-Battut, I. (2010, April 18). Ibrahim al-Battut (part1) – Halit Ibda' (A creative mood) [Video webcast]. Retrieved from https://www.youtube.com/watch?v=G25ooRUW8_4

Al Tawy, A. (2017, November 22). Egypt's Top Satellite TV Channels Set Cap on Guest Fees, Price of Purchasing Series. Retrieved from http://english.ahram.org.eg/

NewsContent/1/64/282017/Egypt/Politics-/Egypts-top-satellite-TV-channels-set-cap-on-guest-.aspx

'Ali, W. (2011, April 19). '*al-Masri al-Yuwm*' tanshur al-nass al-kamil li-mulakhas taqriyr lagnat taqassi al-haqa'eq hawl thawrat 25 yanayir ('*al-Masry al-Yuwm*' publishes the full of text of the summary of the final report of the investigation and facts finding committee regarding the events of 25th January). Retrieved from http://www.almasryalyoum.com/news/details/126472

Althusser, L. (1971). *Lenin and Philosophy, and Other Essays*. London: New Left Books.

Armbrust, W. (1995). New Cinema, Commercial Cinema and the Modernist Tradition in Egypt. *Alif: Journal of Comparative Poetics*, 15(Arab Cinematics: Toward the New and the Alternative), 81–129.

Armbrust, W. (1998). When the Lights Go Down in Cairo: Cinema as Secular Ritual. *Visual Anthropology*, 10(2–4), 413–44.

Armbrust, W. (2011). Political Film in Egypt. In J. Gugler (Ed.), *Film in the Middle East and North Africa* (pp. 228–51). Austin, TX: University of Texas Press.

Armbrust, W. (2012). Dreaming of Counterrevolution: Rami al-I'tisami and the Pre-negation of Protest. *Cinema Journal*, 52(1), 143–8.

Armes, R. (2015). *New Voices in Arab Cinema*. Bloomington: Indiana University Press.

Awad, S. (2013, December 25). Cinema Crisis. *Egypt Today*. Retrieved from http://www.egypttoday.com/Article/4/691/Cinema-Crisis

Badran, W. (2009, May 27). '*Dukkan Shihata*' Bain Abdel Nasser wa-l-Sadat wa-Haifaa' Wahbi ('*Dukkan Shihata*' between Abdel Nasser and Sadat and Haifaa' Wahbi). *BBC Arabic*. Retrieved from http://news.bbc.co.uk/hi/arabic/middle_east_news/newsid_8071000/8071149.stm

Baker, R. W. (1974). Egypt in Shadows: Films and the Political Order. *American Behavioral Scientist*, 17(3), 393–423.

Balaisis, N. (2010). Cuba, Cinema and the Post-revolutionary Public Sphere. *Canadian Journal of Film Studies*, 19(2), 26–42.

Bayat, A. (2013). *Life as Politics: How Ordinary People Change the Middle East* (2nd ed.). Stanford, California: Stanford University Press.

Bazin, A. (2005a). *What Is Cinema? vol. I. by Andre Bazin* (H. Gray, Trans.). Berkeley, Los Angeles; London: University of California Press.

Bazin, A. (2005b). *What Is cinema? vol. II. by Andre Bazin* (H. Gray, Trans.). Berkeley, Los Angeles; London: University of California Press.

Behnam, M. (2014). Independent Cinema in Post-1979 Revolution Iran. *Film International*, 12(3 [69]), 31–51.

Bordwell, D., & Thompson, K. (2001). *Film Art: An Introduction* (6th ed.). New York: McGraw Hill.

Brunow, D. (2009). Representation and Performativity: Methodological Considerations on Film and Historiography. The Example of Baader-Meinhof. In C. Ahlberger (et al. Eds.), *Historier: Artonoch nittonhundratalets skönlitteratur som historisk källa* (pp. 44–56). Gothenburg: Gothenburg University Press.

CBC Egypt (Producer). (2013a, March 28). Abtal film *al-Shitaa illy Fat* (*The Winter of Discontent*'s cast) [Television show episode]. In *Zaiyy al-Shams*. Cairo: CBC Egypt. Retrieved from https://www.youtube.com/watch?v=XpgyPK8Av_Q

CBC Egypt (Producer). (2013b, October 28). Azmit sina'it al-sinima al-Masriya (The crisis of the Egyptian film industry) [Television show episode]. In *Bath Mubashir*. Cairo: CBC Egypt. Retrieved from https://www.youtube.com/watch?v=FVcgLgXxiBM&list=PLdXABTp0M_vygJ6KihqppyiXalmDCqRAD&index=4.

CBC Egypt (Producer). (2014a, August 5). Huwar khas hawl sariqat al-aflam asnaa' 'ardaha (A discussion around the piracy of films during their screening). In *Inta Horr*. Cairo: CBC Egypt. Retrieved from https://www.youtube.com/watch?v=IzdIYsgUDGs

CBC Egypt (Producer). (2014b, November 4). Ma'lumat wa-tafasiyl gadiyda fi malaf qarsanit al-aflam (New information and details about the case of films' piracy) [Television show episode]. In *Inta Horr*. Cairo: CBC Egypt. Retrieved from https://www.youtube.com/watch?v=blLXJKdBhSA

CBC Egypt (Producer). (2016, November 1). Liqaa' ma' mukhrig film *Akhir Ayyam al-Madina* Tamir al-Sa'id (An interview with the director of *In the Last Days of the City*, Tamir al-Sa'id) [Television show episode]. In *Huna al-'asima*. Cairo: CBC Egypt. Retrieved from https://www.youtube.com/watch?v=UIzzA5hw-Ec

Dal, M. H. (Ed.). (2013). *Cairo: Images of Transition: Perspectives on Visuality in Egypt 2011–2013*. Bielefeld: Transcript Verlag.

Dardarkom. *Film al-Kumidiya al-Diktatur 2009* (The comedy film *al-Diktatur* 2009). (n.d.). Retrieved 25 October 2015 from http://maxcdn.dardarkom.com/files/uploads/13746249331.jpg

Dickinson, K. (2012). The State of Labor and Labor for the State: Syrian and Egyptian Cinema beyond the 2011 Uprisings. *Framework*, 53(1), 99–116.

DMC (Producer). (2017, October 19). Ma' al-e'lamy Usama Kamal (With the interviewer Usama Kamal) [Television show episode]. In *Misaa' DMC*. Cairo: DMC. Retrieved from https://www.youtube.com/watch?v=rC4Gysw_1cE

Dream TV (Producer). (2015, November 10). Ma' Wa'il al-Ibrashi (with Wa'il al-Ibrashi) [Television show]. In *al-'Ashira Masa'an*. Cairo: Dream TV. Retrieved from https://www.youtube.com/watch?v=Zk6VOmWnJcA

Egypt Bans 'Zionist' Film Exodus and Cites 'Historical Inaccuracies'. (2014, December 26). *The Guardian*. Retrieved from https://www.theguardian.com/film/2014/dec/26/egypt-bans-hollywood-exodus-christian-bale

Egypt Speaker 'Plotted Battle of the Camel'. (2011, July 15). *al-Jazeera*. Retrieved from http://www.aljazeera.com/news/middleeast/2011/07/201171417215627964.html

Egyptian constitution (2014), Part III Article 67. Retrieved from http://www.sis.gov.eg/Newvr/Dustor-en001.pdf

El Khachab, C. (2017, January). State Control over Film Production in Egypt. *Arab Media and Society*. Retrieved from http://www.arabmediasociety.com/?article=987

El-Nawawy, M., & Khamis, S. (2013). *Egyptian Revolution 2.0: Political Blogging, Civic Engagement, and Citizen Journalism*. New York: Palgrave Macmillan.

Elghamry, K. (2015). Periphery Discourse: An Alternative Media Eye on the Geographical, Social and Media Peripheries in Egypt's Spring. *Mediterranean Politics*, 20(2), 255–72.

Elmarsafy, Z. (2015). Action, Imagination, Institution, Natality, Revolution. *Journal for Cultural Research*, 19(2), 130–8.

Elnaccash, A. (1968). Egyptian Cinema: A Historical Outline. *African Arts*, 2(1), 52–5.

Eltantawy, N., & Wiest, J. B. (2011). Social Media in the Egyptian Revolution: Reconsidering Resource Mobilization Theory. *International Journal of Communication*, 5, 1207–24.

Emerson, C. (Ed. & Trans.). (1984). *Problems of Dostoevsky's Poetics: Theory and History of Literature #8*. London: University of Minnesota Press.

Ezzat, A., al-Haqq, S., & Fazulla, H. (2014). *Censors of Creativity: A Study of Censorship of Artistic Expressions in Egypt*. Cairo: Association for Freedom of Thought and Expression & Freemuse. Retrieved from http://afteegypt.org/wp-content/uploads/2014/04/Censors-of-creativity-English.pdf

Farag, M. (2012). Egypt's Muslim Brotherhood and the January 25 Revolution: New Political Party, New Circumstances. *Contemporary Arab Affairs*, 5(2), 214–29.

Farid, S. (1988). *Hawiyyat al-sinima al-'arabiya* (*The Identity of Arabic Cinema*). Beirut: Dar al-Farabi.

Farid, S. (2001). *Madkhal ila tarikh al-Sinima al-'arabiya* (*Introduction to the History of Arabic Cinema*). Cairo: General Egyptian Book Organisation.

Farid, S. (2012, December 18). '*Harag wa-Marag*' yo'lin mawlid mawhiba kabiyra ('*Harag wa-Marag*' declares the birth of a big talent). *al-Masri al-Yuwm*. Retrieved from http://today.almasryalyoum.com/article2.aspx?ArticleID=364252&IssueID=2718

Farid, S. (2014, May 3). '*al-Khurug li-l-Nahar*' tuhfa min rawa'i' al-sinima tutah li-gumhurha fi Masr ('*al-Khurug li-l-Nahar*' one of cinema's masterpieces available to its audience in Egypt). *al-Masri al-Yuwm*. Retrieved from http://today.almasryalyoum.com/article2.aspx?ArticleID=423130

Film '*Imarat Ya'qubiyan* … dagga wa-gar'a (The Yacoubian Building … noise and boldness). (2006, June 29). *al-Jazeera*. Retrieved from http://www.aljazeera.net/programs/behindthenews/2006/6/29/فيلم-عمارة-يعقوبيان-ضجة-وجرأة

Flibbert, A. (2005). State and Cinema in Pre-revolutionary Egypt, 1927–52. In A. Goldschmidt, A. Johnson & B. Salamoni (Eds.), *Re-envisioning Egypt 1919–1952* (pp. 448–65). Cairo, Egypt: The American University of Cairo Press.

Flibbert, A. (2007). *Commerce in Culture: State and Markets in the World Film Trade*. New York: Palgrave Macmillan.

Forgacs, D. (Ed.). (2000). *The Gramsci Reader: Selected Writing 1916–1935* (1st ed.). New York: New York University Press.

Foucault, M. (1975). Film and Popular Memory: An Interview with Michel Foucault. *Radical Philosophy*, 11, 24–9.

Gabriel, T. H. (1982). *Third Cinema in the Third World: The Aesthetics of Liberation*. Ann Arbor, MI: UMI Research Press.

Gabriel, T. H. (1989). Towards a Critical Theory of Third World Films. In J. Pines & P. Willemen (Eds.), *Questions of Third Cinema* (pp. 30–52). London: BFI Publishing.

Gaffney, J. (1987). The Egyptian Cinema: Industry and Art in a Changing Society. *Arab Studies Quarterly*, 9(1), 53–75.

Gaines, J. (1999). Political Mimesis. In J. Gaines & M. Renov (Eds.), *Collecting Visible Evidence* (pp. 84–102). Minneapolis: University of Minnesota Press.

Ghareeb, S. (1997). An Overview of Arab Cinema. *Critique: Critical Middle Eastern Studies*, 6(11), 119–27.

al-Ghitani, M. (2015, May 10). *Dukkan Shihata ... Laisat bi-l-nawaya al-hasana tusna' al-sinima* (*Dukkan Shihata ... Good intentions are not enough to produce films*). *Civic Egypt*. Retrieved from http://www.civicegypt.org/?p=56900

Ghonim, W. (2012). *Revolution 2.0: The Power of the People Is Greater Than the People in Power: A Memoir*. Boston: Houghton Mifflin Harcourt.

Gilroy, P. (1988). Nothing but Sweat Inside My Hand: Diaspora Aesthetics and Black Arts in Britain. In K. Mercer (Ed.), *Black Film British Cinema* (pp. 44–6). London: Institute of Contemporary Art.

Gordon, J. (2001). Class-crossed Lovers: Popular Film and Social Change in Nasser's New Egypt. *Quarterly Review of Film and Video*, 18(4), 385–96.

Gordon, J. (2013). Chahine, Chaos and Cinema: A Revolutionary Coda. *Bustan: The Middle East Book Review*, 4(2), 99–112.

Grondahl, M. (2013). *Revolution Graffiti: Street Art of the New Egypt*. Farnborough: Thames & Hudson Ltd.

Grossberg, L. (Ed.). (1986). On Postmodernism and Articulation: An Interview with Stuart Hall. *Journal of Communication Inquiry*, 10(2), 45–60.

Gugler, J. (Ed.). (2011). *Film in the Middle East and North Africa*. Austin, TX: University of Texas Press.

Harrison, N. (2007). Pontecorvo's 'Documentary' Aesthetics. *Interventions*, 9(3), 389–404.

Hassan, 'A. (2015). *Media, Revolution and Politics in Egypt: The Story of an Uprising*. London: I.B. Tauris.

Hassuna, A., & al-Asiuwty, M. (2009). *al-Sinima al-Mustaqilla fi Masr* (*Independent Cinema in Egypt*). Cairo: Audio-Visual Development Foundation.

Hedges, I. (2015). *World Cinema and Cultural Memory*. Basingstoke, England; New York: Palgrave Macmillan Memory Studies.

Hernandez, A. (1974). Filmmaking and Politics: The Cuban Experience. *American Behavioral Scientist*, 17(3), 360–88.

Holoquist, M. (Ed.). (1981). *The Dialogic Imagination: Four Essays by M. M. Bakhtin* (C. Emerson, & M. Holoquist, Trans.). Austin: University of Texas Press.

Howard, P. N., & Hussain, M. M. (2011). The Role of Digital Media. *Journal of Democracy*, 22(3), 35–48.

al-Husini, W. (2017, March 6). al-Mukhrig Yusri Nasrallah: Man' 'ard film "*18 Yuwm*" muhawla li-mahw al-zakira wa-muhasrit al-fananiyn (Director Yusri Nasrallah: Banning "*18 Days*" is an attempt to erase memory and besieging artists). *CNN Arabic*. Retrieved from https://arabic.cnn.com/entertainment/2017/03/06/yosri-nasrallah-interview

Ibrahim, S. (2015, January 13). al-Sinima al-Masriya ma'zuma: Zaman al-aflam munkhafadat al-taklifa (Egyptian cinema crisis: The age of low-budget films). *Raseef22*. Retrieved from http://raseef22.com/culture/2015/01/13/egyptian-cinema-economy-1/

Ibrahim, S. E. (1982). An Islamic Alternative in Egypt: The Muslim Brotherhood and Sadat. *Arab Studies Quarterly*, 4(1/2), 75–93.

Jameson, F. (1981). *The Political Unconscious: Narrative as a Socially Symbolic Act*. New York: Cornell University Press.

Jarjoura, N. (2014). The Current State of Arab Cinema: The Stories of Individuals ... An Update on Documentary Films. *Contemporary Arab Affairs*, 7(2), 209–24.

Jarvie, I. C. (1978). Seeing through Movies. *Philosophy of the Social Sciences*, 8(4), 374–97.

Johnston, C. (1973). Women's Cinema as Counter-cinema. In C. Johnston (Ed.), *Notes on Women's Cinema* (pp. 24–31). London: Society for Education in Film and Television.

Kamal, H. (2015). Inserting Women's Right in the Egyptian Constitution: Personal Reflections. *Journal for Cultural Research*, 19(2), 150–61.

Al-Kashuti, 'A. (2017, July 4). Khalid 'Abd al-Gilil: '*18 Yuwm fi Masr*' lam yu'rad 'ala gihaz al-riqaba (Khalid 'Abd al-Gilil: '*18 Days in Egypt*' has not been submitted to the censorship department). *al-Yuwm al-Sabi'*. Retrieved from http://www.youm7.com/story/2017/7/4/3310808/اخلاد-عبد-الجليل-۱۸-يوم-في-مصر-مل-يعرض-على

Kellner, D. (1995). *Media Culture: Cultural Studies, Identity, and Politics between the Modern and the Postmodern*. London; New York: Routledge.

Kenez, P. (2001). *Cinema and Soviet Society: From the Revolution to the Death of Stalin*. London; New York: I.B. Tauris.

al-Khamissi, K. (2010, November 30). al-Sinima al-mustaqilla fi birnamig *Studio Masr* (Independent cinema in *Studio Masr* show) [Television show episode]. In *Studio Masr*. Cairo: Niyl Sinima. Retrieved from https://www.youtube.com/watch?v=uizFPZlaYEc

Khatib, L. (2013). *Image Politics in the Middle East: The Role of the Visual in Political Struggle*. London; New York: I.B. Tauris.

Kraidy, M. M. (2006). Hypermedia and Governance in Saudi Arabia. *First Monday*, 11(7). Retrieved from http://firstmonday.org/ojs/index.php/fm/article/view/1610/1525#note2

Kraidy, M. M. (2014). Media Industries in Revolutionary Times. *Media Industries*, 1(2). Retrieved from http://www.mediaindustriesjournal.org/index.php/mij/article/view/45/87.

Kraidy, M. M. (2016a). *The Naked Blogger of Cairo: Creative Insurgency in the Arab World*. Cambridge, Massachusetts: Harvard University Press.

Kraidy, M. M. (2016b). Revolutionary Creative Labour. In M. Curtin & K. Sanson (Eds.), *Precarious Creativity: Global Media, Local Labour* (pp. 231–40). Oakland, California: University of California Press.

Kraidy, M. M., & Khalil, J. F. (2008). Youth, Media and Culture in the Arab World. In S. Livingstone & K. Drotner (Eds.), *International Handbook of Children, Media and Culture* (pp. 336–50). London: Sage.

Kraidy, M. M., & Khalil, J. F. (2009). *Arab Television Industries*, London: Palgrave Macmillan.

Kraidy, M. M., & Mourad, S. (2010). Hypermedia Space and Global Communication Studies Lessons from the Middle East. *Global Media Journal*, 8(16). Retrieved from http://repository.upenn.edu/asc_papers/248

Lebow, A. (2016). Seeing Revolution Non-linearly: www.filmingrevolution.org. *Visual Anthropology*, 29(3), 278–95.

Lim, M. (2012). Clicks, Cabs, and Coffee Houses: Social Media and Oppositional Movements in Egypt, 2004– 2011. *Journal of Communication*, 62(2), 231–48.

Lutfi, H. (2013, June 20). al-moʻalga fi aflam Khalid Yusif sayeʻa (The treatment of Khalid Yusif's films is bad). *Laha Magazine*. Retrieved from http://www.lahamag.com/Details/3187

MacBean, J. (1975). *Film and Revolution*. Bloomington: Indiana University Press.

Mada Masr. (2015, December, 28). Townhouse Gallery, Rawabet Theatre Closed after Interagency Raid. *Mada Masr*. Retrieved from http://www.madamasr.com/en/2015/12/28/news/culture/townhouse-gallery-rawabet-theater-closed-after-interagency-raid/

Mada Masr. (2017, May 12). Filmmakers Release Film about Rural Egypt Online after Censorship at Cairo festival. *Mada Masr*. Retrieved from https://www.madamasr.com/en/2017/05/12/news/culture/filmmakers-release-film-about-rural-egypt-online-after-censorship-at-cairo-festival/

al-Mahdawi, H. (2014, October 4). al-Sinima ʻal-muwaziaʼ fi Masr ('Parallel' cinema in Egypt). *Assafir*. Retrieved from http://arabi.assafir.com/Article/3669

Malitsky, J. (2013). *Post-revolution Nonfiction Film: Building the Soviet and Cuban Nations*. Bloomington: Indiana University Press.

Malkmus, L. (1988). The 'New' Egyptian Cinema: Adapting Genre Conventions to a Changing Society. *Cineaste: America's Leading Magazine on the Art and Politics of the Cinema*, 16(3), 30–3.

Malkmus, L., & Armes, R. (1991). *Arab and African Filmmaking*. London; New Jersey: Zed Books.

Mamduh, M. (2007). *Dimukratiyat al-wasiyt: Suʻud al-sinima al-mustaqilla fi Masr* (*The Democracy of a Medium: The Rise of Independent Cinema in Egypt*). Cairo: SEMAT for Production and Distribution.

al-Manawi, 'A. (2012). *al-Ayyam al-akhira li-nizam Mubarak: 18 Yuwm* (*The Last Days of Mubarak's Regime: 18 Days*). Cairo: al-Dar al-Masreyah al-Lobnaneyah.

al-Masri al-Yuwm (Producer). (2011, December 29). "al-Ghadibun" yahriqun qism al-'Arba'in ("The angry" burns al-'Arba'in police station) [Video webcast]. Retrieved from https://www.youtube.com/watch?v=2Fhk0vakgZ0&list=PLF7B3E4CF8DDA5F85&index=84

McMahon, S. (2017). *Crisis and class war in Egypt: Social Reproduction, Factional Realignments and the Global Political Economy*. London: Zed Books Limited.

Mehrez, S. (Ed.). (2012). *Translating Egypt's Revolution: The Language of Tahrir*. American University in Cairo Press.

Mehrez, S., & Abaza, M. (Eds.). (2017). *Arts and the Uprising in Egypt: The Making of a Culture of Dissent?* Cairo: American University in Cairo Press.

Mellen, J. (1973). *Film Guide to the Battle of Algiers*. Bloomington: Indiana University Press.

Mirbakhtyar, S. (2006). *Iranian Cinema and the Islamic Revolution*. North Carolina: McFarland & Company.

Mostafa, D.S. (2017). *The Egyptian Military in Popular Culture*. Manchester: Palgrave Macmillan.

Mostafa, D. S. (2015). Introduction: Egyptian Women, Revolution, and Protest Culture. *Journal for Cultural Research*, 19(2), 118–29.

Mukhtar, H. (2016, July 12). Ra'iys al-wuzara': Raf' al-da'm al-muwagah li-sina'at al-sinima ila 50 miliun ginih masri sanawiyan (The Prime Minister: Raising the funds directed to filmmaking to 50 million Egyptian pounds per year). *al-Yuwm al-Sabi'*. Retrieved from http://www.youm7.com/story/2016/7/12/رئيس-الوزراء-جعفر-الدمع-الموجه-إلى-صناعة-السينما-لـ50-مليون

Mumtaz, I. (1985). *Muzakkarat rakibat sinima: 30 'aman* (*Cinema censor's diary: 30 years*). Cairo, Egypt: The Egyptian Public Book Organisation.

Mumtaz, K. (2011). The Fall of Mubarak: The Failure of Survival Strategies. *Strategic Studies*, 31(3), 1–23.

Mursi, A. (Producer). (2011, February 5). al-qabd 'ala ahad al-baltagiyya fi midan al-Tahrir – mawqi'at al-gamal (The arrest of one of the thugs in Tahrir Square – The Battle of the Camel) [Video webcast]. Retrieved from https://www.youtube.com/watch?v=kAHJXDAeaIU

Naficy, H. (2011). *A Social History of Iranian Cinema. Volume II: The Industrialising Years 1941-1979*. Durham: Duke University Press.

Naficy, H. (2012a). *A Social History of Iranian Cinema. Volume III: The Islamicate Period 1978-1984*. Durham: Duke University Press.

Naficy, H. (2012b). *A Social History of Iranian Cinema. Volume IV: The Globalising Era 1984-2010*. Durham: Duke University Press.

Nichols, B. (1991). *Representing Reality: Issues and Concepts in Documentary*. Bloomington, IN: Indiana University Press.

Nichols, B. (1994). *Blurred boundaries: Questions of meaning in contemporary culture*. Bloomington, IN: Indiana University Press.

Nichols, B. (2001). *Introduction to Documentary*. Bloomington, IN: Indiana University Press.

Nimr, D. (2003). *Youth's Perspectives on the Egyptian Cinema*. Unpublished paper conducted in Fall 2003 at the American University in Cairo, JRMC 504 (Research Methods in Mass Communication).

ON E. (Producer). (2012, May 31). Ba'd rugu'uh min Cannes ... Ba'd al-Mawqi'a (After his return from Cannes ... After the Battle) [Television show episode]. In *Akhir Kalam*. Cairo: ON E. Retrieved from https://www.youtube.com/watch?v=hC98VbYAiK0

ON E. (Producer). (2013a, March 20). al-Shitaa illy Fat ... wa-l-rabiy' illy ba'duh (The Winter of Discontent. and the following spring) [Television show episode]. In *Baladna bi-l-Masry*. Cairo: ON E. Retrieved from https://www.youtube.com/watch?v=DcNuzXpRas4

ON E. (Producer). (2013b, June 21). Film 'Asham. al-mukhriga Maggi Murgan wal fannan Siyf al-Aswani ('Asham the film. The director Maggi Murgan and the artist Siyf al-Aswani). In *al-Sura al-Kamla*. Cairo: ON E. Retrieved from https://www.youtube.com/watch?v=BtCTiQCGV1E

ON E. (Producer). (2013c, October 22). Azmit sina'it al-sinima fi Masr: Liqaa' ma' Gabi Khuwri (Film production crisis in Egypt: An interview with Gabi Khuwri). In *Ayuha al-sada al-muhtaramun*. Cairo: ON E. Retrieved from https://www.youtube.com/watch?v=BnkIdo6wIV8

ON E (Producer). (2015, January 29). Nazrat al-dawla li-sina'it al-sinima al-Masriya (The state's view of the Egyptian film industry crisis) [Television show episode]. In *25/30*. Cairo: ON E. Retrieved from https://www.youtube.com/watch?v=JxG3VZfne8c&list=PLdXABTp0M_vygJ6KihqppyiXalmDCqRAD&index=3.

Pang, L. (2002). *Building a New China in Cinema: The Chinese Left-wing Cinema Movement, 1932–1937*. Lanham: Rowan & Littlefield Publishers.

Pendakur, M. (2013). Twisting and Turning: India's Telecommunications and Media Industries under the Neo-liberal Regime. *International Journal of Media and Cultural Politics*, 9(2), 107–31.

Police Reportedly Prevents Screening of 'The Nile Hilton Incident' in Heliopolis Venue. (2017, November 25). *Egypt Independent*. Retrieved from http://www.egyptindependent.com/police-reportedly-prevents-screening-of-the-nile-hilton-incident-in-heliopolis-venue/

al-Qahira wa-l-Nas (Producer). (2014, November 15). Ra'iys ghurfit sina'at al-sinima: 'ayiz a'abil al-Sisi wa-na awaffar miliarat (President of the chamber of film industry: I want to meet al-Sisi and I'll provide billions) [Television show episode]. In *Cairo 360*. Cairo: al-Qahira wa-l-Nas. Retrieved from https://www.youtube.com/watch?v=B4aRqG8zuVc&index=15&list=PLdXABTp0M_vygJ6KihqppyiXalmDCqRAD.

Quinn, A. (2007, September 13). The Yacoubian Building. *Independent*. Retrieved from http://www.independent.co.uk/arts-entertainment/films/reviews/the-yacoubian-building-15-464220.html

Radsch, C. (2016). *Cyberactivism and Citizen Journalism in Egypt: Digital Dissidence and Political Change*. New York: Palgrave Macmillan.

Rastegar, K. (2015). *Surviving Images: Cinema, War, and Cultural Memory in the Middle East*. New York: Oxford University Press.

Reuters/Stringer. (2011, February 11). Revolution in Egypt. Retrieved from https://www.reuters.com/news/picture/revolution-in-egypt-idUSRTXX2EJ

Rocha, G. (1983). The Aesthetics of Hunger. In M. Chanan (Ed.), *Twenty-five Years of the New Latin American Cinema* (pp. 13–14). London: British Film Institute Books.

Roncallo, S., & Arias-Herrera, J. (2013). Cinema and/as Revolution: The New Latin American Cinema. *Observatorio*, 7(3), 93–114.

Rosenstone, R. A. (1988). History in Images/History in Words: Reflections on the Possibility of Really Putting History onto Film. *American Historical Review*, 93(5), 1173–85.

Rotana Masriya (Producer). (2014, October 21). al-Muwagaha al-sakhina al-kamla ma-bayn al-montigayn Muhammad Hassan Ramzi wa al-Subki (The full hot confrontation between the producers Muhammad Hassan Ramzi and al-Subki) [Television show episode]. In *min al-Akhir*. Cairo: Rotana Masriya. Retrieved from https://www.youtube.com/watch?v=oTvXOvd5KS0.

Ryan, M., & Kellner, D. (1988). *Camera Politica: The Politics and Ideology of Contemporary Hollywood Film*. Bloomington, IN: Indiana University Press.

Sabri, M. (2012, May 20). Aflam al-baltaga taghzu al-sinima al-Masriya ba'd al-thawra (Thugs Films Invades Egyptian Cinema after the Revolution). *al-Hayah Economist*. Retrieved from http://www.alhayaheco.com/main/art21295-cat-أفلام البلطجة تغزو السينما المصرية بعد الثورة

Sada al-Balad (Producer). (2014, May 21) Liqaa' al-mushiyr 'Abd al-Fattah al-Sisi ma' al-fannaniyn (The meeting of the Field Marshal 'Abd al-Fattah al-Sisi with the artists) [YouTube Video]. Cairo: Sada al-Balad. Retrieved from https://www.youtube.com/watch?v=UnlLlidAQSU.

Sada al-Balad (Producer). (2015, January 20). al-Ra'iys al-Sisi li- "Ahmad al-Saqqa wa-Yusra": Wallahi la-tithasbu 'ala illy bi-ti'miluh (President al-Sisi to "Ahmad El Saqqa and Yusra: You will be accounted for what you do) [YouTube Video]. Cairo: Sada al-Balad. Retrieved from https://www.youtube.com/watch?v=kajajnjilqk

Sakr, N. (2013). Social Media, Television Talk Shows, and Political Change in Egypt. *Television & New Media*, 14(4), 322–37.

Samak, Q. (1977). The Politics of Egyptian Cinema. *MERIP Reports*, (56), 12–15.

Samir, S. (2015, June 2). Is Egypt's Film Industry Monopolized? *The Cairo Post*. Retrieved from http://thecairopost.youm7.com/news/153715/inside_egypt/isegypts-film-industry-monopolized.

Sanders, L. (2012). Reclaiming the City: Street Art of the Revolution. In S. Mehrez (Ed.), *Translating Egypt's Revolution* (pp.142–82). Cairo, Egypt: The American University of Cairo Press.

Sanjines, J. (1970). Cinema and Revolution. *Cinéaste*, 4(3, Latin American militant cinema), 13–14.

Schochat, E. (1983). Egypt: Cinema and Revolution. *Critical Arts*, 2(4), 22–32.

Schwartz, L. H., Kaye, D. D., & Martini, J. (2013). *Artists and the Arab Uprising*. Santa Monica, CA: RAND Corporation.

Shabab 6 ibril yo'linun al-harb 'ala "*Rami al-I'tisami*" (6 of April youth declare war on *Rami al-I'tisami*). (2008, December 18). *al-Yuwm al-Sabi'*. http://www.youm7.com/story/2008/12/18/شباب-٦-ابريل-يعلنون-الحرب-على-رامي-الاعتصامى

Shafik, V. (2007a). *Arab Cinema: History and Cultural Identity* (New rev. ed.) Cairo, Egypt: American University in Cairo Press.

Shafik, V. (2007b). *Popular Egyptian Cinema: Gender, Class, and Nation*. Cairo, Egypt: American University in Cairo Press.

Sharaf al-Din, D. (1992). *al-Siyasa wa-l-sinima fi Masr: 1961 – 1981* (*Politics and Cinema in Egypt: 1961–1981*). Cairo, Egypt: Dar al-Shuruk.

Shawki, A. (2013, March 31). *al-Khurug li-l-Nahar* … al-sinima al-lati ta'rif gumhurha wa-la ya'rifha (*al-Khurug li-l-Nahar*. The cinema that knows its audience and they don't know it). *al-Yuwm al-Sabi'*. Retrieved http://www.youm7.com/story/2013/3/31/الخروج-للنهار-السينما-التي-تعرف-جمهورها-ولا-يعرفها

Shihata, D. (2011). The Fall of the Pharaoh: How Hosni Mubarak's Reign Came to an End. *Foreign 7 Affairs*, 90(3), 26–32.

al-Shinnawi, T. (2015, October 12). al-akhawat "Rayya wa Sakina" wa-l-akhawan al-Subki (The sisters "Rayya and Sakina" and the brothers al-Subki). *al-Masri al-Yuwm*. Retrieved from http://www.almasryalyoum.com/news/details/825897

Shohat, E., & Stam, R. (1994). *Unthinking Eurocentrism: Multiculturalism and the Media*. London; New York: Routledge.

Snowdon, P. (2016). "Film!" – The Arab Revolutions and the Filmmaker as Amanuensis. *Visual Anthropology*, 29(3), 263–77.

Solanas, F., & Getino, O. (1970). Toward a Third Cinema. *Cinéaste*, 4(3, Latin American militant cinema), 1–10.

Solinas, P. (Ed.). (1973). *Gillo Pontecorvo's The Battle of Algiers*. New York: Charles Scribner's Sons.

Sorbera, L. (2014). Challenges of Thinking Feminism and Revolution in Egypt between 2011 and 2014. *Postcolonial Studies*, 17(1), 63–75.

Sreberny-Mohammadi, A., & Mohammadi, A. (1994). *Small Media, Big Revolution: Communication, Culture, and the Iranian Revolution*. Minneapolis: University of Minnesota Press.

Suter, J. (1988). Feminine discourse in Christopher Strong. In C. Penley (Ed.), *Feminism and Film Theory*. London and New York: British Film Institute.

Street, J. (1997). *Politics and Popular Culture*. Philadelphia, Penn: Temple University Press.

Sturken, M. (1997). *Tangled Memories: The Vietnam War, the AIDS Epidemic, and the Politics of Remembering*. Berkeley & Los Angeles; London: University of California Press.

Tabishat, M. (2012). Society in Cinema: Anticipating the Revolution in Egyptian Fiction and Movies. *Social Research*, 79(2), 377–96.

Tarek, S. (2011, April 19). Bosses, Enforcers and Thugs in Egypt's Battle of the Camel to see Harsh Retribution. *Ahram Online*. Retrieved from http://english.ahram.org.eg/NewsContent/1/64/10293/Egypt/Politics-/Bosses,-enforcers-and-thugs-in-Egypts-Battle-of-th.aspx

Tartoussieh, K. (2012). The Yacoubian Building: A Slice of pre-January 25 Egyptian Society? *Cinema Journal*, 52(1), 156–9.

al-Turki, M. (2009, October). Fi "*al-Diktatur*" al-ra'iys a'id wa-'ibnu bi-yibi' mumtalakat al-dawla bas da fi bambuzia (In "*al-Diktatur*" the President's son is selling the state's assets, but this is in Bambuzia). *al-Yuwm al-Sabi'*. Retrieved from http://www.youm7.com/story/2009/10/1/في-«الديكتاتور»-الرئيس-عايد-وابنه-بيبيع-ممتلكات-الدولة-بس-ده

'Ukiyl, H. (2015, December 29). al-Sinima al-tugariyya tatasadar al-mashhad al-sinima'i al-Masri fi 2015 (Commercial cinema tops the Egyptian film scene in 2015). *al-Arab*. Retrieved from http://www.alarab.co.uk/?id=69503

al-'Umari, A. (2014, April 4). Tasa'ulat bi-sha'n al-sinima al-mustaqilla fi Masr (Questions concerning independent cinema in Egypt). *al-Juzeera*. Retrieved from http://www.aljazeera.net/news/cultureandart/2014/4/11/تساؤلات-بشأن-السينما-المستقلة-في-مصر

Urgola, S. (2014). Archiving Egypt's Revolution: The 'University on the Square Project', Documenting January 25, 2011 and beyond. *IFLA Journal*, 40(1), 12–16.

Wayne, M. (2001). *Political Film: The Dialectics of Third Cinema*. London; Sterling, VA: Pluto Press.

Weibel, P. (Ed.). (2015). *Global Activism: Art and Conflict in the 21st Century*. Cambridge, MA. MIT Press.

Weissberg, J. (2016, February 14). Berlin Film Review: 'In the Last Days of the City'. *Variety*. Retrieved from http://variety.com/2016/film/festivals/in-the-last-days-of-the-city-review-berlin-film-festival-1201705591/

Wheeler, M. (2006). *Hollywood: Politics and Society*. London: BFI.

Whidden, J. (2005). The Generation of 1919. In A. Goldschmidt, A. Johnson & B. Salamoni (Eds.), *Re-envisioning Egypt 1919–1952* (pp. 19–45). Cairo, Egypt: The American University of Cairo Press.

White, H. (1988). Historiography and Historiophoty. *American Historical Review*, 93(5), 1193–99.

Willemen, P. (1989). The Third Cinema Question: Notes and Reflections. In J. Pines & P. Willemen (Eds.), *Questions of Third Cinema* (pp. 1–29). London: BFI Publishing.

al-Wirwari, M. (2008, January). Film "*Hiyna Maysara*" limaza tahawal ila ma'sara li-fariquh? (Why did "*Hiyna Maysara*" the film turn into grinding its team). *al-Arabiya*. Retrieved from https://www.alarabiya.net/views/2008/01/10/44047.html

Yau, E. (1997). China after the Revolution. In G. Nowell-Smith (Ed.), *The Oxford History of World Cinema* (pp. 693–704). Oxford: Oxford University Press.

Youngblood, D. J. (1991). The Fate of Soviet Popular Cinema during the Stalin Revolution. *Russian Review*, 50(2), 148–62.

Yusif, A. (Producer). (2011). Hasri: Ahdaas ma'raqat al-gamal fi midan al-Tahrir al-Masri Yuwm 2 Fibrayir 2011 (Exclusive: The events of the Battle of the Camel in the Egyptian Tahrir Square on 2 February 2011). Retrieved from https://www.youtube.com/watch?v=6yZOQeTchhU

al-Zubidi, S. (2011). al-sinima wa-l-thawra fi Masr (Cinema and revolution in Egypt). *The New Carmel*, 1(Summer), 235–47.

Index

25 January 2011 1, 28, 97, 110, 124
28 January 2011 1, 52, 83, 98, 99, 104, 109
2008 global financial recession 7, 43, 45, 51, 52, 162
2010 parliamentary elections 1, 75
2011 Revolution 4–9, 11–14, 16, 18, 21, 22, 25, 26, 28, 29, 32–4, 39, 40–4, 45, 47, 48, 52–4, 56–8, 60, 67, 70, 71, 73, 77, 79–83, 86, 87, 93, 94, 96–8, 99, 101, 103, 104–6, 107, 110, 112, 117–19, 121, 125–7, 130, 131, 136, 139, 140, 153, 159, 161–3, 165–9

alternative
    aesthetics 8, 31, 34, 39, 41, 62, 68, 71, 87, 105, 132, 134, 135, 139
    production and distribution methods 5, 6, 16, 28, 30, 32, 35, 38, 87, 94, 131, 132, 134, 137, 149, 150, 153, 157, 159, 161, 165, 168, 169
the army 1–4, 53, 97, 105
    Armed Forces 2, 68, 86, 103, 128, 158, 169

Battle of the Camels 98, 104, 105, 106, 115, 165
binary opposition representations 3, 13, 74, 102, 103, 108, 165

censorship 8, 9, 12, 17–19, 21–3, 26, 30, 32, 33, 37, 38, 40, 44, 45, 47, 50, 56–8, 61, 62, 64, 68, 69, 73, 76, 80–2, 84, 85, 87, 91–5, 97, 99, 103, 128, 130, 131, 133, 136, 137, 139, 144, 149, 151, 158–60, 162, 164, 166–8
change
    political change 4, 7, 11, 19
    social change 9, 10, 15, 18, 43, 72, 94
corruption 1, 4, 5, 7, 19, 28, 61, 65, 67–77, 81, 93, 94, 95, 98, 124, 144, 163, 164, 167

counterrevolution 3, 5, 14, 17, 33, 35, 39, 85, 100, 106, 109, 121, 123, 127, 128, 130, 156
Coup d'état 4, 27, 53, 73, 74, 103
crisis
    film production crisis 7, 9–12, 14, 16, 18, 36, 40, 44–7, 49–52, 59, 60, 62–5, 162, 163, 169
    political crisis 4, 8, 10, 17, 43, 44, 50, 58, 65, 70–2, 80, 89, 108, 162, 167, 168
curfews 7, 9, 11, 40, 44, 45, 47, 53, 62, 78, 97, 162

dictatorship 8, 28, 70, 82, 83, 87, 94, 163
digital technologies 6, 8–10, 13, 14, 16, 17, 25, 34, 39–42, 44, 46, 48, 52, 64, 65, 68, 74, 87, 89, 91, 97, 98, 118, 119, 122, 125, 130–4, 136–9, 144, 149–51, 153, 159, 164, 166, 168
dissent 1, 4, 7, 10, 12, 14, 18, 34, 40, 41, 65, 68–70, 88, 125, 163
documentary films 5, 8, 10, 12–15, 21, 26, 33–41, 44, 46, 65, 72, 88, 96–108, 110, 111, 113, 115, 118, 119, 121–4, 125–9, 132, 134, 136, 146, 148, 151, 156, 164, 165

economic deterioration 7, 40, 76, 79, 85, 130, 167
Emergency Law 1, 68, 94, 95

film directors
    Ahmad 'Abd Allah 8, 10, 12, 13, 32, 34, 46, 51, 53, 55, 57, 68, 88, 97, 99, 102–4, 114, 115, 117, 122, 131, 132, 134, 136, 144, 147, 148, 153, 155, 159, 163, 164, 166
    Ahmad Rashwan 8, 13, 47, 58, 68, 99, 102, 104, 119–21, 132, 136, 149, 156, 163, 164, 166
    Aytin Amin 13, 34, 44, 46, 71, 76, 91, 95, 98, 99, 104, 119, 122, 123,

124, 126, 136, 146, 148, 153, 159, 164
Hala Galal 46, 98, 127, 136, 139, 150, 153–5
Hala Lutfi 9, 14, 32, 46, 59, 76, 77, 98, 131, 136–40, 141, 146, 147, 149, 151, 152, 156, 157, 160
Ibrahim al-Battut 8, 10, 68, 69, 87, 92, 93, 99, 102, 104, 109–13, 132, 135, 138, 144, 163, 164, 166
Khalid Yusif 5, 7, 68–71, 73, 77, 79–81, 93, 163
Maggi Murgan 9, 134, 142, 144
Marwan 'Umara 10, 13, 34, 47, 99, 102, 104, 119, 124, 125, 129, 136, 148, 151
Nadin Khan 9, 98, 133–5, 144, 160
Samih 'Abd al-'Aziz 47, 51–4, 56, 57, 63, 98
Yusri Nasrallah 8, 97, 98, 101, 102–7, 138, 164, 165
film funding 8, 9, 11, 43, 46, 52, 58, 87, 93, 94, 122, 130, 132, 136, 138, 146, 150, 159, 166
film genres 4, 5, 7, 9, 10, 12, 14, 20, 25, 28, 30, 33, 36, 37, 41, 44, 60, 61, 62, 65, 68, 69–73, 76, 77, 79–87, 91, 93–5, 129, 132, 134, 139, 144, 146, 148, 159, 163, 164, 168
film industry 4, 7–11, 14–16, 18, 20–2, 25, 26–30, 35, 36, 40–7, 49–52, 54, 55, 57, 58, 59, 62–5, 87, 135, 161, 162, 168, 169
film movement 5, 6, 9, 11, 13–17, 26, 29, 30, 38, 41, 126, 130, 131, 134, 135, 145, 146, 157, 159, 161, 163, 165, 166, 169
film producers
 Hisham Suliman 46, 49, 53
 Muhammad al-'Adl 45, 46, 49, 54, 56, 58, 59, 63
 Muhammad Hifzi 9, 43, 46, 51, 53, 59, 62, 63, 122, 136, 146
 Muhammad Samir 46, 51, 52, 60, 136, 139, 147, 148, 156
 Shirif Mandur 45, 46, 48, 50–2, 55, 56, 59, 61, 63, 136, 151
film theatres/screens 7, 29, 35, 37, 43, 47, 48, 51–3, 58, 62, 64, 71, 80, 81, 88, 97, 99, 103, 118, 122, 132, 142, 151, 157, 159

filmingrevolution.org 104, 126
freedom of expression 10, 76, 158, 166
fundamentalism 5, 70, 79

government/state support 7, 8, 10, 23, 28, 29, 35, 42, 45, 47, 49, 54–6, 61, 64, 152, 162

historicise 8, 10, 13, 34, 37, 98, 100, 104, 108, 113, 161, 164
Hollywood 10, 15, 20–3, 29–33, 41, 59, 70, 71, 87, 132, 140, 162
improvisation 13, 68, 72, 91, 104, 108, 118, 127, 131, 134, 135, 138, 144, 159, 166
independent films
 filmmakers/filmmaking 5, 7, 8–10, 12–14, 16, 30, 32, 34, 38, 42, 45–7, 64, 65, 69–73, 87–9, 92, 93, 95, 104, 126, 130–133, 135–40, 142, 144–9, 153, 156–60, 163, 164, 166, 167
initiatives
 Cimatheque 30, 137, 157, 166
 Hassala 30, 46, 137, 156, 157
 sinima fi kul makan (Cinema Everywhere) 28, 137, 157, 166
 Zawya 30, 137, 156, 157
insecurity 7, 9, 40, 44, 47, 54, 62, 104, 121, 162

low-budget films 4, 7, 9, 10, 12, 14, 32, 42, 44, 45, 60, 63, 65, 93, 132, 162, 168

mainstream filmmaking 8, 14, 16, 17, 28–31, 33, 34, 37, 39, 41, 45, 46, 51, 62, 65, 69–71, 78, 87–9, 94, 131, 132, 134–40, 145–8, 152, 155, 156, 159, 161, 162, 163, 165–7
mainstream media 2, 10, 11, 14, 17, 36, 39, 47, 49, 60, 112, 151, 156, 158, 167, 168
marginalization
 independent filmmakers 39, 40, 41, 45, 46, 136, 159
 working classes 5, 9, 10, 13, 30, 32, 36, 68, 77, 78, 103, 105, 114, 115, 117, 124, 134, 135, 139, 140, 142, 144, 159

Maspiro 2, 105, 107, 112, 120
memory
   audio-visual, cultural memory 5, 6, 8, 10, 13, 14, 16, 20, 33, 34, 97–9, 101, 103, 104, 105, 109, 110, 112, 117, 119–21, 123, 125, 127, 161, 164
Mubarak 1, 2, 4, 7, 12, 13, 19, 52, 67–9, 71, 75, 76, 81, 83–5, 93, 95, 98, 99, 105, 106, 109, 110, 112, 114, 119, 120–5, 128, 130, 144, 154, 163, 167
Mursi 2, 3, 53, 56, 57, 95, 145
musalsalāt ramaḍān 47, 48, 49, 53, 64, 168
Muslim Brotherhood 1–3, 17, 27, 28, 32, 49, 52, 53, 55, 56, 58, 61, 68, 75, 76, 80, 86, 102, 103, 109, 122, 123, 126, 128, 129, 130, 136, 154, 156, 158, 169

oligopoly of production and distribution 9, 12, 43, 45, 47, 50, 51, 62, 63, 64, 162
oppression (as a theme) 12, 16, 20, 34, 36, 38–40, 68, 77, 78, 80, 87–92, 94, 95, 104, 109–11, 118, 128, 133–5, 141, 160

piracy 9, 11, 12, 18, 43, 45, 47, 49, 50, 54, 55, 59, 62, 162, 163, 168
police brutality 1, 7, 10, 12, 65, 68, 70–5, 77, 78, 84, 85, 93–95, 99, 123, 133
political activism 4, 11, 12, 16, 40, 41, 67, 93, 153, 161, 163
political affect 11, 14, 73, 87
political economy 4, 11, 16, 21, 23, 42, 44, 48
political movements
   Kifaya 2, 67
   Six April 2, 7, 67
political satire 5, 7, 12, 30, 70, 71, 73, 81, 82, 85, 86, 93, 163
politicise viewers 16, 86
popular drama 4, 5, 7, 10, 12, 30, 68, 70, 71, 73, 76, 77, 87, 93, 144
poverty 7, 12, 20, 28, 65, 68–74, 77–85, 87, 88–91, 93–5, 115, 117, 118, 124, 132, 140, 144, 159, 163
production, distribution and exhibition 9, 23, 32, 43, 45, 47, 64, 87, 131
propaganda 15, 18, 22, 26–8, 37, 38, 168

protest/protesters 1, 2, 3, 5, 6, 7, 10, 12, 15, 33, 34, 39, 44, 52, 53, 68, 72, 73, 75, 82, 83, 86–9, 94, 97–9, 102, 103, 105, 106–9, 111–15, 118–26, 128, 130, 133, 136, 146, 149, 153–5, 157, 163, 165

re-enactment 12, 61 101, 102, 105, 106, 107, 115, 118–21, 127, 128, 133, 165
realist approaches 6, 8, 9, 10, 17, 28, 30, 37, 41, 42, 68, 70, 72, 81, 88, 93, 100, 130, 134, 156, 159, 165
resistance
   filmmaking 8, 10, 11, 14, 15, 16, 21, 23–6, 28–30, 33, 34, 36, 40, 41, 73, 82, 87–9, 103, 130–2, 133, 134–6, 139, 148, 155, 159–61, 164, 165, 167
   political 5, 19, 21, 130, 153, 154, 155
revolutionary moment 5, 10–12, 14, 65, 96
revolutionary struggle 5, 14, 24, 26, 29, 32, 130, 133, 134

al-Sisi 2, 3, 4, 28, 45, 49, 53–6, 63, 162, 167
slum neighbourhood 74, 77, 78, 79, 85, 140, 144
social injustice 4, 33, 34, 38, 70, 72, 74–7, 81, 83, 87–9, 91, 133, 163, 167
socio-political films 5, 9, 10, 16–19, 25, 29, 31, 33, 38, 41, 44, 49, 65, 72, 73, 77, 79, 82, 109, 131, 135, 144, 145, 161, 163, 165
   socially conscious films 10, 17, 21, 30, 31, 33, 34, 36, 41, 99, 161–3, 168
al-Subki 49, 51, 58, 60, 61, 139

Tahrir Square 1, 2, 10, 12, 13, 34, 65, 86, 97, 99, 100–3, 105–8, 110, 111, 113–15, 117–19, 121–6, 128, 133, 154, 164, 165
television 3, 6, 7, 9, 10–12, 23, 27, 43–54, 57, 60–2, 64, 67, 69, 77, 79, 84, 89, 99, 102–4, 106, 107, 109, 113, 114, 115, 118, 119, 123, 124, 127, 142, 152, 155, 158, 162, 163, 167, 168
Third Cinema 6, 24–27, 30–5, 39, 87, 89, 131, 165

voices 8, 17, 41, 55, 70, 88, 89, 101, 103, 106, 112–14, 117, 119 , 123–4, 126, 127, 135, 155, 163, 165

World Cinema and Revolution
   China 8, 11, 15, 17, 25, 28–31, 35, 157, 162, 163, 167
   Cuba 5, 8, 17, 26–8, 31, 35, 36, 98, 131, 162, 166, 167
   Iran 4, 11, 15, 17, 25, 36–41, 157, 164
   Soviet Union 5, 6, 8, 11, 15, 17, 25–8, 29, 35, 40, 131, 162

young filmmakers 5, 11, 14, 40, 42, 46, 136, 137, 146, 149, 151, 153, 159, 166, 168

www.ingramcontent.com/pod-product-compliance
Lightning Source LLC
Chambersburg PA
CBHW07638300426
44111CB00013B/2162